Blow Away
Your Limits

The True Meaning of Success

To Kathleen and Lorie
A special thank
to two real winners!
Enjoy your reading!

Charles Douy

Blow Away
Your Limits

The True Meaning of Success

Dr. Claude Sarrazin

Translated by Kirsten Bjorn

Canadian Cataloguing in Publication Data

Sarrazin, Claude, 1945-

   Blow away your limits : the true meaning of success

   Translation of : Le vrai visage de la réussite

   ISBN 2-9807697-1-1

   1. Success - Psychological aspects. 2. Self-realization. 1. Title

BF637.S8S27313 2003   158.1   C2002-941715-5

Dr. Claude Sarrazin, Psychologist
Phone : (514) 343-7589
e-mail : claude.sarrazin@umontreal.ca

Cover and book design by Martine Gravel

ISBN : 2-9807697-1-1

Copyright © 2003 by Claude Sarrazin
Legal deposit : 2003
Bibliothèque nationale du Québec
National Library of Canada

Printed in Canada

Contents

PART 3
The Strategy of Champions: See the Direction

PART 5
Living Strategically...

PREFACE

CHOOSE FREEDOM

It is a pleasure and an honor for me to write this short preface for Dr. Claude Sarrazin's book "Blow Away Your Limits: The True Meaning of Success". In fact, I have known Dr. Sarrazin for quite some time, as I was his research director for his doctoral studies in psychology as well as his student when he was teaching karate. Claude Sarrazin is one of those rare people who actually practice what they teach and personify what they write about in their work. He embodies that idealistic and rebellious spirit mentioned in the prologue of his book that is necessary for all scientific creation, but in addition he knows how to combine tenacity with the love of a job well done which are also guarantees of success.

In his book, Dr. Sarrazin shows how the idealism necessary for all human enterprises must be embodied within a solid personal discipline and a staunch determination, before yielding its full share of success. This book comes at a time when people tend to blame others, the system or the government, for their failures and unhappiness. But to want to succeed is not everything. In fact, as young Claude's grandfather says in the prologue of the book "to have will and to forge ahead is not enough, you must also know how to will". What Dr. Sarrazin does in his book is to teach us how to "know how to will". Very few people could write with as much seriousness and conviction as Dr. Sarrazin does. As a matter of fact, his triple education in kinesiology, psychology and martial arts has given him a practical and theoretical perspective that very few possess.

By restoring a sense of honor to the concept of freedom, this particular freedom that everyone should choose to exercise instead of continually placing the blame for their problems on the backs of others, he shows us, step-by-step, how to succeed, how to set and attain our goals while first and foremost distinguishing between a dream and a pipedream. These three strategic principles: lucid will, seeing the direction and staying on course and the following seven keys of success – master the wave, tame change, dream concretely, give yourself a directional map, plan everything even the unpredictable, adjust the mechanics and sustain your spirit – are all unquestionably essential in the training of athletic champions and will interest every trainer, coach and sport psychologist alike. However, what is extremely interesting about these strategies is that they are applicable to any domain in life. They are as appealing for athletes as for businessmen, for artists as for scientists, in fact, they are for anyone that sets a goal and wants to attain it.

They are even relevant to the psychologist as a frame of reference in the therapeutic process. In fact, the strategies for change and evolution that Dr. Sarrazin proposes in his work are founded on the basic principles of human cognitive behavioral psychology and in this sense are appropriate for implementing all types of change. Despite its thoroughness, this book is written in a style that makes it accessible to anyone, it is just as interesting for the professional who's job is to guide someone's efforts toward change, as for people who have decided to change and attain their objectives on their own. Further, it also applies to organizations and to their evolution.

As Dr. Sarrazin says, "Nobody comes into life feeling incapable of achievement or accomplishment…but when we continually hear that we are not capable or cannot succeed, we end up believing it". In his book he illustrates tangible strategies that enable us to break these restraining chains and rediscover our freedom to accomplish and to attain our objectives. Nevertheless, you have to choose to do it, to choose freedom and then want to put forth the necessary efforts. No one can do this for us but if we decide to do it "Blow Away Your Limits: The True Meaning of Success" can teach us how to succeed.

Luc Granger, PhD.
Psychologist
Director of the Psychology Department of the University of
Montreal
Former President of "Quebec Order of Psychologists"

ACKNOWLEDGMENTS

A PROJECT such as this one, spanning close to four years, could not have been realized without the support and help of many significant people.

First and foremost I would like to thank my wife, Lise Péloquin, for her unequaled patience and constant support throughout these last few years. I would also like to emphasize the pertinence and subtlety of her comments and suggestions. Lise made a significant contribution to the achievement of this project and I am extremely grateful.

I would like to thank Mrs. Kirsten Bjorn for the wonderful job she has done with the translation of this book; her professionalism, her availability and her patience were always greatly appreciated. I don't want to forget psychologist Dr. Luc Granger, who read the first version of my book and gave me very positive feedback. My appreciation also goes to my friend and partner Claude Hotte, for his relevant suggestions about the English presentation of this book, as well as for his constant positive state of mind when working together.

I likewise want to thank Mrs. Martine Gravel for her inventive graphic presentations.

Finally, I would like to express my gratitude to all the patients, athletes and managers with whom I've worked with over the course of the last twenty-five years. All those individuals and organizations stimulated my thought process and helped me to justly appreciate the marvelous dimension of the incredible human odyssey.

Prologue

THE WISDOM OF MY GRANDFATHER

It was the spring of 1965. I remember as if it were yesterday; I don't think I could ever forget. I was sitting in a window seat on an old bus, traveling from Montreal to Magog. We were driving along the picturesque route that would take us to the heart of the magnificent Eastern Townships.

It had been a mild spring that year; nature had already begun to offer its abundant treasures of color and smell to those that would appreciate them. Yet, despite the warm morning sun with its silver rays shining on the paved highway, my heart was heavy and I was in no mood for laughing. With my forehead resting against the cold window, I struggled to hold back my tears. I felt cold and empty, as if the life had drained out of me.

The day before, I had called up my grandfather. From the tone of my voice he knew straight away that something was wrong. He immediately asked, "Why don't you take advantage of your Easter vacation and come visit us for a few days? There is a bus leaving early tomorrow morning; take it and I'll meet you at the station. Come, we'll talk, and the fresh country air will do you some good; it really is spectacular this year!"

Without hesitation, I accepted his invitation. At 19 years of age I was in desperate need of getting some fresh air, of leaving my surroundings and of opening up to someone that would listen, understand and help me with my problems. That is exactly what happened. I really had no idea at the time how much these few days would change my life. Never again would life's difficult periods or events, as painful as they can be, affect me in the same way. Never again, would I allow my setbacks or failures to put me into such a state of depression as I experienced at that particular point of my life. Looking back, I realize that I came very close to what is now referred to as burnout. Fortunately, thanks to the wisdom of my grandfather, my overwhelming feeling of exhaustion was transformed into energy and despair would never again work its way into my life.

Hitting Rock Bottom

As I rode along in the bus with my head pressed against the window, I let the countryside pass in front of my eyes without really seeing it. My attention was turned inwards, as for perhaps the thousandth time I went over the events of the last few difficult months in my mind. I was in my last year of study at the now defunct classical college, where I had spent the last eight years of my life. It's not that I regretted my years of college; I had learned a lot both through the academic plan as well as through personal experiences. All my efforts had been worthwhile. No, the problem wasn't there. Several weeks before my graduation, just as my long adventure was coming to the glorious and successful finish I had been working towards, I had the awful feeling that everything was going to end badly. Worse, I felt as if my whole universe was crumbling around me like a house of cards in a stormy night.

During that era, the private college milieu was very intense; competitive spirit and performance were valued above all else. This was where the future elite of society was produced, shaped and groomed. Attending these schools guaranteed success: it opened doors to university, which was the royal way to power, money, success and fame. The college was also the antechamber to what we affectionately, and maybe a bit too ironically, called the 'factory', meaning the great seminary where future parish priests and clergy of the all-powerful church were formed and educated.

For my parents, sending me to classical college was the greatest legacy they could ever bestow upon me. This was especially true since the parish priest had trumpeted this message loud and clear during his Sunday sermons. Coming from a modest social class but being very ambitious, my parents secretly hoped that through giving the Holy Church their oldest son, they would be securing their place in paradise.

It was within this context that I began my climb up the ladder of success. From the beginning, I disappointed no one, completely the opposite. I was altruistic, obedient and devoted: the ideal seminary candidate on the path to sainthood. Moreover, my parents were extremely proud as I exceeded all their scholastic expectations: I was first in my class and was awarded a multitude of medals and honors as well as public recognition. There was only one small problem. I was not only academically applied and studious. I also enjoyed sports and participated in a variety of non-academic organizations. At first, my parents were worried; they were losing control of their eldest. But this small inconvenience was soon forgotten with the soothing salve of validation from the clerical authorities. I was a born leader and a powerful perfectionist, what could be better for the Saint Mother Church? Basically, this was how I spent my first years of classical college. In time, I gained both confidence and importance. I became more and more like the person I was expected to become. A religious career seemed certain, and academic success was confirmed. In my last two years of study, what we called the philosophy years, I became president of my class and the swimming club, head scout and director of the college's summer camp. What more could anyone ask of me? I shined in all my glory!

It was then that my world began to fall apart. Almost imperceptibly, certain inconsistencies began to subtly penetrate my field of consciousness. I began to notice the clergy's talk seemed more and more distant from their actual behavior. I was a complete idealist and I naively expected nothing less than perfection from my teachers. As I grew and learned, my blinders of naivety fell. How could I ignore the sudden disappearance of this good old father confessor that had too frequently asked his young pupils if they had been experiencing some hardening of their "purity organ"? Another event concerned a certain priest who was very jovial and funny in a straight-faced way. As an amateur mechanic, he made us laugh while he repaired his old Citroen car: he would always finish the job with more defective parts than when he started. One day he disappeared in an odd manner. A rumor circulated that he had gone to a detoxification center to regain his health. And how was I to ignore these backbiters with viperish tongues who were eating their hearts out and gossiping about those who could stand tall, trying to belittle them? All these things began to add up, and weigh heavily on me. Without me even realizing it, I began to question my calling to the church.

At the same time, I began having serious problems with the chaplain scout who was also involved with the swim team. It started as a few minor differences of opinion. I became increasingly more aware that he wanted to act in my place as the true head scout and swim club leader. He did everything possible to undermine my leadership. With each passing month, it continually worsened. Eventually, the good father began putting pressure on me to resign. He didn't accept or encourage his docile and humble student wanting to fly on his own wings. Then, one day, I had the grave misfortune of coming across him and one of our young scouts engaged in some overly friendly roughhousing. Warning bells went off in my head and serious doubt began to creep into my mind. A few weeks later, the college superior asked to see me, and by his questions, I realized that my doubts were indeed well founded. And even though I may have been right, it looked very bad to have a chaplain lose face against a mere student. The father superior made it clear to me that he had no choice but to immediately relieve me of my duties as president of the swimming club and head scout. I had been sacrificed for the good of the diplomatic hierarchy.

This was a difficult blow. My image as a respected leader, so dearly acquired and patiently cultivated, had been suddenly destroyed. All at once my illusions of the perfect and just world of religion were being shattered. I had an idea that my call to the Church was just a dream now broken to pieces. I was merely feeling like I was one of the living dead. Everything seemed empty and meaningless, and I no longer felt the desire to pursue a religious career. I needed to reorient myself, but I didn't know toward what, where or why? The pursuit of a new career would require that I take more courses before entering university. I would have to take these courses over the summer, further obliging me to quit my job as head of the college summer camp. Yet another responsibility I would lose. It all started to add up. I became frightened inside, and began suffering from anxiety and insomnia, and my grades slipped. I began spiraling downwards toward a state of depression.

To make matters even worse, just before Easter vacation, I had taken a stand against college authorities concerning a party they'd refused granting permission for. I had united my fellow students together to prepare a letter clearly stating our position to them. We found their objections to be unjustified and unfair so we demanded they change their minds, otherwise we'd be forced to take the necessary measures! I don't think I have to describe the explosive impact this letter had on the administration. It was even recommended by some that I should be expelled. But, due to my excellent record, they decided to tolerate me until graduation, and simply consider me as a lost sheep.

This situation even further exacerbated the uneasiness that had overcome me. I was trembling inside and every time I breathed it felt as if I had a cement block stuck in my chest. I could no longer see clearly and even considered abandoning everything, not taking my final exams and going somewhere far, far away to forget about the whole thing. I was in this state of mind when I called my grandfather; he was my last hope for restoring a bit of reason to the world that had completely collapsed at my feet.

My Wise and Mysterious Grandfather

I was lost in thought when the bus finally pulled into the station. The vision of my grandfather, as he waited for me at the end of the platform with his peaceful and loving smile, seemed to magically rouse me from my troubled thoughts. As I collected my bags, I considered this wise, somewhat mysterious man, and I realized just how important he had become to me.

In reality, Jerome Ovila was not my real grandfather. I had lost my grandparents a long time ago and grandpa, as I affectionately called him, had become the adopted and understanding grandfather that I was dearly missing. We met four years ago, while I was on Easter vacation. I was on a hike with my Rover troupe, enjoying a three-day stopover at the Saint-Benoit-du-Lac Abbey on the shores of Lake Memphremagog. Among the many activities offered, we were given the chance to go on a panoramic in a small Cessna. It was during this unforgettable flight that I met Jerome.

He loved taking off before sunrise. It was to give us a real taste of, as he said, "That magical moment when time holds its breath as if to allow God the chance to marvel at his own creation." As we slowly made our ascent towards the east, above Memphre Lake, nightfall was rapidly fading into the pale light of dawn. Then suddenly, an immense orange ball of fire began to break the horizon of the massive Appalachians. There was magic in the air. The lake under our wings shone in a pale salmon hue, while in front of us, a diaphanous light chased away the last shadows of night in the valley. Time stood still. No one spoke; we were speechless with admiration, contemplating how God was giving life to his creation.

As the feeling of euphoria faded, we all began commenting on the spectacle we had just witnessed. It was as if, insatiably, we wanted to relive that precious moment, over and over again. We took out our frugal breakfasts that we had brought with us, and with Jerome commenting here and there on the view that passed beneath us, we began sharing our interests and preoccupations. His questions were simple and direct and his interest appeared both genuine and warm. He neither judged nor condemned anybody and seemed to understand perfectly what each of us had lived. This was the very first time that I had seen an adult give that much attention, respect and understanding to young people my age. I told him, with great importance and pride, all about the responsibilities that had been entrusted upon me. I was pleased to tell him about the motto I lived by: "for others". The more I demonstrated how I was on the road to success, the more I had the impression that a small, skeptical smile had begun to form on the understanding, warm look that Jerome was giving me.

After we had disembarked from the plane, Jerome took me aside and asked, "So tell me, what do you do for yourself?" I was a bit taken aback and was not quite sure what he wanted me to say. "It is charitable and kind to look after the needs of others, but one should never forget that each of us has only a limited amount of energy. If you always empty your battery without ever recharging it, you could be in store for some unpleasant surprises. Once it is empty, it is extremely difficult, and sometimes even painful, to recharge. Importance, image, perfection and even self-sacrifice, that's all very nice! But you should never forget that once you run out of juice, there is nothing left to give. When you'll need energy, you won't be getting it back from those that have become used to receiving from you. The more you give to someone, the more they become accustomed to it and the more they will demand. There is only one person in this world that can control your flow of energy, and that's you. No one else will do it for you. Eventually, when the time comes, and you'll be needing to receive, very few will be able to understand."

I listened to everything he told me, but I wasn't sure I understood what he meant. I was surprised and even a bit shocked by what I considered a flagrant lack of altruism. As if he had read my mind, Jerome added, "Don't be too quick to judge what I have just said. Take some time to think about it. Don't forget that once empty, a battery will never, without help, recharge itself. Think about your own recharging system from time to time, it's important if you want to continue giving for a long time to come." I was receptive to his advice and understood its logic. But, that could never happen to me, especially not at my age!

Before leaving that day, Jerome told me that I was always welcome to visit him at his home, and that he would be glad to see me again, anytime, under any circumstances. I did see him again after that day, many times. I took every opportunity I got, finding as many excuses as possible to pass by his place and each time I would stop in for a visit. Bit by bit, I came to know him and his wife Elysa, as we chatted by the fire in the chalet he rented by the Saint-Benoit Abbey. Although he spoke very little of his family origins, I did learn that Jerome Ovila was a Quebecois descendent. His family had emigrated to the southern United States a few years before the Second World War, settling somewhere in Florida. As a young adult, he enlisted in the American army and became a pilot, realizing a dream he had since he was young. After Pearl Harbor, he fought as a B-29 pilot, these were super-bombers that were still legendary long after the war ended. While fighting in the Pacific, he found himself in Tokyo after the Japanese surrender. He spent over seven years there, piloting bombers that had been literally transformed into flying meteorological laboratories. His job was to fly into the heart of a cyclone and gather as much scientific information as possible about these extraordinary phenomena. This gave him a pleasure that was out of the ordinary.

Upon returning from Japan, he decided to leave the army, taking advantage of a meteorological recycling course. While working as a Sunday pilot at the small local airport in Fort Myers, he met his future wife, Elysa. She was a financial controller for a business that owned an airline company that shuttled merchandise as well as passengers between the various airports in Florida and the neighboring states. Hit by a case of nostalgia, Jerome took Elysa up to the shores of Lake Massawipi beside Magog, to honeymoon at the magnificent Hatley Inn, known for its enchanting setting. Originally from there, Jerome helped Elysa discover this splendid region. It was September and autumn was showing off its full splendor, having painted the forests in a fiery multitude of color. It was on their honeymoon that they made the decision to relocate there.

Lucid Will

With my bags in hand and my heart already feeling somewhat lighter, I walked towards my grandfather as he waited at the end of the unloading platform. His peaceful and inviting smile drew me towards him even before I felt his strong, warm handshake. "It's a pleasure to see you again, son. It seems like ages since we've seen each other!" Between us, we had developed a warm and affectionate relationship. He called me son and I called him grandpa.

"Well, you don't seem to be in the best of shape", he added, looking me over with his keen eye. "Come. Elysa has some errands for us in town." The rest of the morning passed like a dream. It was such a pleasure and a relief to be able to occupy myself with something besides my troubles! I suspect Jerome planned it that way, giving me time to settle in. As the day passed, I felt my mood lighten, freeing my spirit from the dark emotions that, for the past several weeks, had clouded my thoughts, paralyzing my ability to think straight.

It wasn't until later that afternoon, with the old jeep packed with construction materials, that we finally headed toward home. We left downtown Magog, passing by the old dock and public beach.

This route took us to Fathers' Road, where we turned left toward the Saint-Benoit Abbey. We passed through fields and gradually made our way toward the mountains that surrounded Lake Memphremagog. The drive through the countryside brought back memories of the plane tour I had taken with Jerome several years ago. A feeling of peace and harmony moved through me, after many long weeks of nothing but worry and anguish.

As we came out of a wide sweep, a beautiful stone house came into view. It was on the side of the lake, well removed from the road, and looked very charming with its black gabled roof. An old wood fence surrounded the property. The lawn, trees and gardens, in vibrant harmony, looked like an impressionist painting. A small gravel path led from the entrance of the fence, right up to the house. The path was lined with two rows of hedges resembling respectful sentries guarding the entrance to the enchanted kingdom. The view of the valley, the lake and the city of Magog, was incredible. On the horizon, there was nothing but mountains and the thousand shades of blossoming green leaves, cutting the backdrop of the sea blue sky. The sight was spectacular and simply took my breath away!

As soon as the Jeep stopped, we were greeted by Spotty, the master of the house, all black and white spots, a mix of Dalmatian and English Setter. He leapt around us, jealously chasing away Bordeau and Bourgogne, two great tomcats that had also come in search of attention and affection. The big front door opened and out came Elysa, in a long dress and flowered apron, to welcome us for herself. She was beautiful with her blond hair pulled back in a barrette! Her green eyes, thin face and pale complexion made her look like a proud Scandinavian. As I looked at them, I marveled how the effects of time had seemingly passed over my grandmother and grandfather. Life had only left traces of happiness, peace and harmony on them.

Elysa descended the front steps towards us and embraced me in her arms. I felt welcome, appreciated and comforted. After putting my bags in the room reserved for me, we went to the table to eat. Throughout the meal, the mood was light. Even if I had wanted to, I would not have been able to talk about my preoccupations for fear of ruining that charming and precious moment of enchantment. After dinner, we cleared the table and washed the dishes. The cold spring air made it a perfect evening for a fire, so we lit one in the old stone fireplace. A subtle odor of pine and dry maple filled the room, and reflections from the flames lit up the shiny floor. The moment was right for opening up and talking. As I sipped my tisane, I told my story, recounting all the setbacks and misadventures that had befallen on me over the last several weeks.

My grandparents listened patiently, asking a few questions here and there to make sure they understood, and encouraged me to continue. When I had finished, a feeling of great relief swept through me and I broke down and sobbed freely, without shame, unable to stop. My grandmother held me in her arms while my grandfather, with his hand on my shoulder, told me to go ahead and let go of my pain, to let it all out.

I have no idea how long it took. I felt as if suspended in another dimension. Suddenly, the crackling of the fire brought me back to reality. Jerome had just put on another log, and was poking at the fire. I took another tisane and began to breath deeply and fully. It felt as if a dam had just broken down inside me, releasing emotions that had been blocked for a long time. I was exhausted, but also relieved and content. For a long time no one said a word, as if to give time the opportunity to catch up with me.

Just as the wave of silence had faded away, allowing reality to intrude once again on my consciousness, I heard my grandfather's voice as it gently pulled me from my own world. "Do you feel a little relieved, a little lighter with what you have just released son? It already looks like there is less tension in your face!"

"It did do me good, you're right, to release all that. But at the same time it makes me scared. I feel a bit discouraged. I can't see

23

how I will ever get out of this mess. I don't even know what I want, or where I'm going. I feel like giving up and abandoning everything." "You don't think that's perfectly normal given what's happened to you these last few weeks? Anybody, in your position would feel the same. You are not superhuman. Tonight you are worn out, but give yourself the chance to recover. Have faith in yourself. Give it some time." And then, as if to lighten the mood before we all retired for the evening, my grandfather asked me, in a mischievous tone and with a playful grin, "Do you know the story of the two frogs that fell into a bucket of milk?" Shocked by a question that seemed so completely out of context in the given circumstances, I told him that no, I had not.

"The two frogs actually resemble the two personalities within you. Everything was going well for them. As usual, they were playing in the cowshed, when all of the sudden, they fell into a bucket of milk. They immediately began to jump in an effort to escape from their desperate situation. After many failed attempts, they were both discouraged and exhausted, and had to stop to catch their breath. The first frog, after evaluating the situation, told the second, "There's nothing we can do. It's impossible. There's no way out of here. I have no more energy, I'm sore everywhere, I can't try any longer. Rather than suffer like this, I'm going to give up." Without hope and exhausted, she closed her eyes and let herself sink down into the milk. The second frog, even though she too was exhausted and could see no solution, wouldn't give up. She began to try again, jumping right and left, without stopping, refusing to think, not wanting to let feelings of despair drain her energy. Then suddenly, after many unsuccessful efforts, she began to sense that the consistency of the milk had changed. It had become thicker. She realized that her repeated movements had gradually transformed the milk into butter. A few more efforts and she was able to use this unexpected platform to jump free from her prison. The moral is that we never know what surprises life has in store for us!" That night I slept better than I had in a long, long time. Besides some frogs trying to eat some priests, my dreams were peaceful and untroubled. I woke the next morning feeling as if I had just awakened from a long state of hibernation. After taking a nice shower to freshen up, I went down to join Jerome and Elysa for breakfast. The two of them were fresh and lively, and looked as if they had already been up for a while. They were cheerily preparing one of those morning country feasts that would leave us feeling full and satisfied for the rest of the day.

After breakfast, all perked up from the night before, I said to my grandfather, "I understood the meaning of the story of the two frogs, and I don't feel I'm the first type. I have always tried and I don't think I'll start giving up now and abandon everything. It would not be a good thing to run away and skip my exams and graduation. I'd be letting years of effort slip through my fingers and go to waste. No, I think I'll continue, and at least finish off my classical studies. After that we'll see." As I listened to myself speak, I was surprised at the change in me. I was still skeptical that my depression of the previous day could transform into the desire to face a challenge that was still not well defined. What magic had been worked to help me this way? As if he could hear the thoughts running through my head my grandfather smiled understandingly.

As I looked at him smile, I added, "There are still some things that I don't understand, grandpa. It seems like I've wanted something all my life. I charged headfirst everywhere and into everything. I never let myself stop and I always went forward. So why now, all of the sudden, is nothing going well?" Jerome didn't answer right away. It's as if he was taking the time to re-examine every aspect of my situation and to clearly choose his words so that I could understand without being hurt or frightened. He spoke in a tone that was affectionate and reassuring.

"It's true that you always did have a lot of desire and persistence. You were able to overcome every challenge that blocked your path. And you did all this to the great satisfaction and pride of everyone around you, until recently.

"But all these achievements may have corresponded more with the expectations and demands of others rather than with your own personal choices. It's like homework given to an obedient student. We expect him to complete it according to established standards and rules. You always behaved as this good student, until recently, when you started to question those rules and standards. That's when everything started to go bad, provoking reticence on the part of some people.

"What has happened to you has been more or less inevitable. I have never known a well-established institution that could easily accept confrontation or being questioned. I have the feeling that is where you now stand. It is time for you to define your own challenges, those that will correspond with your aspirations and talents. It is time for you to stop trying to please everyone else and to choose for yourself.

"But it is not enough to have the will and to go for it. You must also know how to will. And that is neither obvious nor easy. It takes both clarity and courage to be able to think for yourself."

At that moment the telephone rang, interrupting Jerome. When he returned a few minutes later, he laughed as he told me, "That was Médé, my neighbor. He was coughing so much on the other end of the line that the receiver vibrated in my hand. It's unbelievable how much he smokes. He's finished with my bench saw and wants to come return it. I told him not to worry and that we would pass by and get it ourselves. It's ironic that he should call just as we were talking about will! Come with me, you'll see, him and his wife are special phenomena when it comes to will power.

My grandfather's neighbors were very unusual. What a clutter their house was! It looked as if a storm had passed through while

26

an earthquake had shaken the area. Everything seemed in disarray. Even so, Médé and his wife gave the impression of being two librarians amidst their well-organized book stacks. Médé gave us the tour and explained, in detail, all the renovation projects that he had done over the last five years. It was all one big unfinished project, from the basement to the attic, including the flower and vegetable gardens. Médé was on fire, bubbling with ideas as he explained to us, between coughing fits, how he was going to perfect this, improve that, add a little something on top or remove a little something on the bottom. He seemed completely incapable of finishing one project before starting another. Never have I heard so many "I should have's" and "I must's" as during that afternoon spent with them. "I should really quit smoking," he would say after turning crimson from coughing. "I should really re-organize the basement...I should really plan my projects before the summer." One after the other, like an endless litany.

Louisa, for her part, appeared a bit less agitated. She explained to us, with eloquence and conviction, her ultimate motto for life. It all had to do with the enlightened teachings of her latest positive thinking guru, who was spreading his good word to the poor, ignorant flock of the region. How wonderful and luminous this holy man was, with his jolly and rubicund picture sitting merrily on the chimney mantel! Life became so simple when you followed his teachings! And then there's the all-powerful visualization. All you have to do is see your goal in your mind and it will magically come true. It was that simple and easy. Flooding me with her marvelous certainties, Louisa showed me her shelves filled with books and brochures written by this saint of a man. She reminded me of an alchemist religiously handling her precious flasks of magical potions.

When I asked her about the other books filling the bookshelf beside, this brought a look of disdain to her face, "Those ones, if you want them you can have them. They are about happiness, positive thinking and other things of that nature. I have read them all, but there's nothing to them, it's not worth your trouble." I was impressed by the diversity of her interests, but also surprised at the clear-cut judgments she had for certain subjects. It was as if she wanted to sweep them from her field of conscience.

On the drive home I asked my grandfather whether his neighbor's wife had always preached her good news with such zeal and conviction. He had to stop himself from laughing at my dumbfounded and abashed look. After composing himself, he explained to me that for as long as he could remember, Louisa had always been a perpetual convert bursting with proselytism. "Her beliefs, while appearing so strong, actually change with the flow of the tide, he told me. Once the elation of novelty has faded, any smooth-talker with promises of guaranteed nirvana will get her to move any which way the wind is blowing. Today it's positive thinking. Yesterday it was reincarnation and past lives. I believe that all her life she's been surfing from one fad to another. She has had to literally change her personality dozens of times over without ever finding true satisfaction. Willing she does. She wants to progress, to better herself, to change, yet she's incapable of stopping and thinking for herself. She's a typical example of what we call **blind will**. She's always on the move, always going somewhere, but never with any lucidity or clarity of mind.

"I have known others like her. These individuals all share the same tendencies. They jump from one trend to another, passing from exaltation to disappointment without ever learning a thing. They are searching for that one magic recipe which requires, on their part, the least amount of effort and change. They have neither a vision nor a plan and rarely see something through to the end, opting instead to change their approach as circumstances dictate. This is brute and blind will.

"Médé, her husband, represents another type of will. All his life he's been saying the same thing, he should have done this or he should have done that. He is a man of wishful thinking. He has always known what he should do to improve himself and better his situation, yet the story of his life is one of unachieved desire. This is what I call **wishful wanting**, will that makes you dream but is nothing more than a wet firework.

"In life there are four kinds of people, each with their own type of will. Firstly, there are those that stubbornly refuse change. They don't want anything around them to move and are unable to see outside of their own little world. This is **immobilizing will**, the acceptance of neither evolution nor progress. Next, you have people like Médé, who would really like to grow yet are incapable of getting beyond that stage of **wishful will**. Third, there are people like Louisa, who move through life with their heads down, giving the illusion of progress with their **blind will**, yet never getting anywhere. Finally, there is the last type and unfortunately they are few and far between. I'm talking about those individuals that have the courage to want with their eyes wide open. These people never delude themselves with illusion, they realize it takes a lot of hard work to grow and progress. They don't wait for others to do their thinking for them. They possess sound judgment, relying on vision and lucidity. They are able to accept the fact that they will make mistakes and know how to make corrections when necessary. These people are not afraid to face life's challenges, yet are never reckless. These people are open-minded and intelligent, disciplined and creative at the same time. They have what I call **lucid will**. They realize that in order to move forward and evolve, you have to understand, to learn and to change. As for you, son, I believe that this is where you have arrived. You will no longer blindly go where others tell you. This is over for you. It is time for you to come to an understanding about what has happened to you and to learn your lessons from it. It is only with this type of clear and lucid will that you will be able to make the necessary changes in your life, and adjust and progress from here."

See the Direction

Over the course of the following three days, we never once discussed my preoccupations. We were drawn outdoors by the irresistibly mild spring weather. Spotty, disappointed that his playmates were too busy for him, watched with an air of resignation as we built a storage shed for the garden tools. The manual labor absorbed my thoughts, and the harmonious panoramic view soothed my spirit. I felt as if my life's concerns were returning once again to more human, more normal levels.

We finished our work late in the afternoon on the third day, and grandfather announced that our project was completed. We were sitting on the terrace, sipping an aperitif, breathing in the warm, tender fragrances of nature, when Jerome asked me where I was at with my thoughts. I responded that, "Things have started to become more clear. I have come to realize that once I started to question an established authority and form ideas and opinions on my own, the consequences would not always be positive. I understand that I must accept these consequences without losing sight of my own value. I also need to make my own choices about my career, regardless of what others will think. It is time for me to change my attitude and to stop depending so much on the validation of others. It is also time for me to define my own challenges and to cease from falling prey to every single request imposed upon me. I believe that I understand all this very well now. I've learned that I need to change my attitude and that I can, from now on, move forward by myself and for myself. My only big problem now, grandpa, is to clearly see where I should go. That is not yet apparent to me. A change is necessary, but for what?"

"You are right, son, grandfather told me. It is always easier to make a change when we know what that change should be. For the moment, you are aware that you need to adjust your attitude in order to feel better and take control of your life. But on the other hand, there is no point in just changing for the sake of change. How will it help to simply adopt new attitudes or behaviors that will, in the end, prove to be no more efficient? But as you say, that is where the difficulty lies. What will help guide you with your new decisions? What will help you choose one thing over another? What will help you to orient your behavior and your decisions from now on?"

I was a bit flabbergasted, faced with all those questions, not being able to see how I could ever work my way through it. As if he understood my feelings of helplessness, my grandfather said, as he affectionately tapped my shoulder, "Don't worry too much about this for the time being. You'll see, everything will work out…just give it some time. For now, you are like a ship's captain who has headed straight into the heart of a storm. He realizes that he must change his course. He knows that he needs to be more careful, cautious and efficient. But in order to ensure that he makes the right course correction, he must first figure out what the right direction is. So this is the point where he'll return to his maps, sit down, think and re-orient himself.

"To have a **lucid will**, is a basic quality, an essential predisposition that will help you make precise and pertinent choices. **To see the direction** is being able to turn ideas into concrete action. This requires taking out your own personal navigation maps in order to define your own course. That, son, is something that very few individuals take the time to do. The majority prefer to simply ride the waves and let the wind take them where it will, hoping that the gods and destiny are favorable. It takes some effort to find a good direction and to see where to go, and this is what scares most people." At this point, grandmother, who had been listening to us for quite some time, announced the end of our break. It was time to prepare the evening feast, one of the great pleasures of each day.

After the meal, while comfortably seated in front of the fireplace, I absentmindedly stroked Spotty. I was chatting with Jerome about one thing or another when Elysa finally joined us by the fire. "This afternoon I was listening as you discussed the importance of finding a direction in order to effectively achieve change. It is essential to figure out where we want to go if we want to have some success. In that sense, let me tell you a story about my father.

"It was during the 1920's, near the end of the great depression which rocked America and the world. Like everyone around us, we suffered greatly during this crisis. My father, who had always been a relatively successful and prosperous farmer, saw his savings melt away like snow in the sun. Not many people could afford to buy his fruits and vegetables; his regular clients had all gone bankrupt. With six children and almost no money coming in, he was forced to scrape the bottom of the drawers in order to survive. My sister, the eldest of the family, was finishing up her degree in engineering while my brother was studying law. Another brother hoped to follow in my father's footsteps, while another was showing artistic talents. The youngest, at 15, dreamed of becoming a pilot. For my part, I was 18 years old and finishing up my collegial studies.

"One Sunday, while gathered around the table for a family dinner, I saw my father lose his temper for the first time ever. Like every occasion of late, we talked about all the difficulties we faced and all the worries that tormented us. The more we discussed, the heavier the atmosphere became and the more depressed we all grew. This is when my father made us all jump up as he slammed his fist on the table. It wasn't that he had something against us, quite on the contrary. But he couldn't stand the situation anymore. 'That's enough, he told us, I've heard enough self-pity. We are not victims here; we are not haunted by bad luck or condemned by destiny! Everyone has been affected; everyone has suffered during this crisis. It is time that we wake up and take charge of our situation.'

"He explained that if we were ready and willing to take charge of our lives, we would never again have to suffer through anything else like this. Never again would we be dependent on an overly captive market, nor constrained by our lack of diversification. This was when he revealed his dream to us. This was also when I discovered that my father was a visionary. He was not a whimsical crank nor a lunatic daydreamer with his head stuck in the clouds. No, he was a true visionary, audacious, lucid and with both feet firmly planted in reality.

"My father dreamed of a true family enterprise, dynamic, diversified, opening up horizons beyond our own little corner of the world. He explained to us that each of us, if we wanted, would play an essential role in the business while still being able to fulfill our own dreams and personal goals. He captivated us with his words. Time was suspended. Something was in the air giving us all the impression that we could move mountains if we wanted.

"Under the patient and understanding guidance of my father, we all outlined the projects that were in our hearts. After intense discussions, the structure of a family enterprise began to take shape. Each one of us clearly saw our place and our role within this undertaking. We already had common objectives for the enterprise as well as our personal goals. We knew clearly where we wanted to go, and at the same time we were conscious of where we had to start from. We had just established a first directional map to guide us towards the dream that had now overtaken all of us.

"A few years later, the dream became reality. My brother, the farmer, had diversified and expanded our agricultural production. The artist had added a horticulture production of flowers and exotic trees, opening up the landscape design market. My sister, the engineer, helped us penetrate the agricultural machinery market by perfecting and adapting equipment according to the client's needs. The youngest did indeed become a pilot. This allowed us to develop an airline company for our products and helped us reach markets that would otherwise have been inaccessible. My brother, the lawyer, took care of the legal side of the business. As for me, I became the financial controller of the whole enterprise and helped my father with the administration and coordination of our family corporation. The business is going very well to this day, and I continue to be involved for both pleasure and passion.

"What I learned most from all those wonderful years working with my father was the importance of finding a direction, of having a vision. In that sense, the strength of my father was his ability to globally visualize all sorts of situations. He never made a decision without considering a whole ensemble of factors, whether relating to our internal operations, our clients, our markets, and the political or economic context…in short, every element that could possibly influence either our evolution or our functioning. What made him a great leader was his global, coherent, intelligent vision that could be translated into a concrete action plan. This enabled us to distinguish ourselves from our competitors and to achieve the success that we did.

"What I also discovered by working with him, was that finding a direction and having a global vision is valuable everywhere, whether it be for an enterprise, in economy or politics…or for an individual. When you know where you're going, it's much easier to adapt because you know that the changes you must make will help you get closer to your dream. Without a clear vision toward your direction, you risk making course corrections that might head you into yet another storm. You'll exhaust yourself trying to get out of it without knowing exactly why you have to do it. You'll end up overextending yourself, using up all your strength and energy, as many people and enterprises do. You'll finally take your flags down, letting the currents overtake your ship, or worse, jumping ship and abandoning it all."

My grandmother's last few comments jolted me. I had been deeply touched by the whole story. How could I possibly disagree with the logical and obvious reality that she had just described? I was excited yet frightened all at the same time. Could I succeed in finding a real direction for myself? Do I have it in me to define a vision that is both global and concrete? As if to calm me down from the doubts that were now running through my head, my grandmother added, "Don't worry too much about a global vision for now. Don't look for perfection right from the start, or else you risk paralyzing your spirit. My father did not become a great strategist overnight. You have to start somewhere, so try to give yourself the best possible direction for the moment. Keenness and experience come with time. The idea is to first figure out how you see yourself as a young adult, for instance five years from now. Take into consideration all the different aspects that are most important in your life, like your career, family plan, social aspects, health, financial plan, friendship, religious dimension…and whatever else. Try to describe how you would like each to be and give yourself objectives to achieve in five years. This will help you decide what aspects are most important for you to develop, those that will become your pillars of success, the key factors of what you want to accomplish. Then set some short-term goals for the coming year. As you can see, the idea is really quite simple. You clearly define where you want to go for each important sector of your life. You look at where you are starting from for each sector, and then, by setting short and medium term goals, you give yourself a directional map to guide your progression. This is what we did with my father when we decided, on one fine Sunday, to buy into his dream!"

Staying on Course

That night, my sleep was restless. I was tormented by a recurring dream in which I was building a house. I had set up the structure, assembled the rooms and erected the walls. Then suddenly, as with each time, the whole thing begins to tremble and shake and finally crumbles to the ground. I am sitting on a rock, feeling completely exhausted and discouraged, when I notice a small hydroplane on the lake in front of me. A man, wearing aviator glasses and an aviator helmet, gets out of the plane and stands on the end of the dock. He then walks towards me, carrying a suitcase. When he reaches me he hands me the suitcase and says, "You haven't consulted your plans, you forgot your pillars. That's why everything fell apart. Take the time to look over your plans, it's important if you want it to stay up." I open the suitcase and take out a bundle of papers, yellowed from time. I look over several sheets, but there is nothing on them. They are all blank.

The shock woke me from my sleep. As dawn was not far off, I decided to take a walk and try to put some order into my thoughts. It was very peaceful outside; the sky was still full of stars, bathing the countryside in a diaphanous glow. The invigorating atmosphere of the coming dawn managed to lift my spirit and my thoughts did become a bit clearer. The vision of what I hoped to become, started to take shape in my head.

I returned to the house as the sun was rising. Upon my approach, I noticed my grandfather on the terrace looking out on the lake and mountains. He was wearing a "gi", the traditional clothing of the martial arts. I knew that during his stay in Japan, he had met several masters reputed for their expertise in karate and aikido. I knew very little about the martial arts and this was the first chance I ever had to truly appreciate the finesse of this art. I stayed a bit removed and I watched Jerome executing a series of movements with the ease and agility of a young man of 20 years of age. His movements were at once a precise ritualistic gesture, a harmonious dance and a fascinating demonstration of concentration and internal strength. I was completely absorbed by the hypnotic chain of movements that unfolded before my eyes. When he was finished, grandfather remained calm and unmoving for a very long while. His breathing was deep and regular and I had the sensation that an intense energy source was emanating from him.

It wasn't until after breakfast that grandfather again brought up the subject of my preoccupations. It was the last day of my visit, and I was anxious to share my morning reflections with him. I understood that the most important thing for me, was not first and foremost to find a profession, to define my social status nor to find my place among the rich and affluent as fast as possible. I was not interested in getting caught up in an adult world that to me appeared to be dull and dimensionless. I needed more; I needed to challenge myself and to explore my limits. I needed to take action and to be physically active. At the same time, I was also overcome by an immense intellectual curiosity that I was determined to satisfy.

When I visualized myself as an adult, a few years from then, it was also important to me that I became very competent in my domain as well as helpful to others. I had the desire and need to continually push myself to my intellectual and physical limits. I also wanted to quickly become autonomous and financially independent. I saw myself pursuing a degree in psychology, but the degree was long and at that time I didn't have the financial resources to follow that course of action. So instead, I thought I might first get my degree in physical education. The curriculum was shorter and the possibility of finding work was very good. I would be able to fulfill my desire for physical training, pursue my university education, and become autonomous and financially independent in the shortest time possible. More specific goals had already begun to form in my mind. I wanted to get my first diploma within two years. Then, I thought I would work for two or three years, save up some money and return to university and study psychology for the next few years. Besides that, I wanted to do some traveling, and take up martial arts, something that had interested me for some time now.

Grandfather listened attentively as I related the fruit of my reflections. After a long approving silence, he told me, "Bravo, that's very good. You have made a great deal of progress in only a few days. When you arrived, you were lost, without hope, in a deep state of depression. And now, you have succeeded in giving yourself a direction to follow. You have in front of you a future reference image that you want to make real, a dream to realize. What's also good is that you haven't just considered one aspect of your life; you haven't grabbed the first lifeline thrown your way to temporarily lift your spirit. You have taken the time to examine the situation in a more global manner. You had the courage to consider your overall needs, tastes and constraints while making your decisions. You have set short as well as medium-term goals for yourself. You have also given yourself a good directional map to guide your course over the next few years.

"All that is very good, but that's not all. This is a great starting point. But you have to ensure this will happen. In life, there is a time to create, a time to structure and a time to act. An artist doesn't just set himself in front of a blank canvas and create a masterpiece from pure inspiration. Unfortunately, we imagine that the inspiration and talents of great artists were gifts from God, and that only those with extraordinary minds can create extraordinary things. These are illusions that allow us to dream of achieving fantastic results without any effort.

"In reality it is not as simple and easy as that. Behind every great masterpiece or work-of-art, there was first a vision. While in Asia, I knew these great masters of pictorial art. Before creating an exceptional masterpiece, they were inhabited by the image, the sensation or the impression of what they wanted to reproduce. In certain cases, the experience was even painful because they couldn't clearly see what they wanted to express. Then, bit-by-bit, the vision would become clearer, it would start to take shape and materialize. This is the stage of pure creativity. In and of itself, this is still only a starting point. Next, come the outlines, the sketches, the plans, to try and give a more concrete appearance to the vision. This is the structuring stage that permits the project to take shape. The general look of the painting begins to emerge. It's not until this point that the artist actually starts working on the canvas, adding details, tones and colors. This is the stage of precise action, where the painting will often be corrected or adjusted until the vision of the start has finally been transformed into a work-of-art.

"Upon returning from Japan, I decided, along with a friend, to realize a dream that I'd had for a long time. We wanted to travel around the world by boat. Before starting anything, we needed to precisely define our project and to develop a clear global vision of the route we wanted to take. Seated in front of our world maps, we made many outlines until we finally came up with a course that we were both happy with. We then gave ourselves a limit of 18 months. After that we set some very specific goals for our itinerary, with specific destinations and time frames. In this way, we clearly defined our vision, and gave ourselves a directional map to guide us through the 18 months.

"This was still just a starting point for our project, the stage of creation. We now had to ensure that we would effectively **stay on course** throughout the journey. So we made a very detailed action plan, taking into account every possible detail, from boat preparations, to traveling from one place to another on the open sea. This isn't to say that everything happened as planned. But without this stage of detailed planning, we would have lost our skin at several points along the way. Finally, once we had come up with an operation plan we were satisfied with, we were ready to put it into action. Each day, throughout the journey, despite the quality and precision of our operation plan, we had to take our bearing in order to be sure we were still in line with our charted destination. This was the only way to stay on course and make the necessary corrections if we wanted to attain our objectives in accordance with our directional map.

"As you can see, son, in order to create a work-of-art, realize a personal dream, or complete any other project, you go through the same steps in order to succeed. You always need a clear and precise vision of what you want and the direction to follow. A clear vision doesn't just happen as many people like to think. It requires time, effort and thought. The vision has to become structured by making outlines, sketches and operation plans, being as precise as possible. This is the only way to methodically trace a route to follow and to assure you **stay on course** once the plan goes into action. Once you jump into action, you'll also need a method for checking your progress, and taking your bearing when you step back and survey the situation. This is the only way to make the necessary and inevitable course changes along the way if you want to attain your goals, to go all the way and turn your dreams into reality.

"You remember the story of Elysa's father. It's the same kind of progression he followed during the development and realization of his dream of a family business. He must have made dozens of operation plans and changes to **stay on course** and achieve his ultimate goal. When Elysa and I decided to realize our dream to live as we do now, we did the same thing. We first came up with a clear vision of everything we needed. We then made a precise action plan of what we had to accomplish in the next five years. We put in the effort and made the necessary adjustments along the way to achieve our goal. As you can see, everything is possible when you know how, and have the will and courage to go all the way.

"It's the same thing for you. You have a much clearer vision of the direction you want to follow and you have given yourself clear objectives. It is important that from this day forward, if you truly want to stay on course, you make yourself an action plan for the next few months, and be as precise as possible. If you want to continue your studies and train in martial arts, you will have to manage your time efficiently. Take care of yourself and make time for relaxation and rest so that you want over-extend yourself and burn out right away. Give yourself some very precise short-term goals so that you can take your bearings on a regular basis and thus stay on course with your studies, your training and your work. If you do this the right way and if you are methodical you will realize all your dreams and aspirations and live your life to fulfill your true potential."

To Live Strategically

The conversation I had with my grandfather and the examples he related filled me with enthusiasm and a renewed spirit. New horizons were opening up in front of me. Anything was possible and life took on that special hue that only intense moments of happiness can confer.

After lunch, Jerome and I took advantage of the time we had left to take one last nature walk in the mild and peaceful air of those first days of spring. A gentle wind caressed us with the spicy humus fragrance of the forest of conifers and leafy trees bordering my grandfather's property. Even though it was still early in the season, we had the impression that it would not be long before the buds would be blooming, sprinkling their tender shades of green against the darker backdrop of the neighboring conifers. The stream that ran along the edge of the property was still swollen with clear, cold water from melting snow. Everywhere we looked, we could sense the sun was working hard to restore life to this still numb world of nature.

It wasn't until late in the afternoon when Jerome and Elysa drove me to the bus station. As we sat in an old shiny armchair in a remote corner of the terminus, grandfather said to me, "Over the course of these last few days, we have discussed at great length how to realize one's dreams and ultimately, let's be honest, how to **achieve success in life**. And the way to do this essentially rests on creating a logical approach to follow, an approach which in turn relies on three major principles: to have a **lucid will**, to change and progress, to clearly and globally **see the direction** to follow and to rely on specific methods to ensure **staying on course**. The secret to effectively employing each of these principles is to remain practical, and above all else, to be methodical. You have to be ready to make the necessary effort, think well before acting and have the guts to go all the way.

"Proper use of a methodical approach gives you a strategy for success. Without an effective strategy, **success** is just not possible...never forget that. There is however, yet another aspect that must not be neglected. A strategy is not merely a method or a systematic procedure. A strategy has a soul and this soul is built on the value and belief systems of the individual or the organization that shapes the strategy. This soul is what gives the shade and tone to your strategy. It is the driving force connecting all the elements together. It will influence and determine the type of vision or dream one will aspire to, the objectives that are set and the methods to employ to attain one's end. Those who primarily long for power will not use the same means, nor have the same objectives as those who thirst for knowledge or creation. Those who yearn for money will utilize a completely different strategy than those who wish for peace and harmony.

"But don't forget, son, that a value system does not guarantee success. It can often have no correlation with accomplishment. You can be a con man or a saint and still reach your objectives and realize your dreams...give yourself the impression of a successful life. On the other hand, if you fail to use a methodical approach or an efficient strategic process, whether a con man or a saint, you have very little chance of success. I am telling you all this because you, especially, should be aware of this threat. You have based your life on what we call a system of positive values. You believe in harmony, peace, justice and the value of others. You want to help people, to develop your potential and to find balance. Never forget that not everyone shares your values and beliefs. Too many people make the mistake of thinking that it is enough to be honest, work hard and have potential in order to achieve their dreams, accomplish their goals and succeed. Nothing is more dangerous than enclosing yourself within this naïve belief, because your strategy also becomes tinted with naivety. Your vision will fail to be sufficiently global and you will be vulnerable to the methods exploited by those in quest of power or money, or by the egotists centered on their own self-image. Never forget that the soul and structure of a strategy are inseparable. The effectiveness of your strategy depends as much on your ability to be methodical as on your lucidness and clear-sightedness."

As my grandfather spoke these last few words, my final boarding call sounded in the waiting room. As she hugged me good-bye, grandmother softly said, "I am happy that you are feeling better and are more serene. I believe that you will emerge from all this very admirably. But, don't try to achieve everything all in one breath. Give time the time it needs to help you to mature. Be patient and have confidence in yourself." Grandfather, for his part, said nothing as he gave me a warm handshake. From his eyes I could sense his internal force and I took a bit of his energy, will and assurance with me.

On the trip home, I admired the countryside as it changed shape and color under the salmon reflections of the setting sun. Everything seemed prettier and more luminous than during my trip out. Although the situation waiting for me at home was still the same, it weighed less heavily on me. My manner of looking at and interpreting things had slowly changed over the course of my stay with my grandfather. I understood that at the heart-of-the-matter, in life, things were neither positive nor negative; they were merely events upon which we placed significance. It is the color of our own internal filter that gives life the appearance of either happiness or sadness. Over the years, I have since had many opportunities to verify this phenomenon, in my personal life as well as in my professional life. My contact with my grandfather forever changed my filter and granted me the assurance that my life was under my control.

I learned another extremely important lesson during my visit: NOTHING IS MAGICAL. Miracle solutions do not exist. I realized that I needed to employ concrete methods to achieve control over my own life. They were right there at my fingertips; all I needed was to utilize them. The beauty of it was the simplicity of the method…but this was at the same time its danger. It is so simple that we sometimes don't take the time or put in the effort to make use of them. The **lucid will** to progress, to **see the direction** and **staying on course**…it was so obvious yet God knows how quickly we tend to forget these three motors of **success**.

By returning to these principles, grandfather taught me how to establish a **strategy** for my life. He helped me understand that I should stop waiting for things to happen to me and that I could shape my very existence on my own. I became aware of the importance of visualizing with lucidity all of life's possibilities, to set my objectives and to apply concrete methods to attain them. It was solely up to me to establish my own personal directional map and to regularly check my progress and make the necessary course corrections when needed.

In deciding to live strategically, I acknowledged that failure no longer existed. There could only be fragments of a strategy that proved to be less efficient, yielding less than the expected results. I simply had to recognize what hadn't worked, to learn from my mistakes and to modify my strategy accordingly. I no longer believed in dark fate or bad luck. Even unexpected events could be regarded as challenges helping me to modify and refine my strategy.

From that moment on, everything in my life became lighter and easier. I effortlessly completed my collegial studies. I even wrote my year-end exams with a smile on my face because I knew it was all part of my short-term and medium-term strategic plan. This is not to say that things were always easy for me since then. My journey has known storms and tempests as well as flat calms.

Never, on the other hand, did these difficult times bring me to the brink of depression or burnout. Discouraging and depressing passes did occur, that's normal. One must live through these times of sorrow. But during these difficult periods, I always heard this little voice inside me saying, "This is nothing more than a bump along the path, even if you see it as huge for the moment, you will end up coming out stronger and more solid than before. This is a challenge to help you grow. Live your sorrow, let yourself cry and digest your pain. Once you have emptied all your disappointment and grief, and erased your self-pity, it will be time to understand, learn and change."

PART 1

BLOW AWAY YOUR LIMITS

Chapter 1

TO CHOOSE FREEDOM

Those unforgettable days spent with my grandfather during the spring of 1965 enabled me to open the door to an extraordinary world where obstacles were nothing more than challenges and limits only existed to be surpassed. This is the world inhabited by those rare men and women who have decided not to wait for destiny and chance to decide their fates. It is a fascinating universe, far from always being rose-colored and easy; but to those that are willing to dive right into it, it brings to them the ultimate gratification of reaching one's potential and realizing one's most fantastic dreams. This unique reality is where exceptional human beings, through work and patience, become true **champions**.

The True Meaning of Champions

Years and experience have given me the chance to meet champions of all kinds. I worked at training them when I was a martial arts instructor. I had the opportunity to help others optimize their performance, both in the domain of sport as well as in the performing arts. I collaborated with people in the field of business, either company presidents or managers, who wanted to push themselves in an effort to attain the objectives they had set. Many times I rubbed shoulders with excellence. Not superficial excellence, bestowed ceremoniously through either titles or dust-collecting trophies that throw powder in your eyes. No, I'm talking about undeniable excellence, the kind that is at the base of all extraordinary achievement. Not like the straw fire, which exists only as a momentary flash of brilliance, but more like the staying power of deep waves, irresistible and potent, which enable us to attain veritable summits. This type of excellence can neither be bought nor improvised. It is forged through time, effort, perceptiveness and tenacity. This is the excellence of genuine **champions**.

For many people, the term champion is limited to the notion of conqueror, the winner of an event, a competition or a contest. This manner of interpretation represents a very narrow vision of reality. It leaves room for only one champion, whoever takes home the victory. It exists in a universe that solely favors officially confirmed records, trophies and medals. Instead, excellence and surpassing oneself are far from being limited by the definitions of a restricted universe. The notion of champion, in my eyes, has a much wider sense, a more fundamental nature. As I can attest, real champions are, first and foremost, remarkable people who throughout their lives have continuously tried to push themselves past their limits. Whether elite athletes, eminent artists, exceptional coaches, accomplished virtuoso or unequaled professionals, they all have one thing in common. They all believe they are responsible for their own success; it belongs to them. Achievement does not depend upon others nor external factors, but upon the will and effort they put toward attaining the goals they have set.

For real champions, success is not just represented by trophies, titles or medals. I don't mean to imply that these extrinsic rewards have no importance or are little appreciated. They are highly coveted prizes as they symbolize the consecration of long and arduous journeys, full of sacrifices and numerous repetitions. But as lusted after as they are, these rewards merely represent the visible point of the process, where genuine accomplishment rests upon the ability of the champion to reach increasingly more demanding goals. It is only through examining the way champions behave in order to attain their goals and **blow away their own limits**, that we can truly appreciate these champions' performances as art and discover the keys to success and the secrets of achievement.

When I knew Kim she was in her early twenties. She was training for her black belt in karate and was taking my course on the psychology of efficiency and performance. Within the course syllabus, each student was required to develop and implement a psychological plan for the optimization of a performance either for himself or herself or someone else. It was at this time that Kim came to talk with me about the difficulties she was having with her martial arts. Over the course of the first four years of training everything had gone well. She was talented and had progressed rapidly. She achieved all her goals, successfully going through each step of her belts and won many competitions. But, at the dawn of her passage to the black belt, everything seemed to become more difficult. She felt less sure of herself and became less successful in competition. With all her potential, her instructors were unable to understand why she was "choking" like that.

Together we examined her method of functioning in both training and competition. Since several weeks, she had lost sight of her methodical preparation plan for each event. She no longer set precise technical and tactical goals as she had done before. She wanted so much to win and placed so much importance on getting her black belt, that she was stuck, having lost the very lucidity of spirit that had made her a champion-in-the-making. Once she understood the possible source of her problem, it was as if an enormous weight had been lifted from her shoulders. The fog began to dissipate. I suggested she design her performance optimization plan to fit her needs and use it to help get her black belt. Together, we fine-tuned a psychological training program to help control her energy level, her concentration and her way of thinking regarding competition. She then put aside thoughts of title and victory and returned to her methodical preparation of setting precise technical, tactical and psychological goals for herself. A few months later she succeeded in passing her black belt and decided to follow her performance optimization program all the way to the world championships. That year she became world champion in each and every category for her style of karate.

On returning from the championships, she told me how it went, saying, "You completely changed my way of looking at karate and my training. I thought the black belt and world championships were the only things worth conquering. I have since realized that both victory and defeat are nothing but two lures, two liars that you must not dwell upon. The real achievement is elsewhere. It is actually linked to each of the objectives that brought me to the point where I could surpass my limits and discover a side of me I never knew existed. Getting my black belt and winning the world championships gave me enormous pleasure, that's for sure. But for me these now represent the events that taught me that I have a long way to go, many things to master and, at the same time, that I have a genuine capacity for achieving them."

In a similar manner as Kim, I can't forget Josée, one of my first patients in private practice. In her late thirties, her face slightly rounded with a look of sheer panic, she came into my office wearing these enormous radio headphones that completely covered her ears. Almost sprinting, she sat down in front of me and immediately told me in a strangled voice, "Doctor…doctor…I have a crisis…" Her eyes then rolled upward and her head fell back. Quickly, I moved behind her, holding her up, and told her, in a voice that was as calming and reassuring as possible, "There is no crisis…you can control it…don't worry about a thing, you'll be OK…I'm here to help you, don't be afraid." I had absolutely no idea what the nature of the crisis was and was in fact worried she would pass out on the carpet or stir up panic among the other patients in the waiting room.

As obvious as it seems, my reaction was the right one. Josée opened her eyes, brought her head back up and calmed down. Then, looking around the room as if she was worried the devil would suddenly appear, she removed her headphones and turned her attention on me. A bit more confident and reassured, she could then tell me what had caused her feeling of helplessness.

Diagnosed as epileptic since quite a while, she had come to control her crises through adequate medication. But in time – and only God knows how all this could have started – she developed a fear of noise. The slightest sound that was even a bit too loud would provoke an epileptic crisis in her, despite medication. She would then faint, lose her urine and embarrass everyone in her entourage. She became so terrified that noise became like the plague to her. The more fearful she became, the more she noticed each sound, convinced it would provoke the very thing she hoped to avoid. She so much wanted to avoid a crisis that she actually prepared herself for it, just by thinking about it, and would suffer one when exposed to the slightest sound. The more time passed, the more she avoided risky situations; she lived like this, confined to her room, at her parents', headphones over her ears, constantly aware of every sound in the house likely to provoke a crisis. You can just imagine the courage it took for her to leave her house, come to my office and sit down in front of me!

Today, Josée is cured. She realized her greatest victory the day she, on her own, walked through her village, passing in front of a municipal mechanics' garage where violent and unexpected noises come at any time, went into the neighboring woods and gathered mushrooms. Josée had learned to overcome her handicap and live with her illness. This victory was her dream. It had been in her head since her first days of therapy. It took many weeks of work and lots of pain, to arrive at this result. But she prevailed, with courage, open eyes and by methodically working to correct and adjust her behavior and her way of thinking. Week after week, she gave herself concrete objectives, continually more precise and demanding. She used practical methods to attain them and break through the limits she had herself created. Because of this courage, this performance and this achievement, Josée will always remain a champion to me, in the same way as Kim who, in her world, worked to surpass her own limits.

Each one of us, like Kim and Josée, can achieve our goals, realize our dreams and reach our potential. We are all born with the capability and capacity to become champions, remarkable human beings. When we don't succeed or blossom the way we would have hoped, it's because somewhere we are blocking our own possibilities, holding ourselves back from where we want to go. Thus we become our own worst enemy. We are transformed into break specialists and obstacle experts, shackling ourselves and blocking our own progression.

Despite their success, champions are no different. They are subject to the same tendencies to shackle themselves. Everyone is born with the capacity to achieve success. But along the way, we learn to build blocks and obstacles and erect the walls of our own prison. The only difference, for champions, is they have discovered the means to break their bonds and escape from their chains of constraint. They have, each and every one of them, found the keys enabling them to open the door of their own self-created jail. With patience and effort they have learned to use these keys effectively. They are free to surpass their limits and to realize their dreams. This is the secret: discover the keys that will allow you to open wide the door of your prison, the prison that you, yourself constructed, little by little, over time.

Freedom or Captivity

Upon coming into this world, there exists within each of us two extremely fertile grounds, both still virgin yet completely different. One is particularly favorable to the seeds of blossom while the other is perfect for the grains of stifling. These two fertile fields will produce fruit in accordance with the coincidences we encounter along our route, the events we live and the people we meet. Once we begin to tame the reality around us, events, circumstances and people become the gardeners of our life. They sow, fertilize and tend to our internal soil up until the point when we are able to gradually take charge of our garden for ourselves.

During these first few years, all sorts of grains are planted, those of stifling as well as those of blossoming. Our two different fields begin to produce. According to the situation and circumstances, when we take charge of our own garden, one field may already be more productive than the other. Despite the condition of our two soils, we should never forget we have become our own gardener. No matter what state our seeds are in, from that moment on, it is up to us alone to take charge of our garden and maximize the blossoming potential of our soil. Nevertheless, despite our desires and will, our choice in life is not an easy one. Nothing is ever conquered or won definitively. Unless we are completely attentive to the state of development of our two fields, the soil favorable to suffocation could always continue to produce, develop and eventually dominate the field favorable to blossoming. Champions have well understood this reality. They never once let their guard down by abandoning themselves to the quietude of their fleeting victories, resting in the false certainty that they have finally reached the summit of an immutable achievement.

During the course of our lives, we are constantly subjected to the influence of gardeners of all molds. Whether it is our parents, teachers, bosses, friends, religious leaders or politicians…it doesn't matter, all these people cross our path, plant their seed and leave us with something. If these people have a champion's mentality, they will sow our garden of blossoming, enabling us to fertilize it and they will implant in us the desire to become champions for ourselves. On the other hand, others will continually seed our garden of suffocation and shackles. I call these people the "limit makers". They become the tyrants of our existence. These despots will constantly be found along our route, it's inevitable. Throughout life, we shall be continuously forced to make a fundamental and inescapable choice. Either we allow the grains of suffocation to overrun our garden, shackling ourselves and becoming prisoners of fate. Or, we separate out the good grain, cultivate all our capacities and possibilities, and strive to realize our full blossoming potential.

As autonomous human beings, this is the most fundamental choice we must make. Live free or become prisoners. Follow the way of champions or let suffocation gradually transform us into tyrants. Life constantly presents us with the choice between these two avenues: one opens toward **liberty** and the other leads toward **captivity**, the way of a **champion** or that of a **tyrant**. It is up to each of us to choose our own direction.

Many people try to bypass this fundamental choice, to avoid this inalienable responsibility that only humans have the conscience to possess. How many times have I heard, "Oh yes, but if my parents had been different…yes but, if my wife or my husband had acted another way…yes, but if my coach had been more competent…if my boss knew how to appreciate me…if only I lived somewhere else other than this damn country…" and more of the same! Too many people put the blame for their unhappiness and troubles onto someone else's back, or on the fault of circumstances, actually on everything outside of themselves. In acting like this, they think they can escape the walls of their prison when in fact they are tightening their chains of constraint. Nothing can ever be perfect around us. There is no such thing as a parent without faults. The ideal job has not yet been created. The irreproachable boss and the always-exemplary employee do not exist. The perfect relationship or friendship is nothing but a utopian dream and paradise on earth is but an illusion. As long as imperfect humans are alive to interact with other imperfect humans, there will be power struggles, conflicts, games of influence and schemes to control or dominate. These are the inevitable remnants of the ancient struggle to survive, gain territory and dominate, having remained implanted in our brains and clinging to our skin since we began to evolve. All these power struggles awake and inevitably attract tyrants seeking to profit from each and every circumstance that comes along. Whether they are parents, friends, teachers, bosses, religious leaders or politicians, these oppressors incessantly attempt to control the very people they say they want to help or set free. They favor ignorance, helplessness, manipulation and coercion to cultivate our suffocation and uphold the chains around our feet. They confine us within our prison, just until, because of their influence and without us even knowing, we are transformed into tyrants in their image.

The Limit Makers

While seated comfortably next to the window, heading toward Paris on a 747, I was immersed in an amicable discussion with Colin, my immediate neighbor. From the start of the flight I easily struck up a conversation with this friendly man, showing energetic traits and a look of keen wit and intelligence. We talked about all sorts of things, our preoccupations, our professions, and ourselves. Colin was a minister of the cult and was educated as a lawyer. He was a respected leader among the black community in America.

This was around the time when the famous O.J. Simpson trial was shaking up the United States. To my surprise, Colin was not wrapped up in the whole issue, contrary to all the talk I'd heard from the black community over the last few weeks. He explained that he had distanced himself from the pressure groups he was once a part of. He no longer felt at ease with certain ideas advocated by Ephraïm, the group leader, and could no longer pretend to agree with positions he didn't believe in. I had the opportunity to listen to Ephraïm speak, a few days earlier, on television. He denounced all the injustices that blacks had suffered throughout the course of history. All that wasn't black seemed to be a threat to his race and his liberty. Everywhere, there were exploiters of his brothers and sisters of color, profiteers that wanted to reduce them to silence and slavery. The only way for them to protect and defend themselves was to become aggressive, attack and fight. The way out of their situation was through confrontation and the control, of course, should go to him, their enlightened leader and uncontestable trustee of this necessary power.

Colin told me he had started to increasingly doubt Ephraïm and all his type who brought up the same arguments, with the same themes, supposedly to liberate their brothers and sisters from secular oppression. "You see, he told me, no one can deny we were subjected to many injustices and inequalities. We knew oppression and it exists still in many forms. It should never be accepted. It should ultimately be denounced if we ever want it to stop. Having access to power is also essential if we want to change things. But, what I'm afraid of is power for power's sake, to be right just so the other is wrong and in the end perpetuating the same errors and inequalities that we have denounced. I'm starting to see through the big mouths that talk the same easy speech. When we look behind their words, they offer no alternatives, no tools to take control of our destiny and define our own futures. They have but one word in their mouth: power. It's all about their own personal power. I do not believe that wanting to kill or eliminate the tyrant that oppresses you is the best solution. That's the short-term and easy way that can blindly lead to wars of power, oppression and injustice. We risk being transformed into tyrants against our brothers. I have witnessed the symptoms of this new despotism. As soon as one among us starts to challenge the ideas of these movement leaders, he is rejected on a plea of weakening or betraying the cause. I don't believe this is the way we will build a more serene future. There is a strong chance that we will be exchanging four quarters for one dollar and become despotic tyrants without improving anything. I can no longer accept this situation and I have withdrawn a step backwards. I need to think. Even though I am brushed aside or, maybe, temporarily rejected, I believe that I must do something. It's time for a little more intelligence to take control of the brute force and oppose blindness. I am ready to take this risk because I don't want us to be back with chains around our feet in this paradise of their own they are trying to sell us."

Colin's decision was not easy. It certainly would take him down a difficult road, going mostly against the tide of a very popular wave gaining more and more force within his community. It brought a lot of risks and potential negative consequences for his career and future. But this was the only decision that he could make, because to close his eyes against the shackles that he saw, was to renounce his human liberty and bury himself alive in his prison of illusions. He had decided to go beyond his limits and, like every champion, was ready to assume the risks and consequences.

The choice is always ours. All along the course of life, we have an awful lot of occasions to exercise this choice, as limit setters are numerous and omnipresent. In my profession, I have witnessed them in action wherever there are human relations, whether it be with family, among friends, in the world of sport or in the milieu of businesses and organizations. It is always fascinating to observe them, and the subtleties of their manipulations – whether conscious or not – will never cease to surprise and shock me.

No matter their mode of functioning – whether they are dominators, profiteers, destroyers, frustrated or narrow-minded individuals, or those blinded by their own insecurities – these limit makers are nothing more than **energy thieves**. In stealing the energy of others, they suffocate everything around them that's dynamic and has potential. Everything they touch ends up weakened, withered, faded or even dead. Whether it is a matter of conserving their power or advantage, preserving their image, their control or their acquired rights, protecting their weaknesses or incompetence, and keeping us within the narrow limits of their insecurity or restricted universe, they will always seek, consciously or unconsciously, to maintain the chains around our feet. Whether by their actions, attitude, behavior, example, influence or constraint, the result is the same: they impede the blossoming of others and limit the capacities for achievement and success of those organizations, businesses, systems or nations subject to their influence.

Champions are no more immune than we are against the influence of these tyrannical individuals. They were all subjected, at one time or another, to their schemes and ploys. But they never entered into the limit makers' games and always refused to be transformed into energy thieves. They succeeded in blowing up the restrictive universe of those who sought to dominate and control them. They have, in their life, made a fundamental choice: that of **liberty**.

Chapter 2

THE SECRETS OF CHAMPIONS

I t is not easy to free ourselves from the influence of limit makers. Throughout our lives, at one time or another, we have all
encountered energy thieves who have left remnants of their influence inside us. In this regard, as human beings, we are all the
same, all equal. Each and every one of us has suffered the impact
of various tyrants who have gifted us with the seeds of shackles
capable of eroding our freedom.

These shackles that restrain us and hold us back are myths we
maintain, ideas we believe in, or recurrent messages we repeat in
our head to confine us within our own explicit limits.

No one comes into this world feeling incapable of achievement or
accomplishment. The notion of powerlessness is acquired gradually through learning and experience. When constantly told we are
incapable or prone to failure, we finally end up believing it. We
internalize these messages and limit our own personal possibilities.

When we constantly hear that the risks are too big, that people will
lose respect for us or no longer accept us if we don't succeed, we
eventually develop a fear of consequences, rendering us unable to
act. If we learned that we always have to be perfect beings in
order to be appreciated or loved, we impose obligations upon ourselves that restrain us, stifle us, and drain our energy. When we
were repeatedly told, while faced with the least difficulty, that we

are unlucky or that, poor us, we deserve to be pitied because of the slightest misfortune, we learn to feel sorry for ourselves. Instead of taking matters into our own hands, we crumble in the face of adversity. When we were persuaded that everything is owed us, that success falls from the sky or that we have to wait for prince charming to make us happy, we were given the gift of "magical thinking". Life becomes a lottery and we enclose ourselves within a dream and utopia instead of creating our own happiness.

When we buy into these messages, ideas and myths of helplessness, and allow them to become instilled within us, we renounce our fundamental responsibility of becoming masters of our own gardens. Once we let ourselves award importance to these sources of ineffectiveness, we heighten the power of our own shackles. When we cease fighting and confronting them, we become our own worst enemy and increasingly confine ourselves within our own internal prison. We block our own blossoming and prevent ourselves from succeeding and realizing our true potential. By submitting to the slavery of our self-made shackles, we end up abandoning the fight. We put down our arms and close our eyes in order to choose the way of compliance. Without even realizing it, we have sided with the **energy thieves** and are gradually transformed into **limit makers** in their image. True champions are totally conscious of this inevitable reality. They fully recognize the implications and risks it represents. They have never denied the existence of these tyrants nor pretended to ignore their influence. Instead they keep their eyes wide open so they can see their games and avoid being taken in by the web of their subtle manipulations. Such is the way of champions. The maintaining of an alert spirit and lucid conscience in order to effectively detect the traps slumbering within us and the shackles some people would want to wrap around our feet. Staying relentlessly on guard, with sharp reflexes to remain conscious of the influence of limit makers that seek to bring us under their thumb. Most importantly, we should never lose sight of the fact that it is up to us, and us alone, to break their influence and free ourselves from the yokes that enslave us under their control and dominance.

The Keys to Success

Once we manage to take charge of ourselves and successfully eliminate the shackles that hold us prisoners within our limits, anything becomes possible. But lookout! I don't mean to say that you can teach an elephant to fly or transform yourself into a champion heavyweight boxer when you stand only one meter twenty and weigh fifty kilos. Champions have well understood this nuance and integrated it into their lives. They can distinguish between a pipe dream and a dream. They recognize and put aside everything that is merely a whim, illusion or utopia. They never behave as if immortal or in possession of unlimited resources. They know, on the contrary, how to accurately define their world of daring and realistic possibilities, and will then jump any barrier or limit that blocks their way. To dream of the inaccessible which is impossible to attain is very simply a pipe dream. This is magical thinking that prevents you from becoming a champion. To put time and effort into discovering one's capabilities, to continually strive to improve and optimize your skills in order to reach your limits, this is both the dream and, at the same time, the challenge of a champion.

I recently listened to a televised interview with the great tenor, Luciano Pavarotti. His parents, people who knew him and even he himself admitted that when he was young, his voice did not promise the extraordinary results he has attained today. However, Luciano Pavarotti believed in his potential. He took the time needed to discover his capabilities and put all the necessary effort and work into developing and optimizing them. When he began to progress, he already had before him other well-respected and well-placed tenors. But he gave himself the challenge of going even further, of pushing himself to the maximum of his abilities.

He never once stopped working or believing in his dream of becoming the great champion that he is today. He never thought that things would be easy or that the game was won in advance. He took the essential steps and, even now, he admitted that he must remain vigilant and work constantly to remain at the apex of his art and continue to produce the kind of performance he always dreamed of.

Luciano Pavarotti is but one example I can recount to illustrate the mentality of a champion. These examples would all be interesting, one as much as the other, but that's not the point. What we should first ask ourselves now is "how does this work?" In other words, what do champions do to break the chains of their shackles? How do they actually and practically realize their wildest dreams? How do athletes transform themselves into world champions and stay at the top of their sport while inspiring the esteem and respect of everyone, including their opponents? How does an administrator or manager succeed at converting his/her organization into a more productive system while at the same time winning the esteem and admiration of everyone? In short, how can we attain the height of our potential, optimally master our skills or our art, in a practical and concrete style, without manipulating or destroying everything around us?

In answering these questions, the wisdom of my grandfather takes on all its significance. I understood, with experience and time, that all champions had a method or approach that was beneficial to them. Each and every one of them utilize specific **keys** that open the door to excellence, free them from their shackles and position them on the way of success. I also observed that from one champion to another, the method and **keys** were very similar and fulfilled the same functions: devise the best possible **strategy** to attain the objectives they had set. In fact, the most remarkable thing about this approach particular to all champions is that it corresponds perfectly with the strategic principles I discovered through contact with my grandfather: **lucid will**, **seeing the direction**, **staying on course**. The essence of their method, that is all the **keys** they use, fundamentally respect these three basic axioms, without which success, satisfaction and achievement are unattainable.

LUCID WILL primarily signifies the desire to understand and learn from life's experiences, then put the necessary and unavoidable corrections and adjustments into action. In accordance with this first strategic principle, champions keep a constant and lucid watch on themselves to fully understand who they are and leave nothing in the dark. In being so aware, they are in a position to fully evaluate and appreciate their way of functioning so that they are then able to appropriately orchestrate the necessary changes.

These two facets of **WILL** correspond with the first two **keys** to the success of champions. The **first key** brings about a self-comprehension that allows them to take charge of their lives. It enables them to straddle the stream of events instead of waiting for circumstances to lead them by the end of the nose. It helps them to MASTER THE WAVE and take control rather than ending up tossed about in every direction and submitting to the weight of destiny.

The second key of success establishes the essential foundation for successful change. By becoming conscious of themselves and their way of functioning, champions are able to clearly recognize their strengths and detect their weaknesses. This leads to the inevitable necessity of self-adjustment and adaptation. This is not necessarily easy because, as we age, we increasingly develop a marked resistance to everything labeled adjustment, correction, modification or change. I have observed this phenomenon in all my clients, whether patients, athletes or businesses. This resistance undermines the very foundation of the desire to progress; it holds us in place and encloses us within our own limits. One of the great strengths that champions possess is the knowledge of how to transform resistance to change into a dynamic ally and move forward. **The second key** of success enables champions to periodically probe their mode of functioning, allowing them to TAME CHANGE in a realistic and efficient manner.

Lucid will opens the door to freedom. It prepares the grounds for the journey ahead. However, this journey is not entered into with closed eyes that cannot see where to go. With experience, I have learned that it is of the utmost importance to clearly **SEE THE DIRECTION** before hoisting sails and going out to sea. This second major strategic principle requires that we clearly identify our desired destination and give ourselves the appropriate navigational instruments to arrive there. Champions know to respect these requirements. Everyone has a dream. Everyone is drawn toward a promised land, a far off paradise that he or she one day hopes to reach. But this paradise need not be a pipe dream. Champions know how to give their dream a tangible form. In other words, they know how to DREAM CONCRETELY. This is **the third key** of success.

In order to avoid navigating blindly and guarantee reaching their promised land, champions have the foresight to PROVIDE THEMSELVES WITH THEIR OWN efficient and precise DIRECTIONAL MAP. This map is the navigation instrument that enables them to keep their destination well in sight. It is their guide toward their personal dream and **the fourth key** of success, which they utilize with meticulousness and efficiency.

Once at sea, the voyage begun, you must then be capable of **STAYING ON COURSE**. If you want to end up at a very specific place, you must first and foremost specify a precise and detailed itinerary to follow. This is what the trainer of a Canadian Olympic team who were long-time world champions was

referring to when he said: "I always try TO PLAN EVERY-
THING...EVEN THE UNPREDICTABLE." A detailed plan that
is rooted in everyday life constitutes **the fifth key** of the success
of champions.

The plan alone, as precise as it might be, is still not enough to stay
on course. The journey requires that you ADJUST THE
MECHANICS along the way. You must properly use your directional map and make the needed course corrections throughout the
length of your voyage. This capacity to adjust is **the sixth key** that
aids champions to continuously progress toward the objectives
they have set.

Finally, once at sea, at the mercy of the elements and at times
trapped in a storm, you must know how to maintain your inner fire
so as to not lose courage and avoid the temptation to give up
everything. Champions never underestimate all these difficulties
faced throughout the daily voyage that can potentially erode motivation and weaken willpower. Champions are extremely adept at
SUSTAINING THE SPIRIT that propelled them onto the way of
success. They use this **seventh and last key**, along with the two
preceding ones, to assure they always **STAY ON COURSE**
toward the horizon of their dream, regardless of the difficulties
they may encounter throughout the length of their journey.

These **seven keys** of success are a champion's vehicles toward
achievement. Together, they form the base of the strategy implemented to realize their dreams. Each of these keys corresponds to
one phase or step of their strategy, which jointly represent a
dynamic cycle favoring a constant progression. The diagram
shown in figure 1, page 69, illustrates this cycle of perpetual evolution that allows champions to continually reach their loftier
objectives all along the road toward success. Over the remaining
course of this book, a new **key** will be introduced with each subsequent chapter. This shall enable you to progressively situate

yourself when you elaborate your own strategy, the one that will help you to attain your highest aspirations.

However, before we go into detail on how to utilize each of these **keys** to success, it is important not to lose sight of the fact that they are not sufficient on their own. For the strategy to be efficient, you must still master the skills needed to draw out the maximum benefit from each of them. In this sense, the strategy of champions is like a powerful ship with hoisted sails. However, in order for this ship to advance and progress, you must know how to master the secrets of wind. If not, your vessel will run aground, regardless of its power and what it allows you to hope for.

Through his wisdom, my grandfather bequeathed me an extraordinary "ship". With experience and time I learned the secrets to mastering wind. I came to understand that in order to effectively utilize the **keys** of success, all champions have the same characteristics in common; they all developed the same know-how and skills.

Figure 1
Diagram of the Strategy of Champions

The Champions' Know-How

Know-how is an art. It is what gives the means we use and the things we undertake, the shade of success. This is what allows champions to give spirit and life to their strategy. The first characteristic that champions have in common is summed up by one single word: RESPONSIBILITY. Champions assume responsibility for their lives, for their dreams, for their difficulties and for their setbacks. They consider themselves responsible for their successes and never look for excuses or scapegoats when things don't go as well as they'd hoped.

Many people have, on the contrary, a tendency to place the burden of their lethargy and miscarriages on the backs of others. "If my parents had...if my significant other had been different...if my employees were more motivated...if my boss was better organized, etc.", all these phrases, all these ideas are nothing more than pretext and side-stepping to escape responsibility. And all this, unfortunately, does not stop there. More and more we are living in what we could call the age of no fault. We allow events or circumstances to explain and even excuse the blunders we commit or the mistakes we make. It is rare that someone says, "If it doesn't go as I would like, it is because I was mistaken..." "If we are there it is because we didn't know how to manage and we need to change something."

Champions don't look for excuses. They first ask themselves what they can do, THEMSELVES, to make it work better and have it change. They don't pity themselves nor drown in regrets, remorse or blame after decisions have been made or actions taken. They assume complete and full responsibility, and take all the necessary measures to adjust, progress and succeed.

The second skill that all champions possess is the ability to situate themselves on a GLOBAL level. A champion thinks globally. When establishing his strategy for success, he doesn't just consider certain isolated and limited aspects of his mode of functioning. On the contrary, he considers all dimensions and components that could affect his strategy and be influenced by it. He takes into consideration the evolution of all factors over time, in a manner that favors the gradual deployment of his strategy.

The preparation of an elite athlete that aims for the world championship or the Olympic medal is a good example of this GLOBAL approach to reality. In building an effective preparation strategy, all internal and external dimensions of the athlete are examined. The material, technical, tactical, physiological, psychological, nutritional, and all other components are considered and planned with great care. Attention is given to the external factors such as the relationship with the trainer and teammates, the strengths and weaknesses of opponents, the characteristics of competition sites, the internal politics of the sport and more of the same. The training strategy strives to help the athlete control and maximize his/her performance with respect to all factors and components for all competitions he/she must face, while making a gradual and steady progression. This capacity to think and prepare in a GLOBAL manner is one of the fundamental characteristics that separates champions from those who achieve less success. It occurs everywhere and anywhere that the standards for quality and performance are synonymous with excellence. I have observed this in all organizations and businesses that continually endeavor to progress and I have noticed this in all individuals that aspire to push themselves to improve.

A third know-how that all champions have in common is their capacity to function at an OPTIMAL level. Champions are very skillful at pinpointing their most favorable state for acting at their best without uselessly wasting energy. We have all heard the expression "too much is like too little". Champions know exactly how to do enough without doing too much. They know how to find what I call their OPTIMAL ZONE. For example, for an athlete, putting out too much energy, or over-activating is just as harmful as not giving enough effort and crashing. "Too much" leads to tension, lack of coordination and anxiety and "too little" leads to loss of power, slowness and apathy. Over-analyzing can provoke paralysis in the course of action while the lack of analysis might entail unconsidered reactions. Too much detailed planning can be a waste of energy because situations naturally evolve and force change. On the other hand, insufficient planning leads to poor decision-making and loss of valuable energy, and more of the same. Examples abound linking inefficiency and lack of success to poor adjustment of the OPTIMAL ZONE, since this zone does exist in all spheres of human life. The margin between "too much" and "too little" is specific to each of our activities. This margin varies according to individuals and their unique needs. The critical thing to know, as champions do, is how to continually adjust your mode of functioning so as to achieve your best results without needlessly using too much valuable energy.

There exists a second facet to OPTIMAL functioning that champions also come to master. For them, quality prevails over quantity. It is of the utmost importance to aim at doing things well, right from the start, in order to achieve optimal quality. To illustrate this here's a remark that a pairs figure skating champion made to me: "For too many athletes, quality is not given enough importance. When they get on the ice they too easily tell themselves that after all it's only practice, it's not serious. And they will repeat their routine several times without ever putting in any care. Us, we have learned with time that functioning like that is nothing but a waste of energy. We treat each training session like a world championship. We give it all our focus. We prefer to execute three perfect programs than do ten that are only so-so. If it's worth doing, it's worth doing right the first time." This mentality of always striving to optimize performance and function within the OPTIMAL ZONE is relevant everywhere. It enables us to make use of our best skills without ever needlessly wasting energy.

The fourth know-how that is a trademark of a champion is the skill of being CONCRETE. This skill makes it possible for him/her to be grounded within reality. For him/her, life, like his/her dreams, doesn't stop at the stage of good intentions. Good intentions are all fine and dandy, but you must strive for something tangible in order to go from the drawing board to the world of reality, of the practical and palpable.

TO BE CONCRETE, for champions, signifies translating what they want to attain or realize or what they strive to modify or improve, into observable and measurable results. I always insist that clients, athletes or entrepreneurs specify what I call "measurable indicators" in order to concretely define their objectives and follow their progress in a tangible manner. Without these indicators, goals would be nothing more than wishful thinking that fall into the oblivion of the comfortable paradise of good intentions. Wanting to control your stress, develop communication within a couple, enhance the image of an enterprise, improve results, performance, concentration or confidence...these are all commendable aspirations! I can give an account of dozens of examples of this nature. These types of wishes are very nice but totally futile unless we know how to translate each of them into indicators that enable us to specify the tangible results we want to achieve. Champions have well understood this requirement of success. For the athlete, stress is expressed as a physical reaction, behavior and/or negative thinking to correct. For a couple it's about attitudes to adopt, messages to better express and moments and places favorable for improving communication. The image of an enterprise can make reference to eliminating production faults, improving speed of service or enhancing market visibility, and more of the same.

The champion knows how to find operational indicators to render concrete his/her wishes. He/she is also capable of choosing appropriate means for bringing these measurable indicators in the desired direction. In other words, any pertinent means or any efficient action should take us closer to the tangible result we have set as an objective. Unfortunately, this is not always the case in our lives. Often we don't know how to clearly specify what we want to achieve and we move a lot of wind to give ourselves a good conscience and give us the impression we are heading toward something. Being CONCRETE is one fundamental quality that enables us to transform our dreams into achievable success.

Champions have a fifth fundamental skill in common: being METHODICAL. This know-how enables them to proceed logically, to follow a precise order of well-defined steps, to attain a determined objective. This skill is very simple to understand, but far from being simple to implement and master. We possess an extremely powerful brain, but it is not always the most methodical. When, in the world of business, I ask a group of participants how they solve a problem, they will instantly name all the essential steps of a good problem-solving method. However, these steps are mentioned in a totally random order, which reflects a non-methodical procedure and explains why they have not been able to obtain satisfactory results in the workshop.

A client, while telling me of all his/her difficulties in therapy, will have the tendency to describe, in a helter-skelter manner, all sorts of events, circumstances or difficulties that mostly have no logical connection with one another. This un-methodical approach reflects the confusion that reigns in his/her head as well as in his/her life. One of the critical dimensions to the art of therapy is to help the patient restore order to his/her ideas and mode of functioning.

Knowing how to be METHODICAL – while not becoming obsessive, which is also knowing how to be OPTIMAL in our approach – is, without doubt, one essential factor of the way of success. When champions choose concrete and efficient methods to reach their goals, they inevitably think along a line of conduct, the steps of which are both logical and methodically organized. They will respect this line of conduct in a manner that maximally benefits the power of their methodical procedure and helps them avoid the errors and needless loss of energy throughout their progression.

To have PATIENCE is the sixth characteristic that champions have in common. We live in a society where short-term thinking is pushed to its paroxysm. Once we catch sight of or desire something, we need it right away and with the least possible effort. Our capacity to wait and our tolerance for frustration have dwindled to the point where we are less and less capable of thinking in the medium-term and, even less, in the long-term. Power and pleasure right now…repercussions and consequences later on and most of all, left for others to face.

The champion, for his part, is aware that success doesn't happen overnight and it doesn't just fall from the sky. A typical example of this capacity for patience is that of a karate champion who faced failure in his first 33 competitions. By creating an adequate and methodical training program that honed his abilities and maximized his potential, he finally got through. He never once wavered along the way and, one day, victory smiled upon him. Knowing how to persevere, being able to accept setbacks and restructuring without stopping and never being discouraged, this is one of the core qualities of a champion.

PATIENCE is also taking the necessary time to exam everything (being GLOBAL) and keeping in mind the evolution of events with time. This is the only way to establish solid action strategies that will remain valid in the medium and even the long-term. This PATIENCE also signifies the power to wait while remaining calm. Unfortunately we expend lots of energy on preoccupying ourselves with what can go wrong. All this energy expenditure is, in the great majority of cases, completely useless because the matters that concern us rarely happen as we fear. It is more pertinent and efficient to learn to tell ourselves: "One thing at a time…you have done all that you could. Be patient now, it will all work out as you wish."

The seventh and last know-how of champions consists of maintaining OPTIMISM at all times. A feeling of failure gradually overtakes many people when things don't go as they hoped, or when they experience a lack of success or a setback. This sentiment takes on more significance with time and, if their bad luck continues, they will perceive negative events as if they were a permanent phenomenon, generalized to their whole life. Failure even becomes, for many, attributable to an inner weakness against which they end up feeling completely powerless.

The OPTIMISM of champions, in contrast, helps them distinguish obstacles and setbacks as passing phenomena. For them, everything can be overcome. Failure doesn't exist. Lack of success is only temporary. It is nothing more than an objective that hasn't yet been achieved, either because it was not well defined or because the appropriate measures were not taken for achieving it.

In this sense, all setbacks or defeats are simply occasions for learning, for overcoming a new challenge and for bringing the necessary course correction to the strategy in place. When champions miss the mark, they will attribute their difficulties to something that can be changed. They always maintain a positive impression of control over their life. This gives them the ability to bounce back and adapt which those that learned to be pessimistic or defeatist, have little or none of.

Matt Biondi, an Olympic champion swimmer, gives us a remarkable example of this capacity to bounce back[1]. Before the 1988 Olympics in Seoul, everyone favored him to repeat Mark Spitz's feat of winning seven gold medals. But as luck would have it, that would not happen. After he performed poorly in his first two events, most of the commentators no longer believed that he could bounce back and predicted he would perform poorly throughout the games. This was not the belief of Martin Seligman, a psychologist who had evaluated the optimistic tendencies of many members of the American swimming team. He knew that Biondi was an irreducible optimist with a capacity for resilience. And this is exactly what happened. Rather than lose courage and spirit, as many others would have done in his place, Matt Biondi recovered to win five gold medals in the next five events.

A Coherent and Efficient Strategy

The seven fundamental skills I have just described constitute the know-how that allows champions to efficiently utilize each of the keys to success. Without these skills, the keys would be nothing more than an empty structure, devoid of spirit, incapable of ever being exploited to its full potential. It's a bit like using an extremely powerful computer for nothing more than simple arithmetic. On the other hand, the know-how itself is not sufficient. Without the support of your powerful computer, even the most sophisticated of software would never produce the anticipated results.

1 The footnotes are at the end of the book.

The keys and know-how correspond to the computer and its application programs. It's only through their judicious interaction that the total capacity of one or the other can ever be exploited to its maximum. To use an analogy of a different kind, it's similar to making bread: we need both the dough and the yeast. "Epoxy glue" would never attain its full strength unless the hardener is combined with the resin. In continuing along this line, the keys and know-how are two components, two essential ingredients that are fully efficient when we know how to use them in synergy with one another.

In presenting the keys to success, I made reference to "the extraordinary sailboat" bequeathed me by my grandfather. I mentioned that as powerful as that sailboat may be, it would never be able to undertake a crossing of any kind if we aren't able to master the secrets of wind. Without the ship AND the art of navigation, we couldn't ever embark on a profitable voyage nor arrive at a fine port. For each of us, life is our voyage, and success is the port that calls to us. Our voyage is sometimes calm, but we will also face rough seas and terrible weather, demanding all our skills to make it through. Along our route we will also face tyrants who, for their own profit, will try to turn our ship back, enslave us and instill doubt and discord within our crew, putting us at risks of losing control over our destiny. It's in these very circumstances that mastering the keys to success and the know-how of champions will make all the difference. This is exactly when our strategy needs to be coherent and effective.

Whether we like it or not, life is like a complex chess match played on many dimensions. We can be manipulated and lose like a beginner, or we can master all the subtle complexities and find a way to win the match. Success, as an alternative, belongs to us. Essentially, it depends on the effectiveness of the life strategy we make use of. And, it is in knowing how to properly combine the keys and know-how that, in the likeness of champions, we will manage to establish this effective strategy.

When I work with elite athletes, elaboration of an effective strategy requires that I devise a "global approach of strategic periodization". Here, the term 'periodization" refers to an extremely precise dose of each aspect of the athlete's training divided into pre-determined periods of time. This "global approach" essentially rests on the utilization of the keys of success and the know-how of champions. In business, the same approach, based on the same principles, makes it possible for us to define a "global approach of strategic management". This type of approach takes into account all aspects of the functioning of the organization to respond to the particular needs of the enterprise. In working with patients troubled by various types of difficulties, I always try to situate my therapeutic intervention within the frame of what I call "a global approach of strategic optimization". This doesn't mean that I push the client into transforming his whole life in an attempt to create the nirvana of blissful psychological happiness that, at any rate, doesn't even exist. Instead, this means that in examining, with the patient, the various aspects of his mode of functioning under the light of the keys to success and skills of champions, it becomes possible to define an effective therapeutic strategy that will enable the client to recapture his autonomy and wellness in the shortest time possible.

The strategy of champions is thus an approach that can be utilized in all sorts of contexts and is valid and effective for all types of individuals or groups. In this approach, the keys of success permit us to precisely define the structure of the strategy we want to use. The skills of champions assure us, on their part, the maximization of the structure's effectiveness. They constitute the fundamental know-how that favors an optimal employment of each of the keys, meaning each constituent step of our strategic structure.

The more I work with champions, the more I realize that their exceptional success invariably depends on the mastering of the same basic skills, utilized within the framework of a remarkably coherent strategy of functioning. This doesn't mean that all champions will proceed in exactly the same way, blindly following the same "recipe". Each of them has originality, a color and a way of doing things that responds perfectly to his or her unique personal needs. The same applies in therapy. The therapeutic intervention strategy that I put into action for each of my patients is never the same from one person to the next. It always aims at responding to the particular needs of each individual. But nevertheless, it is at all times grounded on the same basic principles: establish a coherent strategy for functioning that becomes more satisfying thanks to the support of the keys and skills of champions.

Champions all respect these basic principles, whether consciously or intuitively. I have likewise claimed that the more an individual or organization is skilled at respecting these basic principles, the more they will achieve and the greater their success will be. In other words, the more coherent and complete the strategy is, the more we are able to attain our objectives. In the domain of sport, a very fascinating study of world champions and Olympic medal-lists observed results of the same trend.[2] It was discovered that the top international elite athletes all know how to make use of strategic plans and certain psychological skills; this corresponds closely with what I have observed in champions of all different domains. Further, the best of these elite had mastered their strategic plans and skills to a superior degree than those who had achieved less success. Finally, what is most interesting, they were even more successful when they used a greater number of these skills throughout their preparation and during competition.

The fundamental idea to remember from all this is that achievement and success are out of reach unless we respect to a minimum these ineluctable basic principles. Now, when I look around me and observe the mode of functioning of most of the people I meet, I ask myself if, as human beings, the majority of us have not lost control of their ship within the heart of a storm, on rough seas. Yet all these people would tell me that no one is more grounded to reality than they are. They work, earn a living, raise children, consume, remain active, run around and…exhaust themselves without realizing that time and energy are given in limited quantities. Too often we take everything for granted. We roll along on reflex, automatically, without thinking too much. Despite the symptoms cautioning us to moderate, despite the signals warning us our effectiveness is far from ideal, we continue with our eyes closed. It is a bit like driving a car on the highway with the lights for over-heating, low oil and all the others, indicating we should stop, repair and correct our way of driving. But, despite that, we ignore all these warnings and push even harder on the gas pedal until one day, the inevitable catches up with us.

We behave as if we have lost the "directions" for our marvelous machine we were given at birth. If we don't know how to redis-cover these directions, true success will only be a mirage on the horizon of our dreams. Champions, for their part, are aware they are driving a magnificent Formula 1. They are extremely meticu-lous in how they use it and take care to develop the skills that allow them to maximize their effectiveness. In other words, they behave as "professionals of life" and, as PROFESSIONALS, like a Grand Prix driver, they leave nothing to chance.

If I had to define what a champion is with one single sentence, I would say it is:

A person who strives to maintain his/her optimal state of functioning at all times and in all circumstances, while relying on a strategy of life that is coherent and effective.

This is a definition that can appear very demanding. Yet it reflects nothing less than the mentality of champions. It is this mentality that guides champions on the road to success and enables them to break their shackles and surpass their limits.

A coherent and effective strategy of life is what we will talk about throughout the next few chapters. We will examine, in detail, how champions go about constructing this strategy with the help of the seven keys to success. We will see, at the same time, how they uti-lize their seven fundamental skills to optimize the effectiveness of their strategy. Each of the following chapters will help you better understand and better utilize every one of the seven keys so you can implement your own strategy for achievement and success.

PART 2

THE STRATEGY OF CHAMPIONS:
LUCID WILL

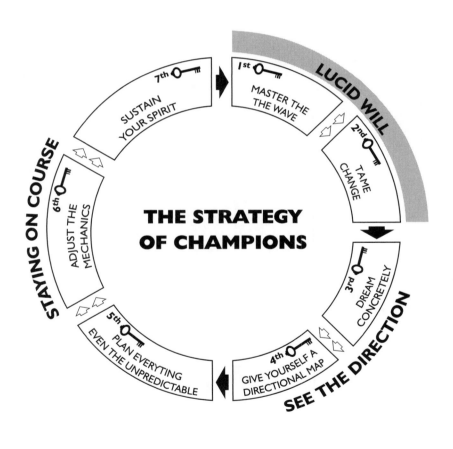

"To will is one thing; to succeed is another. You all might dream of reaching the level of black belt one day. By enrolling in this dojo you have taken the first step. Your will may be huge, but the road is long. During the next four or five years you will encounter many difficulties and few registered here will persist until the end. There will be highs and lows, periods of doubt and questioning. During these low periods you will need to discover your true motivation and understand who you really are. That is what you must learn from your experiences on the training floor. It is during those moments that you must find the strength to adjust and change in order to continue your progress. If you cannot do this, all your willpower will be nothing more than a storm contained within a glass of water. The way to success is not a straight line where it is enough to charge along, head lowered and fists clenched. If you cannot understand this you will end up wasting a lot of energy; you may be able to tear down some walls, but the door to success will forever remain closed to you."

This was what master Nakashima said each time he started training a new group of beginners at his karate school. As with everyone else his words were very strange to me. We wanted it so much... who or what could stop us? With time we understood that he was right. Out of the hundred subjects enrolled at the beginning, no more than two progressed to the black belt five years later. It was the same story for each and every group!

Will on its own, without a lucid mind, is not sufficient. Despite his pious wishes Médé, grandfather's neighbor, let the waves of his life toss him about, hoping that circumstances would take control and navigate the course of his existence. On the other hand Louisa, his wife, belted along, head down, through her own waves, yet all the while she was continually drowning. Médé never managed to make any headway. Louisa tore down some walls yet she was never able to understand or even learn from her turbulent existence. Neither one nor the other ever took charge of their lives or themselves. Neither one nor the other ever successfully mastered the waves of their existences nor discovered a way to alter the course of their realities.

Wishful wanting as well as blind will delude us with illusions. Only lucid will is capable of wisely and efficiently guiding us on the path of success.

Chapter 3

THE 1ST KEY: MASTER THE WAVE

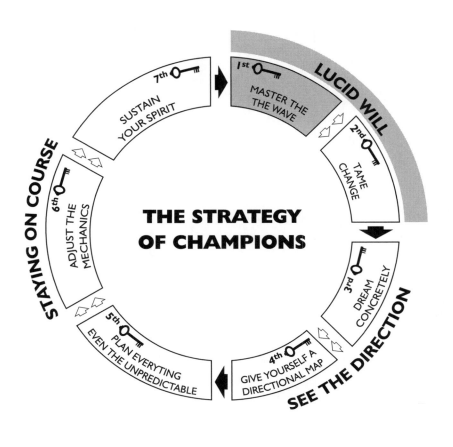

The balmy, late afternoon sun amused us by painting a rainbow with the fine mist projected into the sky by the impressive waves that broke beneath us. A few dozen meters from the sandy shore a minuscule skiff progressed slowly toward the hellish liquid that looked ready to swallow it up. A few feet from me a small group with binoculars was attentively following the arduous progression of this frail distant point on the surface of the bluish wilderness.

Curiously I approached this group. A big fellow with gray hair handed me his binoculars, indicating with his hand the far-off point that was continually growing fainter. It was a surfboard and someone was lying on top paddling with both arms, going head first toward the waves. Suddenly, after one last energetic push, I saw the swimmer stand up on the board just as a monstrous wave simultaneously rolled over him, ready to swallow him whole. That was the beginning of the most incredible ballet I ever had the opportunity to admire. The surfer moved to the front of the wave as if trying to overcome it. He glided onto his flank and flirted with the roll, penetrating its hollow so deeply that his hair seemed to touch the wall of water that was on the verge of crushing him. He emerged to dominate the wave once again, as if they were amusing themselves, partners in a universe where gravity had been forgotten. After a seemingly infinite amount of time the wave was finally worn out, her fiery spirit had been tamed, giving back the euphoria of his liberty to the swimmer.

All around me I heard the "ahh" of relief as if everyone had been holding their breath in fear of breaking the magic unfolding before our eyes. Then someone spoke to the big fellow with gray hair, "Tell me Ron, isn't your son a bit reckless to play with the devil like that? Aren't you afraid he'll one day lose his skin?" Ron burst out laughing saying, "I told you Michael would take your breath away. And yet you have seen nothing!"

Sitting in the sand, his eyes filled with emotion and pride, Ron began to tell us about his son. He explained that as far back as he could remember waves had always fascinated Michael. As a child he played with the surf the way others amused themselves with balls. When he left the water he would spend hours watching the dance of waves as if seeking to unlock the mystery of what animated them. When he got his first surfboard at the age of six it wasn't simply an object received as a gift but a whole universe to discover. He began learning the wave a bit like we learn life... at first he groped along... learning through trial and error. But Michael had a dream and, even though he was young, he was very astute. He soon realized there were others much better than he was. So he started over by sitting down and observing. He sought to comprehend the mastery of those most talented. He then set out again onto the water and, without rest, tried to repeat the dozens of small gestures he'd seen the others execute with such beautiful ease.

At night during the family dinner he recounted his conquests, making everyone laugh as he described the clumsiness that made him swallow a mouthful of water. This was how, by relating his misadventures, he was able to see his errors and learn how to correct them. Nothing discouraged him. It was all pleasure: dream and challenge.

Little by little Michael's mastery grew, as did his reputation. He talked constantly with those more experienced and more talented. He observed them incessantly, seeking to unlock their secrets and learn from their experiences. He avidly read everything about his sport and passion. He formed a small group of buddies who trained together and helped each other out. He even sold them on the idea of registering for different competitions telling them that they would be pushed, stimulated and would learn even more.

One day he displayed his innermost colors. He had earned some success and many recognized his potential. He wanted to become world champion. That summer a surfing school in Hawaii was holding a training camp where an ex-champion was coaching. He gathered his money and he and his friends left on this great adventure, their chests filled with courage and their heads full of dreams.

It wasn't easy. This was serious. It was as if Michael had to start over from scratch. The training was tough, technical and methodical. He had to undo and redo, reprogram the machine to draw out the maximum. They were all discouraged but not Michael. He returned more charged than ever. He had passed to another level. He understood that in order to be a champion he could no longer neglect a thing. He had to adapt and further change to cross the line that transforms the marvel of a dream into a tangible reality.

From that moment on, his passion became his life and his life, his passion. He fully dedicated himself, openly and for everyone to know. He found allies, trainers and experts capable of encouraging him, following him and pushing him. But throughout it all he always remained the master of his own dream and in control of his own destiny. He returned to Hawaii many times. And little by little, from competition to competition, he won the admiration and respect of everyone. One day he won the regional championship, then the nationals, and finally, the realization of his dream: **WORLD CHAMPION**.

For Michael that was not only a passing fancy; a transitory dream that once attained is set aside like a shelved trophy. On the contrary, he was there to stay. And this is the substance of a true champion. He was at the top and had been there for more than five years. He was a master, a bit like a "sensei" in martial arts. Surfing was a way, a living art, and a continual evolution. He knew that one day he would retire from competition and he prepared himself. He helped others realize their dreams, all the while pursuing his own approach. A school, an enterprise and who knows what else... life had no limits except for those he wished to give himself.

Taking the Lead

Michael's story is very similar to those of the other great athletes I have known. It is also reminiscent of the experiences and evolution that many of the high quality men and women I had the opportunity to meet, have lived. Michael uncovers a fundamental secret for us: if we wish to master the wave, we must not wait until it falls upon us before we act. By simply hoping that life will bring us THE solution, happiness with a capital H or love with a capital L, we submerge ourselves within the illusions of the cozy comfort of our inactivity. This is to live at the mercy of events, swaying with the wind.

To successfully tame the wave, Michael charged toward her with eyes wide open. He took the lead, unafraid of diving into her depths in order to gain mastery over her. He emerged, yet stronger, to finally ride her as though she had surrendered to his desires and will. He didn't wait for the wave to foist itself upon him before acting. On the contrary, he took the initiative rather than risk being dominated and overwhelmed.

Take the Initiative

Michael similarly took the initiative in life. He didn't wait for his father to show him how to use his surfboard. He didn't count on someone to teach him how to face the waves. He took steps to provoke competition and improve his skill. Never once did he place himself at the mercy of circumstances.

This type of mentality is characteristic of the way true champions function. Those men and women who have reached the summit never waited for coaches to push them in the back to advance further. They are, on the contrary, fundamentally curious and have a desire to constantly learn more and more. Research has shown us[3] that they have the desire to discover by themselves and appreciate the importance of the basic elements that are the keys to their success.

But how do they do it? How is it possible to take initiative in our lives? First of all we must assume **responsibility** for our own realities. This is the cog in the gear system of initiative as well as one of the basic qualities common to all champions. One way or another they all say: "I'm taking care of it... I will get there... I will do it and I am capable." If these types of expressions are not part of your vocabulary, there is a good chance you are waiting for either life or other people to bring you pre-packaged solutions and take responsibility for your happiness.

Developing initiative requires taking **concrete** actions...another know-how of champions. All great athletes that have achieved success were able to find the time to listen to others as well as listen to themselves. They observe and speak with others. They read everything relating to their field. They consult with top experts. They practice, attempt and experiment in order to enhance their ability to discover and self-adjust. They rethink their way of acting and evaluate the results they obtain. They sit and reflect, make appropriate decisions and continually restart the cycle, until they find satisfaction. By operating in this way, as Michael did, champions know how to take initiative. By reading this book, by making the effort to discover and understand the secrets of champions you will also develop your reflexes for initiative. By following the example champions set, you will take your first concrete steps toward empowering your will, which is essential to completing the journey on the road of achievement. There are no magic tricks. It requires you to, at some point, make the decision to grasp your destiny with your own hands.

When it comes time to actually act and move forward, taking the lead also requires fundamental **patience** and **optimism**. The cycles of continuous progression that champions live demand this kind of patience and optimism; without these they risk abandoning their watch for potential ambushes along the path. It doesn't happen overnight. It takes time; never allowing slowed progress or setbacks to discourage you. Observing, reading, experimenting, seeking advice, reflecting, adjusting and starting over, all these are elements that can help you make your own dreams come true. Without this process nothing will ever hook you; no far off shore will grab your attention and you will never undertake a voyage of true value. We shall see with the third key of success how to make your dreams more concrete. But, before getting there, it is important to clear the ground adequately, to give yourself a solid foundation capable of awakening and nurturing aspirations suited to your potential.

Endure or Act

Why take the lead? Why spend all that energy in an endless search to move forward? Well in a way life gives us no choice. It is precisely so as to not uselessly waste too much energy.

In martial arts there's an old adage that states, "The best defense is still to attack". I'm not saying that in order to take the lead you must become aggressive, dominant or overpowering. The simple message here is that by waiting for an opponent to strike before acting puts us constantly on the defense, in a position of weakness. We exhaust ourselves with the continuous effort to defend, dodge and block. We burn up our energy without ever having constructed an efficient offense to score our own points. We have surrendered to the battle instead of controlling it.

To achieve success we must act for ourselves, devise an attack strategy and be prepared, as in the martial arts, to use the adversary's own moves to gain mastery over him. It's the same in life. Throughout the span of a lifetime we face all sorts of hits and assorted influences that threaten to stagger us. If we are unprepared, if we have not yet taken the initiative to define our own strategy, then those influences and blows will drag us wherever they want. We will wear ourselves out in our attempts to endure and react to them, sparing us no energy to realize, let alone dare to have, our own dreams.

The distinction between enduring and acting is similar to the difference between being **reactive** and what we term **proactive**. Reactive individuals wait for events to happen without preparing. They hope everything turns out for the best but never make any efforts to ensure they do. They are affected or disturbed by all sorts of things. The temperature makes them moody and environmental stimuli influence them. Other people's comments can make them defensive. And the list goes on. Proactive people face these same types of stimuli or events but they are in control of their responses. They have taken the initiative to develop a life strategy that enables them to economize their energy and attain their desired results.

Proactive individuals realize they possess all the essential means for shaping their own destiny. Instead of waiting or hoping, they take charge of themselves and progress forward. Rather than let events or people frustrate them, they understand that nothing or nobody can touch them unless they grant them permission to. They know that everything depends on their strategy and their decisions.

Being proactive is taking the lead in your personal life; no longer allowing circumstances or others toss you around. It is the decision to act according to a well-developed line of action rather than allowing oneself to be subjected to the desires of fantasy, circumstances and time. When athletes become overwhelmed by stress and perform poorly as a result, they find themselves caught in situations of "reactivity". These athletes have submitted to events and pressures. The art of therapy is to help them rediscover their own means of controlling their reactions to stress. They need to redefine their strategy and retake the lead over events and pressures.

In the world of business there's an old saying: "if it ain't broken, don't fix it". This is actually the best excuse for powerlessness and incompetence that I have ever heard. All CEO's and managers who have lived by this motto had but one thing on their minds: don't move, don't make waves lest things turn out badly and wait for problems to present themselves before taking action. This situation serves to stimulate the "fireman's panic". These types of businesses find themselves in a perpetual state of emergency, incessantly obliged to put out fires. The majority of their energy expenditure is instead directed toward repairing, remaking and patching. The waste of time and money becomes enormous and the situation escalates until it becomes impossible to adjust without turning to draconian solutions: partial closings, discontinuing products, massive lay-offs and so on.

Champion enterprises hold a completely different mentality. They know how to make things move their way and for the better of their organization. They have learned to take the lead, take initiative and be proactive. They employ clear and precise strategies to orient their actions. This is the only way to do it: either master the waves or else endure events and finally disappear.

Think for Yourself

In order to develop initiative and bring an end to the practice of enduring reality, you must also develop a fundamental aptitude called autonomy of thought. In sports we found out that high-level athletes demonstrate high levels of independent spirit[4]. They tend to live their life according to their own set of principles. Another interesting phenomenon worth noting is that the longer athletes were able to maintain a high level of performance, the more they manifested the traits of autonomy and independent spirit.

I have observed the same trend within the world of businesses and enterprises. Successful leaders and managers are those men and women capable of thinking on their own. They depend neither on the approval of others nor on the continual blessing of their superiors to take initiative. They form their own opinions and assume the risks associated with acting according to one's convictions.

The significance of autonomy of thought also has many implications in therapy. In my experience I have noticed that those patients who have personal opinions regarding their evolution and manner of functioning are better able to expediently and swiftly re-establish their personal balance. On the other hand, those patients that constantly seek my advice and tend to wait for the approval of the "specialist" before acting, stay in therapy longer and find it more difficult to overcome their problems.

The capacity for autonomous thought is not an inner gift. It is developed and learned. It is accessible to everyone. To develop your initiative you need to have a basic curiosity and you need to take concrete actions. Then, throughout, it is important that you keep a certain measure of "reasonable doubt": never take anything for granted or accept everything you hear, see, read or observe as absolute fact. This doesn't mean you should reject everything or become relentlessly negative or arrogant. An appropriate balance can be found. Furthermore you must, as in the example of a champion, know how to be **optimal**. Neither be naïve nor gullible nor yield to total refusal or nihilism. To think for oneself is to consider all the facts and elements (be **global**), verify their truthfulness and examine the logic. It is to confront reality and draw your own conclusions. Everyone is capable of doing this, but it requires energy, so not everyone is ready to make the necessary effort. It is undoubtedly easier and safer to return to relying on our so-called thinkers, gurus of all kinds or licensed specialists. Many find the idea of taking charge of themselves and breaking free of their personal shackles both demanding and frightening. But the benefits are worth the effort. The feelings of autonomy, competence and self-determination become an extremely powerful motor of life. This is what enables us to go that additional mile, to give that little bit extra which can make the difference between an ordinary life and a successful existence.

Understanding and Learning

To think for yourself in order to take the lead and become proactive doesn't mean lowering your head and mindlessly charge without thinking. Taking the lead and mastering the wave definitely do not entail, as with Médé, grandfather's neighbor, waiting for life to magically arrange itself for you. Neither does it mean, as with Médé's wife Louisa, jumping onto the train of hasty dead ends to cherish the illusion of being in control of your life.

Michael, Ron's son, was ambitious and driven. Yet he was very aware that in order to tame the wave without it swallowing him up, he first needed to completely understand it and then gradually learn to master it. He spent hours examining the wave, studying it and keenly observing those who already knew how to control it. Next he tried, practiced and took risks, sometimes succeeding, sometimes failing. From this starting point he subsequently reflected, analyzed and eventually came to understand and learn; without respite, he worked at refining his mastery and sharpening his control until reaching the point where he felt completely autonomous and competent.

In order to take the lead in an intelligent and lucid way, this progressive cycle is unavoidable. We must stop ourselves in order to know who we are, how we function, what we live, then we can draw out the appropriate lessons in order to progress. Lucid will is precisely that: understanding to facilitate learning and take the lead and control of our own lives.

Understanding makes reference to knowledge. Having a clear idea about things. It is the ability to distinguish and perceive all the subtle nuances of reality while grasping their logic and complexity. Understanding is essential to progress and evolution. It is an inherent condition of efficient learning and achievement. Of course, understanding in and of itself is not enough. Just because you understand how to execute a tennis serve doesn't mean you

can correctly perform the skill. However, if you have fully examined the stroke and grasped its technical detail, you will certainly learn more efficiently. Observing, making attempts, feeling the
movement, looking at the results, analyzing, understanding and
learning to correct and adjust is the best and only way to do it.
What is true for this simple technical gesture is equally true in
every domain of life. This seems obvious when we think of the
tennis serve. Yet we so easily lose this perspective when worrying
about our own lives. We don't understand who we are or how we
function. We rarely take the time to stop and orient ourselves, analyze our situation and learn from ourselves, yet despite our neglect
we still expect that "our serve" will always be effective and always
guarantee success!

***

When I met Flavio, a short Belgium man of Italian descent, he had
just been named head of the frame assembly department of an
important factory that built heavy-duty machinery. We were at the
beginning stages of a vast, factory-wide, efficiency improvement
project. During the first three or four months many departments
charged ahead in a hurried effort to correct their production flaws,
but not Flavio. He said to me: "Don't worry, it will come. First off
I want to clearly monitor what is actually going on." He took the
time to observe and gain a complete understanding of his new
department's functional dynamic. He looked for allies inside his
department and quietly prepared the ground for change. Along
with his team he completed a **methodical** examination prior to ini-
tiating the transformation phase. Flavio **patiently** considered all
operational aspects of his department. He understood the need for
a **global** evaluation. He searched for **concrete** facts about what
was needed to improve the situation. He established priorities in
an **optimal** manner and targeted those areas most critical to
obtaining immediate success from the implementation of his
action plan. Throughout he remained **optimistic**, even when others regarded him with an air of skepticism because he took his
time getting off the ground. Flavio always assumed **responsibili-**

ty for the risks incurred in taking the lead, setting himself in a class of his own in comparison with the approach taken by most of his colleagues.

In other words, Flavio had the courage to face reality right from the start and gain a full understanding of all the components of his new situation by adeptly using the seven great skills or fundamental know-how of champions. Thanks to this, he was able to masterfully employ a strategy that would assure his success. He knew how to draw maximum benefit from the first key of success, which enabled him to master the wave of change that broke over his enterprise. This served him well. Even when the results of many of his colleagues, those who had originally appeared more ambitious, began to fall off, Flavio's results never ceased to astound. The defects, returns and waste in his department dwindled in front of everyone's eyes. Lost time diminished and best of all, the work atmosphere became more positive. At the end of the project's first year, Flavio was awarded the prize for best manager in recognition of his achievements. Everyone appreciated him. He had carved a place for himself amongst the ranks of highly prized leaders and champions.

***

Within a business context the first key of success is to clearly outline the organization's **PORTRAIT OF STRATEGIC FUNCTIONING**. This is the first step in a global approach to strategic management. Without a methodical and lucid understanding of the enterprise's operation within the whole ensemble, all efforts for improvement or correction would be mere drops in a bucket. Without this fundamental step all procedures targeting change would eventually turn against themselves, provoking new problems and inefficiencies. In the long run these efforts would be given up and put aside to reside in oblivion.

Regarding therapy, in the context of psychological intervention, the first key of success refers to the simple preliminary question I ask all clients: **"WHAT IS THE PROBLEM ?"** For individuals who have come seeking consultation, their principal preoccupation is the true problem. One must fully examine this problem from every possible angle. This is what the patient is expecting. They wish to rise above their undesired situation. In fact, they want to understand what has happened so they can free themselves from the difficulties in their life. They have not merely come to "stretch out on the sofa" and hear: "Hmm, hmm... that's nice... continue, I'm listening." They seek help. They yearn to see more clearly. They want to reach a point where they can master the wave and pull themselves out. One must be able to give to them this help. Not to make their way for them nor to fish for them, of course, but to show them how to fish. Help them understand, thus facilitating their efforts to retake control of their lives and subsequently improve their overall situation and well-being.

In order to reach this point and actually assist people with grasping the inner meaning of their troubles, it is important to help them re-situate themselves to gain a better understanding of their way of functioning and behaving. Going back to the preceding example, if Flavio hadn't fully understood his department's mode of functioning, he never would have been able to implement those efficient adjustments. Each time I do an intervention with an enterprise, we first examine the organization's dynamic of functioning. Only once we have reached a consensus of understanding of this dynamic can we, in the same way as Flavio did, complete a useful and pertinent evaluation that will guide us. The same is valid for patients in therapy. Methodically, we consider how they function on the psychological dimension and work to improve our understanding of their difficulties within this frame of reference. This enables us to make an efficient and useful evaluation that will orient the therapy.

The same principle is presently valid for you. If you wish to optimize your way of behaving and actually set yourself on the path of success, it is important to truly know yourself and understand your actual mode of functioning. Having achieved this type of under-standing you can then more easily orient yourself and prepare for the process of change (next chapter, second key to success) that will enable you to lucidly take the lead onto the way to success.

Knowing Yourself

For many of us the task of getting to know ourselves, through an honest and **concrete** examination of our mode of functioning, can be an imposing and arduous task. Our own personal reality is com-plex and diversified. Many aspects need to be considered and the greatest difficulty often resides in the fact that we don't know where to look or where to start. Beware! Don't let yourself fall into the trap of thinking you must move the whole mountain in one shot. An elephant cannot be swallowed in one gulp. It is eaten small mouthful by small mouthful. The whole idea is to know how to manage it and start off on the right foot.

When I look into a patient's problem, I first examine the apparent manifestations that occur in my client's daily life. Along with my patient I go over a list of the most evident symptoms with regard to each of the many components or spheres of activity of his or her life. I try to understand how the problem affects my patient's behavior and activity from various points of view: marital, parental, professional, interpersonal and others. When clients tell me there's a problem, that they are stressed or even depressed, they have told me everything, yet they have also told me nothing. To see more clearly, we must first accurately identify the different reactions this individual manifests in a crisis situation.

The process is essentially the same for an athlete at the beginning of a four-year Olympic cycle. We first examine the athlete's level of functioning with respect to the specific technical, tactical, phy-siological and psychological components of his or her sport. To help effectively, we must achieve a full understanding of all facets in each of these individual spheres of the athlete's particular sport. Once an enterprise's portrait of strategic functioning has been established, we then take a critical look at their behavior on the market. We need to have a clear understanding of what is most successful with respect to their products and services, keeping in mind the types of clients they serve and the types of markets they touch.

In other words, to reach an improved knowledge and understanding of self, you must first examine your behavior within your daily reality. This basic concept entails making a clear and honest judgment of your way of being within the diverse spheres of activity of your life. It is in trying to be more conscious of your reactions, attitudes and behaviors that you will truly learn about yourself and be able to progress more effectively toward attaining your objectives and your dreams.

Once you've become conscious of how you behave, it is then important to consider the various external agents likely to influence or orient your mode of functioning. What events, circumstances, material factors or people play a role or have an influential impact on your reactions and behaviors? This means learning to recognize external causes or stimuli capable of either helping you or hindering you along the course of your everyday life.

When working with patients, this means examining the many diverse facets of the reality in which they evolved. We try to identify those individuals and external factors that influence their mode of functioning, potentially provoking a manifestation of symptoms. In the case of businesses, we must take into account the political, social and economical influences as well as any others that could affect the company's output. The impact of their various competitors, suppliers and raw materials used must also be taken into consideration. With athletes, we examine the many components of their sport environment, social or human as well as the material, economical or political factors that potentially help or hinder their performance. In each case, it is essential to fully understand the play of external causes on the actions or behaviors of a person or an organization.

External factors are not the only likely sources that can influence our reactions and behaviors. As I've already mentioned, existing inside each and every one of us are all kinds of learned tendencies or predispositions, being more or less efficient, that collaborate to shape and even bias our actions and behaviors. These are the internal factors that orient the personal dynamics found at the base of our own modes of functioning.

For organizations, these internal factors refer to the habits or methods of doing, which again are more or less efficient, that prevail within administrative and manufacturing processes of enterprises or systems. It is essential to understand how sources of internal inefficiency affect an organization's output with respect to its markets and products.

For human beings – whether patient, athlete or anyone else – gaining a better understanding of the internal causes of our reactions, attitudes and behaviors forces us to question our personal sources of internal ineffectiveness. What types of shackles do we fasten around our legs to slow or even stop our own progress? What obligations or irrational beliefs do we feed on that uselessly waste our vital energy? Have we learned that we must always say yes to everyone, take care of everyone and be constantly perfect in order to be appreciated by others? Do we believe that we must absolutely be liked, appreciated and accepted by everyone around us to have worth? Are we obliged to work, without break, without rest, to be well respected? Do we endlessly repeat messages of powerlessness that limit our horizons? Do doubts, worries and uncertainties restrict our projects and our dreams? Do certain recollections of our past haunt our memories, filling us with remorse, reproach, regret or blame?

On the other hand, what personal qualities and internal forces do we possess that could help us take charge of our lives, countering the influence of our shackles and our sources of inefficiency? Do we possess or already master certain aspects of the great qualities or abilities of champions? What yet unexplored or hidden potential slumbers within, waiting to be activated and propel us beyond our limits, onto the way of success? By becoming conscious of all the various dimensions of your inner self, you will be able to more clearly see who you are and how you function in terms of your internal dynamic.

In order to move forward with your life, become more proactive and **MASTER THE WAVE** of events and circumstances that otherwise seek to toss you around in every which direction, take a step back. Give yourself some time to take your bearings and define your portrait of strategic functioning. Take advantage of this opportunity to get to know yourself better and pinpoint those elements most important to your actions and behaviors in your daily life; also examine the different external factors likely to influence you and take a lucid look at the diverse internal characteristics that steer or drive your mode of functioning.

To facilitate the task and not become overwhelmed by the scope of this exercise, don't consider all the different components or facets of your life as one. Follow the example set by champions - be **methodical** and **concrete**. The global examination of the complexity of your existence is too vast a field of exploration. I suggest subdividing your life into more precise domains or spheres of activity, which are important to you. Here are some examples of possible spheres of activity.

- o Marital: wife, husband...
- o Parental: your role as father or mother, grandparents...
- o Professional: profession, career, work, studies...
- o Interpersonal: friends, parents, colleagues...
- o Spiritual: religion, spirituality, existential questioning...
- o Intellectual: artistic interests, culture, philosophy...
- o Personal: leisure, rest, diverse interests, organization of life...
- o Bodily: health, nutrition, physical fitness...
- o Material: investments, economy, spending, possessions...
- o Others: according to your needs and your reality...

These spheres of activity are practical suggestions that enable you to split up your life experience and avoid having to consider everything at the same time, jumbled in a helter-skelter manner. If these suggestions don't correspond with your life, adapt them to fit your needs or add other domains if your reality is more complex.

To assist with your reflections, I propose you complete an exercise that will help you examine your profile of functioning with regards to your behavior, your external influences and your internal dynamic.

Close your eyes and imagine yourself in a hospital, lying on a bed, alone in a big room. All is calm and peaceful. You have been in an accident; a hit to the head has put you into a coma. For the moment, nobody knows if you will ever come out of it. As for you, which can happen with comas, you can see and hear everything going on around you. But, you can neither move nor communicate with others. You have the impression of floating in space, while being perfectly conscious of everything happening around you. You see yourself with a great lucidity and you can easily remember everything that has happened to you in your life. Next, people enter the room and sit down by your bed. Since they don't know if you will ever come out of the coma and because they think you can neither see nor hear, they speak freely. They give their impressions of who you are; they make all sorts of comments that you may have never suspected. Everything comes out, your good points as well as your bad. You hear it all, you observe everything and you forget nothing.

For this exercise to be most effective, don't bring everyone in at once. Go one at a time. For each sphere of activity identify one person, or a few people, that are very important and significant to you, individuals who know you well. Then, for each sphere, separately let these people come to your bed and listen closely to how they express themselves, to what they have to say. Watch carefully and try to gain as much as possible from your observations or the likely commentary on your way of behaving, your sources of external influence and the components of your internal dynamic.

Once you have examined each of your life spheres in this way, try, along with the results of your own reflections, to complete the best possible description of your mode of functioning with respect to your way of acting, your external influences and your internal dynamic. Those seeking to take their reflections even further can draw on the practical questions asked in the following section. These questions could help pinpoint your profile of functioning. By answering these questions you give yourself the opportunity to truly get to know yourself and better understand your personal dynamic, thus improving your ability to build a strategy of success that is perfectly adapted to your demands and needs. Each of the chapters dealing with the keys to success will be similarly concluded with a practical note to assist those individuals who wish to take the lead and go forward, to realize their dearest dreams with greater ease.

Putting it into Action

1. To fully define your behavior within each of your spheres of life, identify the principle tasks, functions, jobs or actions that you need to accomplish. Which are your most important responsibilities? What are the essential roles you must play? What duties, jobs or work must you accomplish? For all these roles, work, tasks or responsibilities, what is your way of acting in daily life? What reactions do you manifest or what attitudes do you let show through in undertaking these roles or tasks?
2. Considering the reality outside of you for each of your spheres of life, which events or circumstances interact to influence your way of behaving in your daily life? What material factors are likely to help or hinder your behavior? Who exerts an influence over you that affects your behavior?
3. To clearly examine the various aspects of your internal dynamic, look at your personal shackles or sources of inefficiency

that hinder your mode of functioning within the various spheres of your life. What messages of helplessness or useless obligations could potentially break your momentum and slow your progress? What irrational beliefs or internal myths do you hold that could needlessly drain your vital energy? What doubts, worries or uncertainties do you embrace that hold you back from acting and moving forward? What memories haunt you and possibly paralyze you? What regret, remorse, reproach or blame do you hold over your own head to crush yourself and diminish your own potential?

4. To complete the lucid portrait of your internal dynamic, don't neglect any of the personal qualities liable to prop you up and help you within each of your spheres of life. Which champion-like abilities do you possess, partially or totally, that could facilitate your task on the road to achievement? What capabilities or specific talents could you exploit to assist your progress? What internal forces live within you, at your disposal to help keep you on track throughout your progress? What special qualities characterize you and distinguish you from everyone else?

Chapter 4

THE 2ND KEY: TAME CHANGE

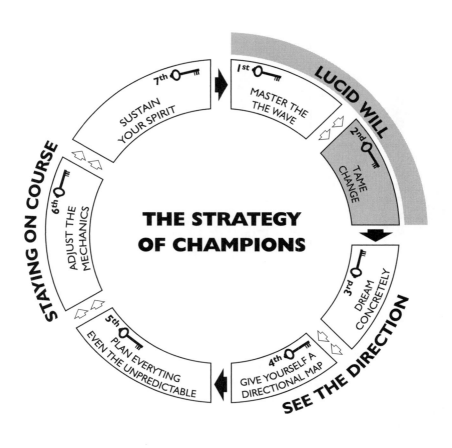

L UCID WILL is the real sparkplug of an efficient and rewarding strategy. Without a mindful and enlightened purpose, no serious undertaking or constant progression will ever be possible along the path to success.

The ideas presented in the preceding chapter can help you initiate your strategic procedure and take the first step. You have made the decision to look yourself straight in the face, get to know yourself better and discover what's on the inside. Now you should take advantage of this knowledge and learn from your own life.

The first key to success helps you become aware of how you really behave. It assists you in illustrating the ins and outs of your own personal dynamic. It enables you to familiarize yourself with the different poles and components of your lifestyle. Once done, the door to the process of change opens before you, with the promise of an improved standard of well-being and greater satisfaction. However, becoming conscious of your lifestyle and behavior is not sufficient, in and of itself, to propel you toward the achievement of your procedure for change.

In golf, understanding the game's fundamental techniques will not transform you into a champion overnight. You must take it further and integrate your knowledge and understanding in order to learn from your own experiences. After having tried and practiced, faced both triumph and disappointment, it is imperative to stop and examine your failures and dissatisfactions. Analyze your productivity and learn from the lessons that have been imposed on you, search for a way to continually adjust until you are satisfied with the end results. In other words, you cannot pass from understanding to satisfaction without going through a learning process, a period of adjustment and **CHANGE** which can only be effective once you've completed a lucid appraisal of your behavior along the course.

The second key of success illustrates how to **TAME CHANGE** by learning from your own life. It forces you to examine the picture of your mode of functioning to identify your successes and failures, your satisfactions and dissatisfactions within each different sphere of your life. The second key of success inspires you to question your strengths and weaknesses as well as search for the root source of your satisfactions and dissatisfactions. It guides you in the evaluation of your personal dynamic so you might effectively orient the necessary adjustments.

With the strategic processes of an enterprise, the second key of success corresponds with an organization's **APPRAISAL OF STRATEGIC FUNCTIONING**. To extract the appropriate lessons, here we must analyze the internal and external strengths and weaknesses of the business. The idea is to learn from the organization's own experience, to properly prepare for and integrate those changes relevant to improving overall output and efficiency.

Within the context of therapy, the second key of success helps patients become conscious of the dissatisfactions they suffer with respect to their psychological symptoms. We analyze their strong points and weak points as well as any external influences that help sustain their symptoms and dissatisfactions. We assist our clients as they learn from their own personal experiences, preparing the field for the necessary course adjustments or corrections essential to rediscovering satisfaction and well-being. We help patients become aware of the impact of their shackles and limits and ask the question: **ARE YOU READY TO CHANGE**?

Before you can learn and progress, you must first assess your mode of functioning. This is the only efficient way to achieve change and find desired satisfaction or well-being. Change is an integral part of learning. To improve my efficiency at work, I must modify certain habits and learn how to profit from my errors and frustrations. To improve my relationship with my spouse or children, I need to learn, from my own experiences, how to understand, listen and speak to them better. If I want to improve my health and feel better in my own skin, I must examine my lifestyle; discover a way to correct my behavior and master new habits, which will make me happier... and so forth.

What it means to **TAME CHANGE** is having the ability to learn from a deeper understanding of our dissatisfactions. This is the most effective way to rediscover satisfaction and success. It sounds so simple and obvious! So why don't we all do it? Why do we stick with old, inefficient habits rather than stopping to **MAKE OUR APPRAISAL**, adjust ourselves and live life at the height of our desire? The answer is as simple as the necessity for learning: learning means adjustment and adjustment means change. In fact, no phenomenon of change exists without its counterpart...

Resistance to Change

At the beginning stages of a reengineering project for an important manufacturer of heavy-duty machinery, I had the overwhelming impression that I was facing a suicidal challenge. Although the enterprise's CEO had endorsed all project details, nothing could be taken for granted. After our first meeting with various departmental directors, it was quite apparent that we were perceived as troublemakers. The message was loud and clear: "We have neither the time nor the energy to invest in a project of this sort. We don't want to hear about yet another way of functioning that will ultimately fail to yield tangible results. We already have our own improvement programs and, in any case, we don't believe in your approach."

The same skepticism prevailed among personnel. Over the last few years, the company had launched a range of quality improvement programs under the guidance of various external consultants. These efforts yielded very few substantial results and each time, after months of wasted effort by the participants, the programs were gradually abandoned. Needless to say the general attitude toward management and us, as external consultants, was something along the lines of "we're not going to let you booby-trap us yet again with another hopeless fad".

It took time, diplomacy and tangible results to slowly change this mentality. It took us a year to transform the situation, but in order to do this we had to patiently and skillfully come to terms with the **resistance to change**. This is what we faced at the onset of our reengineering project with this enterprise. I have encountered similar experiences in numerous diverse environments. Any organization attempting to improve its output cannot escape this type of reaction. Even though processes of evolution and progress may naturally develop with time and practice, inevitably a point is reached where course corrections and adjustments are needed. This is the moment where difficulties surface and the **resistance to change** emerges. The manifested reaction is protective and defensive. This is a conservative mentality, installed and polarized around such ideas as "we have always functioned this way and it has worked up to now... so why should we change?"

The same phenomenon is true for individuals. Every system, whether it is an organization or a human being, holds within itself the seeds of its own failure. At the beginning of its life cycle, a system develops efficient responses and behaviors that favor adaptation, progress and survival. In humans, these responses represent complex networks of neural patterns that are stored in memory. The more often a response is used and practiced, the stronger the neural pattern grows and the more difficult and costly it becomes to modify and replace it. This is one of the main reasons that as we age, we become more and more reluctant to modify our habits even when internal circumstances (health problems, for example) or external circumstances (increased cost of living for instance) urgently demand immediate adjustments. Rather than face this head on, we prefer to search for excuses and invent all sorts of false rationalizations that justify our inertia. At this moment we have given our shackles the latitude they need to hold us prisoners within our own limits.

The trend is identical for groups and organizations. Within the business world, responses and behaviors refer to the various manufacturing and administrative processes that are organized into operational and management networks, which often become complex and entangled. The longer these processes have been employed, the more powerful they grow, the more those individuals, rooted within their functioning, become resistant to change. Nothing moves even though countless internal factors (for example, increase in number of defects, lost time, etc.) and external factors (for example, new competitors, dissatisfied customers, etc.) indicate a pressing need for change.

When a system resists change, it is essentially trying to avoid the energetic cost of modifying habits and behaviors that it had previously made a huge effort to acquire and perfect. It simply wishes to protect its integrity. But in so doing, it mistakes preservation of its present mode of functioning for a guarantee of survival. This is when individuals, as well as organizations, become most vulnerable to irrational decisions and quick fixes.

The relentless necessity for course corrections, combined with a natural aversion to change, drives people to search for a magic pill. We seek our desired paradise in a quick, effortless fix, which, we hope, will allow us to bypass the cost and effort required to adjust habits and efficiently achieve change. Unfortunately, too many consultants, specialists of all types or supposed experts profit from this vulnerability and abuse their distressed clients by selling them every promise and miracle they're willing to buy. The risk associated with this type of adventure, is endlessly walking from one approach to another, surfing on the popular trends, never facing the true problem, until the point where draconian remedies become inevitable. Once this point of no return is reached, the survival of the system often requires emergency surgery. In the business world this means cutting personnel, closing down subsidiaries or discontinuing products that had been successful up until then. The organization might survive but it will never be what it once was. Its past prestige, power, prosperity and market share are now only memories. Recapturing yesterday's position and influence, at this point, will demand considerably more energy than it would have to adjust and modify a few inefficient responses and behaviors when there was still time.

This type of problem is also found at the individual level. Athletes who have neglected to find proper methods for controlling their reactions to stress because they are hoping for the magic pill to pull them through, will be unable to endure competition in the long run and will consider quitting. People who let their worries and fears run wild rather than trying to face them and adjust, will eventually be incapable of functioning normally in everyday life. Excessive behavior, bad habits and lies we entertain about ourselves, all under the pretext of profiting from life, are attempts to escape the effort of change. The illusion can be maintained up until the time when the critical point is reached, and suffering, sickness and disease come to claim their due. Climbing back up the hill is extremely tedious whereas it would have been much easier and less costly to make adjustments back when we still had energy and time.

Examples of the search for easy solutions or magic recipes abound in all spheres of human activity, whether it is groups, individuals or enterprises. All these fixed ideas hold the system within the illusion that the safeguarding of its functioning, which had appeared suitable until then, is guaranteeing its longevity, satisfaction and survival. In reality, this does nothing but delay the moment when we must face the real problems and make the required corrections.

Our flight from making course adjustments is an attempt to avoid the effort and energetic costs associated with change. It requires extreme prudence to evade this trap and escape our system's natural reaction. Thoughtful control is essential in making sure that our endeavors to improve and adjust our mode of functioning will not provoke the opposite effect, the resistance to change, which holds us on the path to failure and inefficiency until the point of no return.

The 10 Golden Rules for Successful Change

In order to change, fundamental principles must be respected. In my experience, I have found that the success of change is controlled by ten golden rules. When we fail to respect these rules and neglect these basic principles, any procedure of change will eventually stall, lose momentum and sink into the abyss of its own inertia.

Rule #1: Be Convinced of the Advantages of Change

If we fail to perceive the necessity of change and remain unconvinced of its advantages, we then cling to the comforting benefits of the status quo. When attempting to convince ourselves of the advantages of change, there are three dimensions to consider:

° The risks and disadvantages of not changing;
° The benefits of changing;
° The benefits of not changing.

Suppose you are increasingly dissatisfied with your physical fitness and health, numerous signs indicate your general condition is slowly deteriorating. Thus you decide to take charge of yourself and correct the situation by modifying certain habits. You decide to quit smoking, drink less alcohol, eat better and start exercising again.

Those are all great intentions! But will you really modify each targeted habit? To see whether you're being realistic, examine each intention under the light of the three dimensions just mentioned. So, if for quitting smoking:

1. You are not inconvenienced and have only a small risk of cancer;
2. You see no other benefits besides an improved odor in your apartment;
3. You take enormous pleasure in each cigarette you smoke,

hence, chances are strong that you will not persist to the end of the road of change for this habit! You are not being realistic or, put another way, it will be incredibly difficult to vanquish your own natural resistance to quit smoking.

If on the other hand, your evaluation showed that:

1. You cough ever more frequently, have lots of difficulty breathing and your doctor already considers you a walking corpse;
2. You remember a time when you were able to breathe comfortably, walk and play golf. The pleasures of that sport would once again be accessible if you quit smoking;
3. You no longer find gratification in smoking and just the mere thought of a cigarette turns you green from head to toe,

so, here the probability is much stronger that you will see your decision through to the end. In this case, you'll have an easier time convincing yourself of the advantages of change and thus be able to overcome any hesitations that might linger within. It is realistic to believe that you will tame your resistance to change.

This type of reasoning is valuable for any and all habits you wish to modify. When attempts to change are unsuccessful, somewhere, inevitably, exists a benefit that we still cling to and therefore we resist the change.

From a practical point of view, this benefit is invariably the avoidance of all modifications or adjustments where the advantages of change fail to outweigh the required effort and energetic cost. In other words, to modify a comfortable old habit, we must first perceive the benefit, or else we won't move. The positive value of change must outweigh the inconveniences associated with carrying it out.

You must never under-estimate the importance and repercussions of this first golden rule. In every domain and for all cases where adjustments are required, the advantages of change need to be clearly demonstrated. If I cannot persuade my patients of the full beneficial value of a particular psychological intervention tool or technique, they will gradually discontinue their efforts so as to return to the status quo of their habitual functioning. Athletes will never participate in a stress control or mental preparation program unless they are convinced of the positive consequences that would compensate their hard work, trials and tribulations. No enterprise or group of workers will want to modify their habits and work conditions if the advantages of change fail to thoroughly surpass the benefits of changing nothing.

Rule #2: Count on Your Allies

Further to avoiding effort and energetic cost when these elements surpass the potential advantages of change, a system's natural tendency is to continually maintain the mode of functioning that has always, in the past, been satisfactory. In other words, a system instinctively seeks preservation of the internal equilibrium that guarantees its well-being. In this sense, all open systems (large organizations, enterprises, human beings, cells, etc.) favor homeostasis[5] in comparison to change.

Unless driven to the brink, a system will rarely take the initiative and risk modifying its habitual functioning to head towards some so called well-being. Being convinced of the advantages of change is not an absolute guarantee that a system will vanquish the natural resistance engendered by its tendency for homeostasis and maintenance of stability. Left to itself, a system is inclined to spon-taneously slide, often without even being aware, toward its old reflexes. It will seek to revert to the security and comfort of its most familiar universe.

One of the most efficient ways of avoiding this trap is to get support, to search for allies that will help us stay on the road to change. For certain people self-help groups (e.g.: alcoholics anonymous, depression anonymous, weight watchers, etc.) give them all the support and comfort they need to progress and persist. Others need someone closer, a trusted parent or friend. Some might also consider the possibility of getting professional help from competent experts (e.g.: psychologists, doctors, social workers or other specialists) who have the know-how and training to skillfully assist with the process of change.

It doesn't matter what type of support you seek, external assis-tance and social support are precious assets that will help you avoid the trap of returning to your old reflexes. In the business world, there are a wide variety of consultants whose capabilities are suited to helping organizations get back on track. The best ath-letes never hesitate in turning to a gamut of experts to help them correct and improve their performance. Why don't we do the same when it comes to our own difficulties and well-being? In psychol-ogy, social support has, for quite some time, been recognized as one of the most important factors in helping us face and adapt to problems of stress, illness or psychological difficulties[6]. External assistance furnishes us with precious allies who will support us in difficult moments and help us persist when the pull of our natural tendencies threatens to engulf our efforts to change.

Counting on your allies is not uniquely limited to the external support or social support we might rally to facilitate our task. There exists as well, inside every system, living forces that, in order to be of assistance in our progression, merely require being tapped. Unfortunately, these treasures are too often neglected or ignored under the influence of everyday habits that seek to maintain the status quo. Within the business context, I have often witnessed that, voluntarily or otherwise, we have overlooked the potential of individuals whose competence, dynamism and good will should have been taken into account for the greater good of the organization. Either caught up in the power of routine or blinded by the fear of change, we have neglected those very assets that were valuable to the survival and optimization of the enterprise.

From an individual point of view, the same blindness causes us, too hastily, to overlook our inner strengths and qualities, those that would help us with our project for change. Within us, there exist idle resources that, when the time comes, we don't know how to exploit to help us break our vicious cycle of inefficiency. Let us return to the example of changing life habits. An efficient and brilliant businessman, despite all his abilities and successes, did not take himself suitably in hand concerning his general health. He has, among other things, tried to quit smoking on many occasions, but always started up again after only a few weeks. He nevertheless felt that the advantages of quitting were greater than the effort required to do so. At that point we examined his strategy within a more global perspective, taking into account all the golden rules for a successful process of change. From that moment he began to realize, in his personal life, the kind of satisfaction and success that contented him in his business life.

One of the first things that surfaced from examining his strategy is the fact that he had never, up until then, searched for allies to help him with his goal of improving his health. He never looked for any external support nor appealed to a professional for assistance with his development. Yet, at work, he never thought twice about finding allies or consulting with experts when it came to adjusting his aim and progressing.

We identified the personal strengths and qualities that allowed him to succeed in business. It was surprising to discover that he didn't know how to use these superb capabilities when it came to correcting his personal failings. This self-examination inspired him to modify his approach to personal change. From this point on, he looked for allies within his life. He sought the support of a friend who'd quit smoking over six months ago. He consulted with a medical expert to seriously evaluate his health and a nutritionist to analyze and adapt his dietary habits. By seeking my own expertise and assistance he successfully put together a more realistic approach for optimizing his procedure for change.

On a personal level, he began exploiting the internal qualities and strengths that had always assured him of success in the business world. With his enterprise, he persistently had a global vision of the situation and problems. He was methodical, concrete, patient and optimistic. When he began a course of action, he persisted right through to the end never contemplating the easy way out that only offered the fleeting illusion of satisfaction. All these qualities henceforth became internal allies, which he could count on for support. Inspired by his winning attitude in business, we were able to initiate an efficient strategy to truly modify his life habits.

Rule #3: Bring Over the Opposition

When a system – an individual, organization, enterprise, etc. – wants to change its manner of functioning, it will invariably confront opposition resisting its efforts to progress. Similar to allies, the source of this opposition can be internal as much as external. Whenever a government decides to make cutbacks to reduce the national debt, all individuals and groups affected will vehemently oppose the cuts despite a general consensus that action is long overdue. The same holds true for cabinet ministers and elected officials. We should make cuts to others but not to us! When a corporation adjusts its products, services or internal operations, there will always be clients or beneficiaries who oppose the change or employees or managers who resist. The organization is in bad need of rescue but don't touch our services or operations!

Opposition to change is inevitable and comes in numerous forms. This is not the problem. The problem resides more in the fact that we don't take our opposition seriously enough. We don't take the time to sufficiently examine all of its implications and significance. We too easily neglect its impact of inertia and the danger it poses to the survival of the system.

To put an efficient strategy for change in place, it is imperative that you consider all aspects of internal and external opposition that you will encounter. Every facet must be examined in order to discover the one approach that will win over a maximum number of opponents. This means knowing how to humbly yet powerfully build allies from those who would otherwise threaten the system's survival.

The same principles apply on an individual level. Within your entourage, there will always be those affected by your change. Your new habits might upset their way of doing things or disrupt their thinking, forcing them to adapt in some way as well. Unless you know how to cope with the repercussions generated by your adjustments, all your efforts might become stifled. In underestimating the impact of the wave created by your desire for change you will surely sink the very progress you strive for.

Further, you must not forget that the consequences of change are not just external in nature. Each time you consider modifying your way of being, you are threatening all your old beliefs, shackles or values that were extremely satisfied with your old, inefficient attitudes and reflexes. Similarly, your system's internal opponents won't simply disappear. Therefore, it is important to accurately identify them so that you can understand their influence, neutralize them and eventually transform them into allies for your dynamic of change.

Referring back to the case I began telling you about, this is what our businessman had to do. He knew if he quit smoking for good, he would upset certain people. His wife and son smoked in the house; his principal associate and his secretary did the same at work. He no longer wanted to breathe their nicotine, but at the same time, he didn't want to provoke any conflicts nor arouse any aggressive or tenacious opposition. He needed to explain, negotiate and define rules for the game, which would satisfy everyone. It wasn't easy but with goodwill and an open spirit, he was able to form allies from those who could otherwise have nipped his efforts for change in the bud.

On an internal level, this man didn't like to hide the truth from himself. He quickly became aware that he had a certain tendency toward magical thinking and ignorance, which maintained his bad habit. He naively believed that sickness was for others. He embraced the idea that, despite the fact that he smoked, one little cigarette every once in a while would not hurt him. He, too easily, allowed himself to contemplate the pleasure of gently inhaling his drug of choice. Once he became conscious of his internal dynamic, he was able to achieve true progress. We worked at modifying and restructuring his way of thinking about this subject matter; subsequently he was able to create allies from those ideas that otherwise would have been powerful enemies against his will to change.

Rule #4: Commit to Change

Once the door to change has been opened, it is no longer time to step back. Each renunciation, each abandonment nourishes a feeling of learned helplessness, amplifying the weight of inertia that holds us prisoner within our own limits. This is another reason why it's important to clearly see the advantages of change. Once this is clear in your mind and your will is genuine and lucid, it is time to dive in and get wet.

Diving cannot be done halfway. In order to move forward, we must assume complete responsibility for change. By relinquishing the burden to others, we are trying to keep an exit open in case the amplitude of the risks and efforts becomes too big. Lucid will to change implies unambiguous commitment, as much to ourselves as to others.

Within the business context, I have seen managers throw out orders for important modifications, then squarely place the responsibility for change on the shoulders of their assistants. This way they can distance themselves and if difficulties should arise, they have the leisure to cry out, loud and strong, that they neither asked nor wished for the situation to sour. Thus, they were the first to renounce their initiative and let down those who were compromised for them.

This is the surest way to squash the dynamism of an entire organization, killing the desire of the most progressive elements. Within an enterprise, one of the essential conditions for moving forward with a project necessitating change is the uncontestable support and formal commitment of upper management. This means upper management should never hesitate to compromise itself within plain view of the whole organization, it must reveal its true colors and explain the why and the how of change to all personnel. It must also display its will to back what it claims, all the way to the end, while actually engaging in the process and continually following the progress. Without a commitment of this sort, the risks are enormous that good intentions, which had been so obvious at the onset, will be transformed into pious vows, a mere smoke screen for good conscience, without risk or effort.

On an individual level, the problems associated with change are the same. To avoid the trap of false perspective and evade the refuge of easy excuses, we must not be afraid of making an unambiguous commitment. Being able to affirm what we wish to attain, knowing how to explain ourselves and having the courage to hold onto our assertions are all qualities that can help us achieve change. For certain people, this poses a problem. Some of us are afraid to openly express our wants or desires. In certain cases, a superstitious attitude is maintained within shadows along the course of change: "The mere fact that I hope for it, think of it or express it, is enough for it not to work!" In other cases, the fear of not succeeding, of disappointing ourselves or others, of looking like an idiot or a weakling in someone else's eyes, drive some people to avoid any commitment using potential risks as an excuse. These fears may often be based on bad experiences and, in this sense, appear perfectly legitimate. We must never lose sight of the fact that, behind these attitudes, we are often hiding a protective barrier erected by our irrational shackles. Irrational beliefs like "you must always be perfect" or "you must never make mistakes" certainly don't favor a firm and honest commitment to a process of change where difficulties and risks are rarely avoidable.

Avoiding commitment very often equates to giving free reign to the influence of our shackles. The more freedom this influence has, the more vulnerable the change becomes to suffocation. Meanwhile, this doesn't mean we should shout out our commitment from the rooftops nor harshly impose it on others, with neither discernment nor restraint. We must not forget that our commitment is part of a global strategy intended to ensure our success. It is important to become lucidly engaged in this strategy, keeping in mind that allies will need to be found, opponents will need to be brought over and, sometimes, adversaries will need to be out-maneuvered.

Once he had decided to quit smoking, the businessman of our example never hid this fact. He clearly explained the situation to the significant individuals within his entourage. He was unafraid of affirming his will to change despite both his previous failures and the fact that his pride could be hurt in the event that, once again, he was unable to persevere. This marked the first occasion where he took such measures and committed himself to such an extent. In contrast, this time his strategy was clear and he had given himself concrete methods to see him through to the end of his process.

Rule #5: Don't Tackle Everything at Once

Once we've committed ourselves on the road to change and believe in the promises available to us, we can easily become impatient to reach our objectives. We want everything to happen as soon as possible and too often are ready to hasten the process by attacking everything at once.

This impulse is a common error that could rapidly sinks a strategy for change. Any undertaking, lacking order or method, will exhaust our energy without, the majority of the time, realizing any significant or tangible results. When I work with patients or athletes, first we put all the targets of their process of change in order. If, in order to increase their control over their reaction to stress, they need to reduce their muscular tension, improve adjustment of their activation, correct their attitude, enhance their concentration and restructure their negative internal dialogue, it is completely unrealistic to attack all these targets at the same time. We need to know where to start and establish our priorities. This obliges us to choose the elements of change that will most likely produce important and significant results in the short term. If we've chosen well, our short-term success will rapidly boost our confidence in our capabilities for improvement. We will therefore have the desire to continue and persist. There is also a good chance that we have indirectly improved our situation concerning the other targets that haven't yet been worked on directly.

The dynamic is entirely analogous within the realm of business. At the onset of any process of change, an organization often has the tendency to want to resolve everything at once or attack the problems that appear easiest to correct. With this attitude, we quickly return to the fireman's reflex, meaning we are continually extinguishing fires but never making any fundamental changes. Nevertheless, there is a wise principle, which states that solving 20% of the most important, sensitive issues yields an 80% improvement of the overall output[7]. To identify those few difficulties with the greatest impact, we need to take the time to set priorities.

The fourth key to success (chapter 6) gives a detailed explanation of how to efficiently and tangibly establish priorities. Continuing with the example of our businessman, it soon became clear that it was unrealistic to try and improve his health by tackling everything at once: smoking, alcohol consumption, dietary habits and physical exercise. The steps were too high. He would have rapidly become disheartened, discouraged and would have given up everything, resulting in yet another sense of failure. To avoid this, we established priorities. His most important victory was to quit smoking. Next came physical exercise, dietary habits and, lastly, alcohol consumption. This table of priorities enabled us to outline a working calendar to which we added, one after another, his four targets for change. Through each successful step, within a prioritized order, he was able to rebuild his confidence and gradually attain all of his objectives.

Rule #6: Identify the Real Causes

In order for a change to become effectively established, momentarily attaining our objective is not sufficient. The correction should not be merely temporary. It is important, on the contrary, that the obtained result be sustained; that the new habit persist and that which was once just an objective becomes a permanent standard of functioning.

One of the essential conditions for achieving permanent change is to attack the real causes of our difficulties and problems. If my car engine has overheated and I've added coolant to bring the temperature back to normal, I might have the impression that I've solved the problem. But, is this really the case? If the car repeatedly overheats, and I regularly add more liquid, I have decisively solved nothing. I modified something (constant addition of liquid) to make myself feel better, but I did not eliminate the source of the problem.

When athletes take medication to reduce their anxiety or stress throughout the days leading up to a competition, they've merely attenuated their symptoms. Nothing has been resolutely solved; the same reactions will surface from one competition to the next, often with a growing intensity. When an enterprise attempts to reduce costs by cutting personnel in one grand sweep of the broom, in the majority of cases they have not actually eliminated the problem. Inefficiencies of administration and production persist and continue to cause unnecessary costs, perpetually endangering the organization's survival.

A similar problem exists concerning the treatment of individual psychological problems. Too many specialists, in the domain of psychology, essentially focus their intervention on the incessant examination and virtual obsession of what they consider the deep-rooted cause of their patients' malaise, meaning their childhood experience and their resulting internal dynamic. But, is this the true cause? If this were the case, an examination of this nature would produce positive and permanent results. This is far from the truth. I have seen numerous patients who had already spent two, three and even five years in therapy and had changed nothing in their lives. They have endured intensive examinations. They know the details of their internal dynamic by heart: conflicts with their father or mother, frustrations they've experienced, poorly digested interdictions, reproaches suffered, a lack of valorization, abandonment, rejection… everything. Nevertheless, they were still just as unhappy! Invariably, the classic excuse of any specialist was that more time was needed, that the patient had not yet understood everything nor sufficiently integrated all the facts to achieve an effective change.

In calling attention to these aspects of psychological treatment, it is not my goal to foolishly and blindly criticize neither introspection nor the psychodynamic approach to therapy. The fundamental question I ask, as with the other examples I've provided, is: have we identified the true cause of our problems? Have we put our finger on what needs correcting to achieve an efficient, satisfying and permanent change? It is not necessarily a bad thing, in and of itself, to examine the past history of our patients and help them understand their internal psychodynamic. On the contrary, this step is valuable in helping us choose the appropriate tools for treatment, in knowing how to use them effectively and thus enabling us to adapt the therapy to suit the needs of the client. But in order to do this, the introspective exam must lead to the intervening techniques best suited for correcting the real causes of our unsatisfactory functioning.

How do we define what a real cause is? First of all, it is a cause that is found at the source of a problem AND is always active in sustaining its negative effects. For our example of the overheating car engine, the drop in coolant could be due to a leak in the radiator, which could have been caused by the impact of a previous accident. Thus, the source of the problem is the accident, but it is no longer active in the present. That which acts directly on the recurring loss of liquid is the puncture. This is the real cause, where we must focus our efforts to solve the problem. The accident can never be eliminated.

Similar logic also applies in the treatment of psychological problems. The primary source of any difficulty might very well be traced back to conflicts with parents, a lack of valorization or neglect, whatever. These undesirable elements, just as in the case of the accident, are in the past and cannot be changed. What we can rectify is how these past events affect our definition of the world, our expectations, our beliefs, our values or what psychoanalysts call our *symbolization* of reality[8]. Through repairing the radiator leak, we eliminate the problem. It is only by adjusting or correcting the flaws of our internal functioning – the contents of our memory, our *symbolization*, representation or transformation of reality – that we can successfully solve our problems. In other words, by targeting the active source - that which is still responsible for the existence and maintenance of our present difficulties - we attack the real root of our problem.

Another important dimension should be taken into consideration when focusing on the **real** cause of our dissatisfaction and discontentment. It's about how much **control** we actually have when attempting to bring about change. There are three categories of situations or circumstances: those over which we have total or direct control, those over which we have an indirect or partial influence and those that altogether escape our control or influence.

All that touches our own personal behavior, reactions or functioning, falls into the first category. We can always directly, or even totally, control our way of behaving, our technical execution in a sport or our production quality within an enterprise. It is up to no one else but us to take the appropriate measures and do it. We might indirectly or partially influence the behaviors or reactions of others, depending on our mastery of interpersonal relations. Finally, there are situations over which we have absolutely no control, like the type of competition site for an athlete, the present temperature, rising cost of living, and so on. For all these elements outside our control, we must learn to live with them. We must adapt our attitude and reactions and adjust as well as possible to maintain our optimal state of functioning.

When working on our problems or eliminating our dissatisfaction, it is imperative that we clearly recognize the nature of each cause. We will only be able to successfully provoke change by attacking that which is within our total or partial control. A desire to alter the past is out of reach. It is a useless waste of energy to scold ourselves for the accident that punctured the radiator. Holding the strong competition on the international market responsible for the difficulties encountered by the enterprise will only bring the organization to the brink of the abyss without ever solving the internal problems that actually undermine its efficiency and productivity.

Identifying the real causes of your dissatisfactions and problems thus means detecting the primary sources:
1. which are at the root of the problem and continually active in the present...
2. over which you have total or partial control...
3. which will enable you to make a significant and durable change.

When the businessman in our example decided to attack his smoking, lack of fitness, dietary habits and consumption of alcohol, he targeted the real causes of his poor state of health. Each was the source of his dissatisfaction and was always active in his daily life. He had direct or total control over every target and by mastering each one he could hope to improve his health in an important and decisive manner.

Rule #7: Think of Tangible Results

Working unceasingly, without respite, and never seeing any tangible results is another sure-fire way to discourage the living forces prepared to invest time and energy to optimize a system's productivity. The attainment of concrete results in the short term, if possible, is one of the most important means of building intrinsic motivation. Results and success help build self-confidence and the perception of competence, which, in turn, encourages participation and persistence, leading to yet more results, success and motivation... and so on. Contrarily, if there are no tangible repercussions or if results take too long in coming, motivation fades and the flame goes out. Participation and persistence decrease, efforts quickly run out of steam and the efficiency problems become greater and greater, to the point of threatening the integrity and survival of the system.

Thinking in terms of concrete results is essential for successful change. It is important that gradual progress be observed and obtained as quickly as possible. This does not mean we should be giving ourselves the impression of improvement; it is essential that we respect our priorities and stick with the most fundamental difficulties and problems if we wish to maximize positive outcomes. Planning for concrete results in the short term is, essentially, defining small steps for our priorities that we could gradually climb, one by one, with success. This is how from accomplishment to satisfaction we finally reach the top of the staircase with a fulfilling and successful feeling of change behind us.

The planning of small steps to create obvious, successive results is a tool that must be manipulated with care. It is not always easy to translate our desires and wishes into tangible terms. How can I concretely define a better relationship with my spouse or children? For an athlete, what type of practical results would demonstrate improved confidence or better concentration? What does it actually mean to create a better image or improve the work climate within a business?

Before beginning a procedure for change, it is imperative that our desires and wishes are operationally expressed. This means that every one of our chosen intentions should be defined by a series of practical actions, which, at each step, yields observable and tangible results. Without this effort, any procedure of change becomes nothing but wishful thinking. Each objective we set should be described in terms of practical as well as measurable results to be attained. Every action we perform should generate concrete consequences, producing continual progress that takes us closer and closer to the practical objectives we are aiming at.

We will learn, in chapters six and seven, how to translate our desires and wishes into practical objectives and concrete actions. For the businessman of our example, tangible results were relatively easy to set. For smoking, it meant going from more than two packs a day to quitting completely by a set date; this was done gradually over the course of a month. The improvement of his physical condition through exercise was translated into precise measures of cardiovascular efficiency, muscular force and joint flexibility. His nutritional habits were expressed by quantity and quality of food, taking into account both calories and the essential food groups of a balanced diet. Alcohol consumption corresponded to a specific quantity of milliliters per week that was gradually diminished until a desired level was achieved. Each of these practical measures enabled him to express his process of change in terms of tangible results, allowing him to follow his gradual progress with time.

Rule #8: Deliver the Goods

One of the major obstacles I faced at the start of our reengineering project with the aforementioned manufacturer of heavy-duty machinery, concerned management's credibility for keeping promises. Employees were too often given the impression of being pressed into procedures of change that rapidly ran out of gas and were then put aside into the realm of oblivion. None of these previous undertakings ever delivered the results as promised, dangled before them by zealous advertising. For the great majority, at the heart of the organization, new projects meant wasted effort. Because they had no choice, people gave the impression of participating while trying to stay out of trouble and do the least possible. It took a lot of patience and a firmly defined strategy to eventually vanquish the weight of inertia that stalled any significant progress.

I witnessed a similar phenomenon play out at the heart of a sports team. The coach had always pushed his athletes to work harder and harder, while endlessly dangling the promise of getting all sorts of experts and specialists to come help optimize the team's performance. He had outlined many projects of this sort, each more interesting than the other, until one day his athletes realized he had never once delivered the goods. The flame went out, the team collapsed and the coach was blamed. The damage had been done. It took some convincing before I could gain enough credibility, in the team's eyes, to help them rediscover that dynamism essential to their success.

Empty words and broken promises always come back to haunt us. It is the same on an individual level. Every time we give up on ourselves, our self-esteem and confidence in our abilities to change and create a better situation, diminish, become extinguished and are even transformed into paralyzing inertia. Each time we make ourselves believe that we will achieve this or that, without ever actually tackling anything, we sow and keep strong within ourselves, the very inertia that will turn us into daydreamers for whom life becomes nothing more than a timeless mirage where illusion is the rule.

To avoid this trap, we must be sure to **deliver the goods**. To do this, first we must define a series of precise action plans taking even the unpredictable into consideration. Next, we must make certain that we will follow through with these plans, by coming up with a systematic follow-up process that won't let us quit before we reach our ultimate goals. There are no magic solutions. There are only concrete, efficient and precise methods that can guide us onto the way of successful change.

With the fifth and sixth keys to success (chapters 7 and 8) we will see, in more detail, how to build action plans and assure ourselves of following them through to the end. This is what the businessman, from our example, knew how to do. Before working on each of his targets (smoking, exercise, nutrition and alcohol), he established a precise action plan to achieve the concrete goals he had set. In each case, he clearly determined what he had to do, how he would do it, by what deadline, and who would be involved. He then established intermediate objectives (the small steps of the previous rule) so he could methodically follow the evolution of his progress. He also solicited my support and coaching for the duration of his strategy for change, to help him stay on course.

Rule #9: Psych Yourself Up

As I mentioned in explaining rule number seven, working unceasingly, without ever seeing any results, is neither encouraging nor motivating. Setting concrete results and objectives, reaching them and observing the gradual evolution of our progress, is one of the most efficient ways to spark our interest and incite us to follow things through. However, all this is not enough to persistently sustain us in times of darkness and pain.

Motivation is a complex phenomenon and is often fragile, for the individual as much as at the heart of groups and organizations. When difficulties arise, during times when pressures are heavier and tensions more strained, we have the tendency to go back to our old reflexes, which up to then have always assured our success. Successful change is strongly credited to the motivation of the participants. Underestimating the cunning and force of the phenomenon of "demotivation", when it surfaces, is to essentially run straight toward our own failure before we even have time to realize what's happening. The only efficient way to protect against this trap is through prevention.

Many methods are used to ward off a drop in motivation and preserve the living flame that animates us at the beginning of a procedure of change. For all projects commenced within a business context, we carefully examine every component that is likely to help the organization maintain its spirit. In each case we put a system of recognition into place that acknowledges not only the results obtained, but also the competence and effort of those involved. In addition, we aim to make these same people responsible, to empower them to take an active part in the established decision-making processes and follow the course of the project. We endlessly search for a new way of proceeding that is dynamic, stimulating and interesting. We continually readjust our motivation tools along the way, to make sure that habits, familiarization or boredom do not create an environment conducive to the development of the phenomenon of "demotivation".

What is true in the business world is valid everywhere. Valuing the efforts and competence of athletes is just as important as rewarding their results. Learning to reward ourselves for the same reasons is also extremely fundamental. Too often we forget to appreciate our true value, especially when trying to overcome our dissatisfactions. We look at the path ahead and see all the work that still has to be done. But why not also recognize the road already traveled and enjoy it for what it is: a step climbed and another success that deserves being praised. Gaining a sense of responsibility with regard to ourselves, following the evolution of our own progress, modifying and adjusting our approach when boredom and routine overcome us, these are sure enough methods to counter the trap of "demotivation".

With the seventh and last key to success (chapter 9), we will take a detailed look at the diverse motivation techniques we can use to more effectively **encourage ourselves** and sustain our spirit along the way of change. We used some of these techniques with our businessman for optimizing his chances to reach the end of his process. For each small step climbed, we had, among other things, anticipated particular rewards (e.g.: going to restaurants, concerts, trips, etc.) that he would not have obtained if he hadn't satisfactorily reached his objectives. He also put tables of results up on his office wall, where all his commitments to change could be easily observed. This was his way of giving himself social recognition, while stimulating his pride and motivation. Finally, we regularly revised his system of encouragement by adjusting all the motivational factors that were less efficient or had lost their appeal.

Rule #10: Assume Leadership

The tenth and final golden rule of successful change is to assume leadership right through to the end of our journey. The decision to change must come from within for our will to be clear and lucid. Even though we may be influenced by the surrounding environment or by external incentive and encouragement, even though there may be outside pressure, the undertaking must still be rooted in our own personal motivation and internal awareness for it to have the slightest chance for success. For those patients or athletes who come to me in order to satisfy external pressures from their parents, trainers or anyone else in their entourage, I refuse to commit to their therapy. I tell them that they must first decide for themselves whether they wish to continue; otherwise they would be wasting their money and time as well as my own time.

Unless these individuals are ready to assume leadership of their undertaking, they will not commit themselves through to the end. They will search for a myriad of excuses in order to avoid the work or efforts involved and tend to endlessly attempt to prove that they don't need help nor even need to change. The same phenomenon appears within groups and organizations. If, within an enterprise, management, with neither explanation nor justification, unwisely imposes a change, its employee base will never willingly assume a leadership role in the process. Regardless of the nature of the project, as interesting as it may be, it will encounter nothing but resistance and rejection. It is extremely important, at the organizational level, that a sound marketing plan is put in place to justify and sell any change process. Unless we've motivated a critical mass of individuals to commit towards the project's goals, not much will actually take place and nothing of significance will ever be achieved.

The value of assuming leadership is not limited to the beginning phase of a change process. It is equally vital to preserve mastery and control throughout, right to the end. There are two dangers to watch out for here: external tossing and internal tossing. The former is a consequence of being reliant on the external influence of anyone and everyone – advisors, consultants or experts – without sufficiently preserving a critical eye toward the direction we should follow and the actions to undertake. Patients, who are overly reliant on my support and passively submit to my opinion and expertise, have a harder time overcoming their difficulties than those who question my input, would like to understand the process and want to be actively involved in the orientation of their therapy. Those clients or athletes, who run from one specialist to another and continually modify their beliefs to align with those of their current expert, have just as tough a time surmounting their troubles. They are never able to take themselves in hand and choose a course of action they can follow, on their own, right through to the end. A similar phenomenon occurs within enterprises that employ a varied range of consultants and experts, with no one on the inside having any kind of coherent, global vision of what they wish to achieve. When leadership makes this serious mistake, the procedure for change becomes so scattered and divided that inner meaning is lost and a situation that was already dismal, deteriorates even more.

Internal tossing, for its part, surfaces when we fail to devote adequate time and care to becoming aware and mastering the internal influences that try to lead us around to their liking and changing fancy. For individuals, this signifies underestimating and neglecting the negative impact of our shackles, weaknesses and other ineffective facets of how we define our world. Despite initial good intentions, the change process will be disrupted and slowed by those internal factors on which we have yet to enforce our leadership.

The same is true for enterprises where the top management, having initiated change, possesses neither the clairvoyance nor the courage to hold up against all the demands and pressures and maintain a constant and coherent line of action. I worked with a plant manager who had such an intense need to please and be accepted by his colleagues that he never made any important decisions unless he had the absolute consent of each and everyone. If one single manager expressed disagreement, he would cancel or postpone his decision on the grounds of failing to achieve a unanimous consensus. During this period, his lack of leadership cost his company tens of thousands of dollars per day in inefficiency and loss of production.

Without clear leadership, without an "iron fist in a velvet glove", the probabilities are very slight that a change process will be successful. The businessman from our example was always able to grasp this truth. Once he made the decision to improve his health, he assumed complete responsibility for all his efforts. First off, he wasn't doing it in order to please someone else or in response to any demands or pressures from his entourage. He realized that the path would not be easy but, for him, that was part of the process and he was ready to pay the price. Throughout our work together, he always maintained an autonomous and critical spirit regarding my support and suggestions. He wanted to understand things and assure himself that everything suited his needs and would actually help him optimize his process of change. He never gave up his leadership to abandon himself to the influence of others or become dominated by his own shackles. He faced his reality in a strategic, coherent and lucid manner. By respecting the ten golden rules of successful change, he was able to achieve all his objectives and design for himself the type of health he had wished for after neglecting it for so many years.

Hints for Taming Change

As I mentioned before, to be able to putt successfully in golf, it is not enough to understand the technique. We need to attempt the stroke, and then analyze our execution in order to continually correct and **change** those elements that aren't working until we are satisfied with the end results. The process is the same in life. We have lived diverse experiences and learned numerous habits, but we are not necessarily happy with how things are or who we've become. If we desire complete fulfillment, we need to stop ourselves and evaluate the situation so we might adequately reorient our approach regarding **change**.

With the first key to success, we gained awareness of the most important components of our lives. Our reflection enabled us to separate those factors, internal as much as external that are linked to our modes of functioning. To go further, we must profit from this examination. It is time to learn from our experiences to steadily pass from comprehension to satisfaction.

To reach that point of satisfaction, the most relevant approach consists of establishing, from our individual profiles of functioning, a personal, lucid and honest appraisal of what is satisfying and disappointing within our lives. This means taking stock of the reasons behind our satisfactions and dissatisfactions, our successes and failures, so we may correctly orient those action plans that will enable us to improve, adjust and progress. This is the actual implication of **TAMING CHANGE**: preparing a favorable field for the course adjustments that will help us satisfy our hopes and expectations. This is the purpose of the second key to success of the strategy of champions.

To concretely and efficiently tame change, we must rely on the first three golden rules of successful change: convincing ourselves of the advantages of change, counting on our allies and bringing over the opposition. Each of the other seven rules will be integrated, at an opportune time, with the other keys to success. This gives our life strategy an essential effectiveness that enables us to face reality and adapt to change.

In order to complete our personal appraisal, while respecting the first three rules of successful change, we must revisit our different life spheres. We need to consider our various responsibilities, roles, tasks and functions and identify our satisfactions and dissatisfactions within our life perspective. We must distinguish those elements we appreciate and want to conserve from those we wish to modify with respect to our activities or ways of being.

Next, we should ask ourselves which dissatisfactions are we truly ready to change? Don't mistakenly assume that everything is equally desirable and easy to correct. Be aware of the effort and energy demanded by each course adjustment. Learn to respect the first golden rule of successful change.

Once we are certain of what we truly want to improve or change, we need to identify that which, for us, is fostering each of these dissatisfactions we are prepared to modify. Which shackles, sources of inefficiency or other personal weaknesses generate or favor these particular dissatisfactions? We must also consider that which, with others or in our environment, might be creating or maintaining each of these dissatisfactions. In other words, as suggested by the third golden rule of successful change, we must get a clear picture of all internal and external opposition that could possibly be the source of our dissatisfactions in life.

To complete our appraisal, we need to take into account our qualities and personal strengths as well as any external allies we will count on for support. We should identify everything, found either within us, with others or within our environment that could assist us in our efforts to correct our dissatisfactions and ensure our successful progress. We must learn how to utilize, as effectively as possible, the second golden rule of successful change.

In so establishing our appraisal of our mode of functioning, we have given ourselves the chance to learn from our personal experiences. This provides us with a solid foundation to build upon. The field is being prepared for lucid, pertinent and efficient action. We sharpen our **WILL** so as to **TAME CHANGE**, which is critical to the success of our life strategies.

For those who wish to create a more precise and detailed personal appraisal, there are some practical questions, at the end of this chapter in the **putting it into action** section, designed to facilitate the process. Nevertheless, before skipping ahead, here are certain suggestions that could help with effectively employing the first three golden rules of successful change.

Properly Evaluate the Benefits of Change

When it comes to evaluating the advantages of change, it is important to go beyond a superficial or abstract level. Unless we force ourselves to be practical and concrete, we will not be able to plainly judge whether the positive repercussions of change surpass the effort required to produce the change. If this point is unclear, we will underestimate the difficulty of our task and ultimately be incapable of either progressing or persisting. We should never lose sight of the fact that the more an effort for change weighs in relation to its benefits, the harder it will be to succeed and the greater the need for a proficient, wise and rigorous strategy.

To assess the advantages of change in a practical manner, first, as suggested by the first golden rule of successful change, make a comparison of the risks of not changing, the benefits of changing and the benefits of the status quo. For each dissatisfaction, we should consider the practical aspects associated with our way of behaving and the effects on our physical and mental well-being. Also examine potential impacts along other levels: material, financial, interpersonal, social and others.

These specific factors will allow us to clearly outline the positive consequences of our change process. We can gain a deeper insight into any dissatisfaction we may wish to correct, by weighing the perceived advantages against the perceived disadvantages based on the following evaluation scheme:

1 = no advantage   5 = great advantage

2 = very weak advantage   6 = very great advantage

3 = weak advantage   7 = enormous advantage

4 = moderate advantage

Once we've gained a thorough understanding of the advantages, we must then examine the associated dimensions of effort and energetic cost. We have to consider the same practical factors as previously examined with each of our dissatisfactions. From this concrete reflection, we can similarly evaluate the dimension of effort by using an analogous scale to the preceding one:

1 = no effort	5 = great effort
2 = very weak effort	6 = very great effort
3 = weak effort	7 = enormous effort
4 = moderate effort	

By comparing the results of these two evaluations, we can calculate the level of difficulty and risk for each of the dissatisfactions we want to correct. If the effort required is greater than the advantages, we must question the realistic aspect of our intentions. If effort and advantage come out equal, we should face our strategy for change with extreme prudence and meticulousness. If the benefits clearly surpass the necessary effort, the scales are tipped in our favor and our chance for success is good as long as we know how to lucidly and strategically plan for change.

Carefully Select Your Allies

The second golden rule of successful change highlights the importance of selecting allies. This means knowing, among other things, how to solicit adequate social support to sustain us and facilitate our persistence during the difficult moments throughout the course of change. However, social support is not a magical method for solving all our problems without any effort on our part. We must take the greatest care and be especially shrewd in order to avoid becoming dependent or, in certain cases, keep from being swallowed or even exploited. To prevent this, it is crucial that we respect certain guidelines when seeking external help.

The first principle is that we must have clear in our mind what it is we want. In other words, what are our expectations towards our friend, support group or expert? Do we just want someone to listen to us and allow us to freely express ourselves so that we might more clearly see within? Is a support group enough or do we need someone with a more extensive know-how and expertise? The more explicit and precise we are in defining our needs, the better we'll be at choosing the appropriate support.

As a second guideline, we should not commit to the first expert, group or person that comes along. If we need a friend or close family member, we should take the time to select the individual who's most appropriate, taking into consideration the knowledge and experience of those around us. For groups and professionals, get information, seek references and find two or three possibilities to explore further.

When meeting with a potential resource for the first time, whether it's a group or an expert, ask for details. We shouldn't be shy or afraid. If they hesitate or avoid our questions (often with an offended look!), we should not be uncomfortable. On the contrary, we should take this as a good indication that this is not the best external resource for us. We must inform ourselves of the approaches and methods utilized by the group or expert. What techniques are employed? What concrete results can be expected? Can they provide examples of these results? What is the cost and duration of an intervention? Do they want to keep us dependent as long as possible or do they intend to make us autonomous within a reasonable amount of time and at a lower cost? Do they want to sell us stuff "on-the-side" (for example: books, brochures, cassettes, complementary treatments, etc.) for the benefit of the expert or group, but to the detriment of our wallets? We should prepare our questions beforehand and list any elements we want to verify so we won't forget anything. With the answers we get and the information we gather, we must take our time and compare the various external resources to eventually make a well-informed decision.

Another significant guideline is to express our expectations to the person, expert or group and see how they react. Verify the extent to which they listen, understand and respond to our expectations. Do they offer concrete methods for satisfying our needs? Can our objectives and desired results be achieved with these means? Do we have our say along the way? Put another way, will they work WITH us or mostly try to impose something that doesn't suit us.

Once we've decided, next, we must proceed with the external resource that best suits us, while never committing for an unlimited length of time. Set yourself a reasonable trial period after which you should take the time to examine your obtained results as a function of the objectives you set. It is only in the light of such tangible data that we can decide to keep on going with the help of a specific external resource. If we choose to continue, again, we should only do this for a pre-determined period, after which we must once more verify if it still suits us or not.

In closing, once we've attained our objectives for change with the support of an external resource, we should never abruptly and definitively terminate this assistance. For a certain time, provide yourself the opportunity of follow-up meetings spaced further and further apart, to assure that you maintain your achieved results. Once you've determined that the change persists and appears to be well installed, then you have become autonomous and independent.

Understand the World of Others

In our attempts to bring over the opposition (third golden rule of successful change), we too often try to make others see our truth, convince them of our point of view. We forget that others also have their own truths, experiences and points of view.

I remember William, a competent engineer and experienced manager, hired to run a manufacturing plant. Over several months he tried to implement a quality-improvement program to resolve the multiple production problems he faced. The project had been put in place, accepted by his management team and the majority of executive personnel wished to go forward with it. All he had left to do was justify the project to the union management and convince them of the advantages so that they'd ultimately become allies in his project's implementation.

The meeting was held early one morning. William was in a good mood; we could feel his inner fire. Calm and relaxed, he explained to the union directors the advantages of the project, the positive repercussions on working conditions, the marginal benefits to employees, the improved relations and enhanced positive climate that would result, he laid all his cards on the table to really sell his idea. All this was wasted effort. The more he talked, the more involved he got, the more opposition he encountered. The union directors jumped on everything, scrutinizing the minutest details and drawing out every possible irritant from what had seemed so positive.

As more time passed tension continually mounted and what had been considered a sure success, transformed into a war of trenches where frustration and bad faith permeated. After more than three hours of discouraging and disappointing discussion, William called for a break to think it over before reaching any conclusions. He told me that, at that point, he saw no hope in the situation and thought of abandoning his project in order to content himself with smaller, insignificant adjustments and feared the worst for the future of his company. It was then that I realized we'd poorly implemented one of the fundamental rules of successful change. We were so convinced of our project's pertinence and merits that we had tried to bring over the opposition by preaching to them! But what did we know of the visions and opinions of others? We hadn't the slightest inkling why they'd been resisting. We had the clear impression of bad faith when we knew nothing of their true motivation. We wanted to be understood before making an effort to understand.

Following my comments, William immediately changed his perspective and tried to adapt and make an honest attempt to understand before being understood. He discussed things over with his management team, now placing the focus on the audience once they rejoined the discussions. From this moment, everything was different. To start, he took the initiative to apologize for the restrictive attitude he had manifested. He explained our conversation and openly affirmed that he would put the project aside to first completely examine the union director's position before attacking the modifications as planned. He then asked them to explain how, from their experience, they themselves saw the situation and what were their ideas for improvement. This is where the union's true hesitations were brought to light: too many projects of a similar nature had already been put into action without ever yielding any results; the previous managements were not consistent and never saw their ideas through to the end; too much effort and too few results; the experience and know-how of employees were never taken into consideration, and so on.

William listened carefully and showed understanding. He had noted all pertinent points as highlighted by the union members to consider before undertaking any project. He proposed, in accordance with his management team, to re-outline the quality-improvement program while including the union managers in the global management group that would oversee the project. Finally, he gave them the time they wanted to define their participation modalities and not feel like their arms were being twisted yet another time.

Their reaction was more favorable. In less than one week we had an agreement on principle and the basis for a mode of functioning that satisfied everyone. We still had all the fundamental elements of the initial project with, as a bonus, a dynamic and positive work climate.

You can never lose by understanding the world of others, to know how to listen before trying to be heard. All humans have their vision of reality and their own personal motives. When we ignore them or fail to take them into consideration, we are trying to dominate, showing no respect and digging a ditch of resistance between them and us that will engender opposition and rejection. If on the other hand we attempt to honestly understand and respect the values of others, we can transform even the most stubborn opponents into allies for the greater good of each and everyone.

First of All, Change Yourself

When it comes to counting on allies or bringing over opposition, the change we envision may demand the efforts of many people. If we want these people to follow along and collaborate with us, we must start on the right foot by demonstrating our good intentions right at the beginning of the process of change. Set the example for everyone. We can't expect from others to commit themselves, respect us or get involved if we are unable to demonstrate our own good faith and will to progress.

I have often seen this type of problem surface within marital relationships. Both parties are convinced that the situation needs improving, but most of the time, each believes that nothing can be done until the other makes an effort. Together, they remain fixed on the spot and wait for their spouse to take the first step. Meanwhile, the situation deteriorates and may even reach the point of no return. On the other hand, all it takes is for one of them to take the first step, modify his or her own attitude and thus put the process of change into motion, leading the problem in a new direction. Certainly, this requires, on the part of both of the spouses, lucid will and fundamental honesty. It is enough that one of the two sets the project into motion and makes the decision of where to begin, for progress to occur and for the situation to improve.

Conversely, I knew a coach who incessantly demanded more and more of his athletes, pushing them to modify their habits in order to improve as well as adapt to training conditions that were ever more challenging. When his athletes asked him to modify his training slightly and make it more interesting and stimulating, he retaliated by claiming he had neither the time nor opportunity to do so. He demanded that everyone else progress and adjust, but felt that he did not have to improve or change on his part! With this kind of attitude, the team atmosphere eventually deteriorated and the athletes' performances suffered the consequences; the coach was forced to abandon his functions.

The businessman, who's case we've been following throughout the ten golden rules of successful change, always knew that he should start the process of change for himself before demanding something of others. He reduced his smoking consumption and quit for one week before negotiating the reduction of air pollution and improving the living conditions around him with the other smokers. If he had made demands before beginning the journey for himself, it would have been more difficult to get everyone to cooperate.

William, our engineer and manager, also fully understood this principle. By changing his attitude on the first hand, trying to understand before being understood, he demonstrated for the union leaders that he was capable of setting an example and taking the first steps. It is through his courage to transform himself at the outset that he set off a veritable ground level movement thus converting his factory into a field conducive to successful change.

Let it be Advantageous for Everyone

The final suggestion I will make concerns the type of relations we establish when trying to make allies or bring over the opposition. In every situation, it is crucial that each and everyone finds profit, pleasure and advantage. Unfortunately, this is not always the case when it comes to our real life relationships with friends, our spouse, within our family or in business. More often, I see domineering-submissive dynamics (or vice versa) develop than genuine relationships of equality, equilibrium or mutually beneficial help.

Nevertheless, each time a relationship depends on a domineering-submissive dynamic, we have something to lose. For those who play the dominator role, we have the impression, in the short term, of winning. We tend to utilize our position, power or authority to obtain what we want. We may succeed for a while, but along the way we spread dissatisfaction, frustration and hurt, which will ultimately be transformed into opposition or resistance whenever the need for collaboration or change arises.

Certain people, for their part, enjoy playing the submissive role. They enter into relationships motivated by their principal need to please and always accommodate. But this type of relationship is doomed from the start. A ceaseless desire to please will lead to unhappiness. We end up hiding ourselves, enduring and suffering. Whether we want to or not, we cannot prevent frustration and hurt from accumulating and the consequences are often destructive. Psychosomatic illness is common among submissive types and the phenomenon of burnout can sometimes be the only way out.

Regardless of how we look at it, whether a domineering-submissive relationship or submissive-domineering one, both are equally ineffective. Both are established on personal insecurities. Both types of individuals bring their own problems to the relationship, which end up transformed into shackles along the road to well-being and success.

The only true way to develop effective relationships is to aim for equality, equilibrium and open and honest collaboration. In order for a relationship to help us progress and surpass our limits, it must be profitable to everyone involved. It must foster a winner-winner dynamic, or as Stephen Covey put it so well, a *win/win* relationship[9]. Without this mentality of winner-winner, without the desire for a sincere, mutually advantageous relationship, it will be too difficult to find true allies, bring over the opposition and ultimately **TAME CHANGE** and successfully bring to conclusion your life strategy.

Putting it into Action

1. Considering the responsibilities, roles, tasks or functions you identified within each of your spheres of life in the preceding chapter, what aspects or elements satisfy you most and that you wish to maintain as they are?

2. Which activities or components, within those same spheres of life, are less successful, disappoint you and that you wish to modify?

3. Inspired by the suggestions in the section titled **Properly Evaluate the Benefits of Change**, which dissatisfactions are you truly willing to correct and change? Take into account the advantages and efforts associated with undertaking these changes.

4. Which aspects of your internal dynamic (shackles, sources of inefficiency, faults or particular weaknesses, etc.) provoke or favor each of the dissatisfactions you really want to change?

5. What, in others or in your environment (events, circumstances, material factors, etc.), is likely to generate or maintain each of these dissatisfactions?

6. Which strengths or personal qualities (abilities of champions or other positive aspects) can you count on to help correct the dissatisfactions you truly want to change?

7. What, in others or in the environment (events, circumstances, material factors, etc.), is likely to support you or assist you in changing these particular dissatisfactions?

PART 3

THE STRATEGY OF CHAMPIONS:
SEE THE DIRECTION

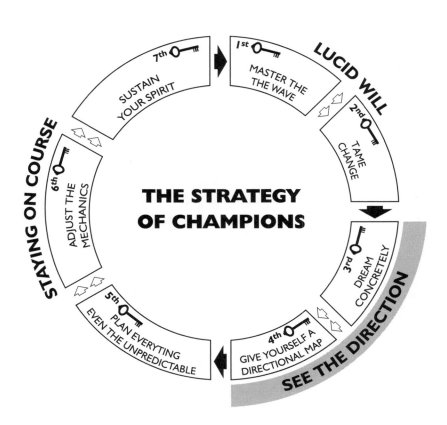

The desire to undertake the voyage in a lucid manner right from the start while being fully aware of our strengths and weaknesses, our allies and our opposition, is a preliminary condition essential to the success of all strategies. It is the first unavoidable step when setting foot onto the path of success.

We have prepped the grounds and completed our personal appraisal. Now we must figure out where we want to go from here. We now know a little more about how to maneuver our ship. We have come to better understand our difficulties with our navigation and are ready to learn and adjust in order to journey farther still along the path toward our dreams.

But, what is the exact nature of these dreams? What far off horizons draw the captain and his or her crew? What is this land that fascinates them, enticing them towards it, through stormy days and heavy winds, driving them to push beyond the limits that previously held them back?

It is this land of predilection, this realm of our dreams that we now need to find. This is what **SEE THE DIRECTION**, the second phase of the strategy of champions, enables us to achieve.

Chapter 5

THE 3RD KEY:
DREAM CONCRETELY

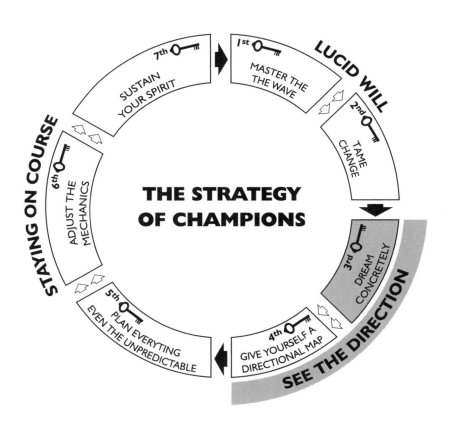

THE STRATEGY
OF CHAMPIONS

1st — MASTER THE THE WAVE
2nd — TAME CHANGE
3rd — DREAM CONCRETELY
4th — GIVE YOURSELF A DIRECTIONAL MAP
5th — PLAN EVERYTING EVEN THE UNPREDICTABLE
6th — ADJUST THE MECHANICS
7th — SUSTAIN YOUR SPIRIT

LUCID WILL
SEE THE DIRECTION
STAYING ON COURSE

On that balmy evening of June 24, Montreal was gently drifting into the mild twilight that gradually closed in upon it. Mount Royal was adorned with all the various tinges of greenness that had come to life with the rebirth of another summer. The city at its feet had abandoned itself to the calm stillness of the night that furtively poured onto its streets but nevertheless it was a time of celebration…the evening of the national holiday.

For the past few hours anyone full of passion and life had been converging upon the mountain as if visiting a temple to celebrate its gods. And there, up above everyday life, as if to shake up a reality that was sometimes too heavy to bear, a motley crowd vibrated enthusiastically under the magic touch of its stars.

Right from the start of the show there was magic in the air. And now Fabrice was singing. What a voice she had! What emotion she communicated! Once she came on stage, it was just as if a tidal wave flooded the audience. Everyone got up as if carried by a current that even galvanized the singer herself with its wild undertow. Happiness danced in her eyes and she seemed to float outside of time, as if suspended by the words she cast out into the air, charming the astounded crowd at her feet.

Her performance infused her with life. Everything appeared easy for her. She gave the impression of infinite vitality and of a destiny fulfilled. But yet such fragility lay buried inside Fabrice. Her enthusiasm apparently camouflaged a tormented heart and spirit. A week never passed where she didn't pour out her heart to a tabloid paper or entertainment journal about all the disappointments and tragedies that afflicted her. She was in her fifth marriage. Each time it was the same story: the love of her life, the happiness they had, finally her soul mate and then… small disagreements, difficulties, frustrations, separations and depressions. There were also miracle diets to help her lose excess weight, followed by anger and resentment of deprivation, all that to return to her favorite dishes and preferred restaurants to the great displeasure of her recently renewed closet. The world of friendship had also been full of waves and jolts, exciting and heart-wrenching at the same time, as if fate had taken a wicked delight in tempting her only to torment her all the better.

In fact, nothing went well in Fabrice's life. She nevertheless offered herself everything she desired. She was an immense success and had a legion of adoring and appreciative fans. Many people would have paid dearly to walk in her shoes and experience, for only a moment, what appeared to be a life filled with fame and success.

As she aged Fabrice became continually less and less happy. Psychosomatic troubles appeared and she complained of all sorts of small aches. Her health problems were becoming more severe. Eventually it all overwhelmed her and nothing satisfied her anymore. Only one thing could make her happy: PERFORMING. Once she entered on stage, she forgot everything. When she sang, her disappointments, misfortunes and even her physical pain disappeared. She began to live and vibrate again. But it didn't last. As soon as the curtain fell, as soon as the magic disappeared everything resurfaced and it became more difficult to endure. Depression consumed her more and more and, during the day only alcohol and medication could relieve her tortured spirit.

Anxiety grew within Fabrice's entourage and those who cared about her were worried. It's not that Fabrice never knew what she wanted or where she was going. Since the age of five or six her voice and talent were recognizable. She was immediately aware of it. Since that time she never stopped talking about how she would become a great singer. Her ambition was obvious and she devoted all her energy towards it. She had fully attained her goal but still she always felt a void, an unease of spirit that relentlessly bubbled inside her and consumed her. Despite all her success, regardless of what appeared to be a glowing achievement, suffering and sorrow flooded her existence.

Be Lucid When Choosing Your Direction

Fabrice had an ambition in her life, a very precise goal. She knew where she was going and she wanted to get there with all her heart and energy. However, her life was very fragile, like a house of cards at the mercy of a strong wind.

Lottie never had any grandiose ambitions, but she nonetheless knew where she wanted to go with her life. Her family was important. One of her greatest aspirations was to create a positive, warm and happy atmosphere within her home. It was equally important to live comfortably without ever becoming a slave to false needs. Taking a bite out of life in order to learn and discover, progress and improve made up the thread of her days. She always had a smile, a radiant look on her face and a hint of laughter on the tip of her lips. However, Lottie was neither well known, nor famous, nor rich. She had had her share of worries and difficulties. At the age of 71, suffering from arthritis and osteoporosis, she learned she was afflicted with a tumor next to her heart. Without an operation she would have soon died. With surgical intervention, at best she was given a 50-50 chance of survival. Full of courage and optimism, she charged ahead and came out okay. Better even. Today at 77, she always has a smile and despite her arthritis she has the gait of someone barely 40. Every day she walks 8 km on the treadmill followed by 12 km on the stationary bike. Then, after a few flexibility exercises, she returns home on foot all the way up to the 17th floor. This is all part of her life, the choices she has made to live a long, happy and fulfilled life. Maybe her ambition wasn't grandiose but her direction was clear.

When I was younger I had the chance to meet a talented professional hockey player who played for my favorite team. He had just started playing in the national league and was promised a bright future. He dreamed of becoming one of the greatest players in the history of hockey and he disappointed no one. He knew where he wanted to go and took all the means necessary to get him there. Today he is in the Hall of Fame because of the success he achieved. Nevertheless, for this man, his hockey performance was not his only dream. He was also known as one of the league's greatest gentlemen. He never displayed his private life in public and zealously protected it. The end of his career and his retirement were planned with care and effectiveness, in contrast to many other players who didn't know how to face this difficult reality. He remained associated with his professional team and was able to build one of the most enviable reputations in the world of business. Honesty, forthrightness, lucidity of spirit and respect for others had always been his trademarks. His fame never stopped growing; he was even offered one of the most sought after political posts in the country. He examined the proposition but politely refused like someone whose needs were situated on another level. This hockey player had always been gifted with a potential suited for grandiose ambitions, but he never let his ambitions lead him by the nose. He certainly experienced difficult moments and had problems like all the rest of us, but he knew how to maintain a lucid focus while constantly and clearly keeping the direction he wanted to follow in his mind.

Having an ambition, a precise goal in life is not everything or is it enough. For this goal to take us beyond our limits, for this ambition not to turn against us, we must be able to clearly see within ourselves and know how to dream in a lucid and concrete manner. When a captain pulls up his anchor and hoists his sails, he has a precise idea of the direction he wants to follow. He knows the shore he wants to reach, the orientation he wants to take and the road he wants to follow. Even when Columbus discovered America he didn't leave blindly hoping to find an undiscovered continent by luck. He was searching for a new route to Japan and China from the west. His orientation was clear and his destination was precise.

When, as young scouts, we left for several days on an expedition into the woods, we didn't close our eyes and thrust ourselves into the middle of the wilderness. With the help of our maps we precisely determined the location we wanted to reach and the route that would get us there. Using a compass, we chose the azimuth we would respect, the orientation line to follow in order to successfully reach our desired site without losing our way. The same principles are valid in our everyday existences for the incredible adventure that is known as life. Whether or not we have a determined ambition or a specific goal, it is important to clearly see our direction, to sustain our dreams in a lucid and concrete manner. Even though we have precise aspirations, we should never overlook the impact, implications or repercussions that could affect the rest of our lives. Wanting to become a famous singer like Fabrice, winning a gold medal or becoming the head of a huge multinational corporation does not happen on its own. There is always a price to pay, both a positive side and a negative side to the medal. There are inevitable risks and potential ill-fated repercussions that could affect other aspects of our lives. To snap one's finger in the face of this reality is to run, eyes shut, toward a precipice that will inescapably engulf us.

The effort to clearly see the direction to follow is just as important and essential, even though we might have the feeling that within our own lives, we don't have any established ambitions or specific goals. I have frequently encountered patients who have felt lost and complained of not knowing where they were going. They envied this person or that because they had an objective or were drawn by a dream. These patients thus had the sentiment that nothing motivated them and that they needed to discover some great passion in order to put their machines into action. This type of attitude is just as delusional as allowing, as Fabrice did, a grandiose ambition lead you by the nose. These patients are too often waiting for "life" to bring them a dream without realizing that they are primarily responsible for the dreams in their own life. And a dream, just like anything else, can be created and given a form; it's within our reach, our capabilities and just as determinable as the destination of the ship's captain or the azimuth to follow for the expedition into the forest. First we must want to define it and then take the adequate measures to accomplish it. Nothing is magical. Just like the champions, we must feel **responsible** for our dream; it is up to us to create it while examining our life in a **global** manner to assure ourselves that it responds well to our requirements and needs; we have to be **methodical, optimal** and **concrete** in defining it so that this dream can be attainable and feasible; it is also important to arm oneself with **patience** and **optimism** to have the courage and lucidity to go all the way with our strategy.

Clearly seeing the direction we have chosen is an essential condition to our satisfaction, our success and even our survival. This is particularly true for those enterprises that have inadequate strategic orientations, imprecise or random directions that could signify the decline and even the death of the organization. The clearer and more precise the direction, the more concrete the dream becomes and the greater our chances of achieving our potential, attaining our objectives and going to the limit of our capabilities. If the direction is unclear, the shore we wish to attain might not be the right one and the compass we would use might not be as effective as it should be in enabling us to achieve well-being, satisfaction and success.

As with the expedition in the forest, in the same way as the ship's captain, we must carefully identify our destination, specify the direction to follow and adjust our compass so we don't get lost along the way. This will enable us to complete the third key of success: **DREAM CONCRETELY**. In the world of business and organizations, the third key corresponds with the **STRATEGIC ORIENTATION** stage. With a patient, this is the moment when we ask the question: **WHAT DO YOU WANT TO BE?** In each case the procedure is similar. It requires specifying, as concretely as possible, what the person, the athlete, the team, the organization or enterprise wants to become and achieve in equipping itself with a compass for orientation. This compass will help us maintain the chosen direction for reaching our destination. It will enable us to respect and adjust the course we follow. It will facilitate the task of sticking to the strategy that will guide our decisions, actions and choices on the way toward the shore of our dreams.

Identify Your Strategic Motives

For each crew that goes to sea, the direction can vary. The ports will be different and the paths will not necessarily be identical even though, at times, the destination is the same. The difference is that which motivates, attracts or goads the crew. Considering the realization of an exploit, a personal heroic deed – like traveling around the world as fast as possible – there's a good chance the chosen route will be far different than that of a family embracing the adventure of traveling for pleasure and discovery. If profit guides a merchant ship, its trajectory and ports of call will not be the same as those of an educational ship wanting its young crew to experience all the various conditions of the sea. At the heart of the matter, under everyone's directions, hides a guideline, a motivation and a reason for being, which we value, something we find good and desirable.

It is the same everywhere, in all spheres of human activity. Take the example of a singer like Fabrice. She can be drawn by pleasure, glory and fame. But her motivation could also be to spread a message that she holds dear to her heart. Other singers might primarily live for the expression of their art, perfection and beauty. For others still, money, wealth or spending might guide the orientation of their careers. In other words that which seems noble, good, well and desirable, that which orients our course varies from one person to the next. It is the same on the level of groups, organizations, enterprises, cultures and societies.

There is invariably, at the base of our behaviors, an intrinsic background that guides our decisions and choices. This background is composed of fundamental motivations and basic values that are found at the center of our lives. We can call this our guiding system[10]. This system develops little by little throughout our education. It can be shaped by the influence of both the champions and tyrants we have encountered. It is molded in the melting pot of our society's collective values. It is found at the base of our definitions of good and bad, desirable and undesirable for which we seek on one hand to attain and on the other, to avoid. With time, this guiding system can become more complex, deepening and enhancing itself. But it can also become paralysing or restrict itself to an extremely severe, limited and narrow guideline.

Regardless of what it is, our guiding system constitutes the **strategic motives** of our lives. Even if we are not always aware of it, there exists within each of us a collection of motivations and values more or less well organized and structured according to the case, that serves as our guide and reference for our conduct and our judgment. Whether or not it's efficient, our life strategy is based on these motivations and values, on these strategic motives rooted in our memory.

All that you have experienced up to now, all that you have realized can be grafted to these central strategic motives. If you are unhappy with the result, if you feel unsatisfied, this could be because of the negative influence of your sources of ineffectiveness, of your weaknesses or your shackles. But this can be equally due, and for an important part, to the confused direction of an insufficiently coherent or unclearly defined guiding system. In such a situation, your strategic motives might leave you prey to the tossing about of life's hazards or yet lead you in directions that are incompatible or even opposite. This therefore provokes within you a feeling of dissatisfaction, confusion and inefficiency.

To avoid this, to give yourself a clear and precise direction, it is important to clearly discern and understand the motivations and values that have guided you until now. It is essential that you become conscious of the **strategic motives** that have oriented your life. If this driving force is inadequate and no longer satisfies you, it is time to sharpen it and adjust it.

Among the fundamental motivations and basic values prone to orienting our behaviors and modes of functioning, are the searches for pleasure or well-being, health and all positive aspects related to friendship, love, family or marital life. For some, religious values, work or the need for social interaction hold important positions. For others, profit, power, consumption and material possessions take the lead. Certain individuals search for prestige or appearance while others are attracted by creativity, discovery or personal realizations. For some the search for autonomy or independence is sacred, while for others still, belonging or identifying with a group becomes the motor of their existence. Principles and virtues guide the steps of many while the lack of morals or ethics characterize the functioning of some.

No matter who we are, fundamental motives and basic values are often varied and multiple. They don't all have the same importance or priority from one person to the next. Nor are they all organized with the same logic or coherence within each of our inner guiding systems. The **strategic motives** they determine vary enormously from one individual to another, taking on the particular shade proper to each of us. Before going to sea and orienting ourselves toward the destination of our dreams, we must honestly and lucidly examine the foundations that, up until now, have guided our navigation. Assure yourself of clearly seeing your own motivations of life in order to recognize the fundamental values on which your way of acting and behaving is founded.

Define Your Personal Compass

By becoming conscious of the driving forces that move you, the goal is to set your motivations and values in order so as to make your guiding system coherent and efficient. This will allow you to adjust and harmonize your strategic motivations to equip yourself with an effective **compass** that will orient your direction throughout the length of the voyage you've decided to undertake. This compass will help you to clearly and lucidly determine the best path for achieving your objectives. It will inspire you to choose the most desirable mode of functioning for finding satisfaction, success and achievement.

The compass created by your strategic motives also represents what some authors call a personal **mission**, which is the particular significance we attribute to ourselves within our reality. In this sense, it is the most important navigational instrument you will utilize for finding that shore you dream of reaching. Without a clear and precise **mission**, without the help of a well-adjusted **compass**, you will never be able to arrive at the right port. You will be hit by all the winds and swept away by all the currents, not knowing where you are or being able to stay on course toward your desired horizon.

Concerning strategies in the business world, it is fundamental to clearly define a managerial profile or mission statement that takes into account the strategic motives of the organization. This type of mission becomes the reference point for all administrative decisions, choices and orientations of the production of the enterprise as a whole. If lucidly and methodically defined, it will orient, at every level, the most important aspects of everyone's mode of functioning. If it has translated and valued the driving forces of the organization's strategic orientation, it will give the enterprise the lead it needs to assure its own success and leadership within its market sector.

It is the same on the individual level. If your mission is clear, if your compass has been properly adjusted in view of your strategic motives, your conduct will be lucid, harmonious, effective and efficient. You will know which road to take and your decisions, like your choices, will be coherent with your strategic orientation. To further clarify this notion of **mission** or **compass**, here is the example of a very high caliber athlete, an Olympic medallist and world champion, at the time she was preparing for her last Olympic games. As she was considering her eventual retirement and asking lots of questions regarding the orientation of her life, we first made a global strategic assessment of her mode of functioning, including her satisfactions and dissatisfactions as well as her strengths and weaknesses. Then, after examining her fundamental motivations and basic values as well as determining her strategic motives, this athlete gave herself the following **mission statement** or **compass** for the three years leading up to the Olympics,

"I am an elite athlete for whom personal accomplishment, for the moment, is of the utmost importance.

The pleasure I get from competitions and challenges is enormous and holds a very important place in my life.

For the next three years I accept that all my energy and efforts will foremost and above all be directed towards my training in order to attain the ultimate objectives of my career.

For this I am ready to take all the necessary means and time required to discipline myself, motivate myself and optimally prepare myself physically as well as psychologically.

I will also put time and energy toward my studies, as my university diploma will enable me to succeed professionally at the end of my athletic career.

During the next three years I am aware it will be difficult, because of my commitments and objectives, to maintain a stable romantic relationship; I accept relegating this part of my life to the second level for the moment.

I accept I will live with a more restricted budget and will not be able to do what men and women of my age can do, because of their salary and their work.

Even if my personal objectives are very high, I will never let my coach or the other guys and girls on the team down. I will never take advantage of others and will never use them in a selfish manner to attain my goals. Friendship, loyalty and fidelity are all very important values in my eyes and I will act accordingly.

I will follow my objectives and my career plan with respect to my body and my health, without using drugs or other artificial means to enhance my performance.

Despite the stress imposed by my athletic career, I want to maintain a mental balance that will enable me to be positive, optimistic and in control. I want to come out of this experience more solid and more experienced to be able to face, with eyes wide open, all the challenges life will throw at me, respecting others, society and myself."

The **mission statement** this athlete gave herself, the **compass** she equipped herself with, served her well throughout the months where exhilaration and turmoil rubbed shoulders without break. Each time she experienced hesitations, doubts or dark moments, she returned to this mission statement to rediscover her courage and enthusiasm. Thanks to her compass, she reconnected with her direction and gave a sense to her everyday life. For her, what she wrote was a firm and official commitment to go all the way with her dream. She showed and explained it to her family and her coach, whom she trusted greatly. She stuck it on the wall in her room and inside her gym locker. By behaving this way, she wanted to always keep her fundamental values in her spirit as well as the path to follow that would respect and achieve them. Her mission sustained her right to the end, just up until the day where a world championship and gold medal had become reality.

Our mission enables us to give sense to our daily lives. When we are in the heat of action, nose stuck in the necessities of life, the spirit sometimes becomes trapped in the banality of our routines, and we have the tendency to lose sight of our reason for being and our objectives. At other times, when the wind howls hard or the tempest explodes, doubts appear and our faith, convictions or confidence are shaken. It is in the storm, as in the calm flat, that the mission becomes most meaningful. It is during these times when the shore of our dreams seems like a mere mirage that we need to rediscover our spirit, inner meaning and the courage to go all the way.

This is how a father and business executive expressed his mission at a time when his work took on a greater amplitude and his small family demanded all his attention.

> "My wife, my family and my business are the three most important spheres of my life.
> No matter what my preoccupations are at work, I want to give my wife the love, support and understanding she deserves from her husband. I want her to feel like I'm close to her, with a positive and warm spirit.
> I want to participate fully in the education of my children and give them attention and understanding. It is important for me to be patient, fair and equitable towards each of them. I want them to see the most fundamental values, which my wife and I hold dear, in action. I want to create a home where it is good to live, where my children feel accepted and valued and where they have a chance to progress and blossom.
> I also want to take the necessary means for my enterprise to progress in a dynamic and positive manner. I want to stress the quality of our products and the efficiency of our service. I will work to improve our productivity, without ever losing sight of the fact that the key to our success is the respect and commitment of our employees.

Throughout all the efforts and time invested within each of my three fundamental spheres, I do not want to neglect my health and my equilibrium. I will try and stay in good physical condition and prevent sickness. I will force myself to maintain a lifestyle that is harmonious with the values I hold dearest.

The need to make money will never become my master. Material possessions will remain practical methods to assure us the minimal comfort and the tranquility of spirit we need to attain our objectives. Our home will be open to our friends yet never become a refuge for those who would take advantage of us. We will be ready to help, understand and support, never forgetting that life is not a one-way adventure but an occasion for exchange, sharing and mutual support.

Finally, I want to remember that behind this reality hides a more profound significance that I want to grasp better and discover. I want to pass my passion for learning, my love and my respect for life onto my children. I want, around me, by my example of honesty, fairness and justice, to give others the desire and taste for a better life that is more harmonious, responsible and positive."

The mission this good friend gave himself made it possible for him to clearly see the priorities in his life. As he told me, he had the impression that... "Now, as never before, I can clearly see where to go. When I reread my mission, each day becomes meaningful because it enables me to move closer to the fundamental values I believe in. I finally have a tangible line of action in my life."

Once your mission becomes your compass, your ship should stay on course. However, defining a mission is not easy. It is not a matter of simple words hastily scribbled on a table corner. It means putting in the required thought and the necessary time.

Just as for a nation, our mission represents, in some way, our own personal constitution. For a country, such a constitution does not develop overnight. It is essential that those working on it properly embody the whole ensemble of their society's values and driving forces. It is the same for each of us. To provide us with an effective compass, mission or constitution that will act as a prudent and lucid guide, we must first determine our own values and identify the fundamental motivations that constitute our strategic motives. It is only when these strategic motives become clear and obvious to us that we are able to adjust our compass to effectively orient us throughout the journey we have chosen to undertake.

Render Your Ideal Tangible

Our personal **mission** shows us the route to pursue, the standards to keep up with as well as the principles to observe if we want to satisfactorily attain our objectives. It guides our decisions when we have choices to make and orients our behaviors and actions in the reality of everyday life. It acts as a national constitution, which serves as the ultimate reference for legislation and as a supreme guardrail for the orientations and projects of each politician as they succeed one another at the country's helm.

Missions as well as constitutions are thus basic terms, standards, or rules to respect that will keep us on the right track. As beautiful and noble as they may be, they do not necessarily tangibly define all aspects of the shore we wish to reach. With the same constitution as a frame of reference, a country's various political parties can entice the population with vastly different dreams. These dreams can be translated into the diverse spheres of socio-economic activities through very different objectives and achievements. Put another way, while serving as a guide, the constitution leaves some latitude for shaping reality, but this reality needs to be defined as specifically as possible if a country wants to go somewhere. This is what we call a good political **vision**, something that is regrettably lacking from the great majority of our politicians.

We find the same phenomenon on an individual level. Having principles and values does not necessarily mean we know where we are going. To find a clear direction our compass must also orient us toward a well-defined shore. We must have a specific idea of the objectives we wish to attain. It is essential that we render the ideals we wish to achieve into a tangible and precisely determined personal **vision** of our future.

If we refer to the examples of missions given, how do we define, from a concrete point of view, the ultimate accomplishment of our athlete's career? How is the realization of her dream translated within a professional sphere? What is the targeted economic situation at the conclusion of her three-year cycle? And so on. In other words, to precisely define where she wanted to arrive at, our athlete had to practically define what she wanted to achieve in the different domains of her life. A gold medal at the Olympics or a world championship corresponded to the desired objectives of her athletic career. A specific job with particular responsibilities within the enterprise of her choice constituted her professional goal following the Olympic Games. Accumulating savings and a specific starting salary were her goals for her economic situation, etc. By specifying her dreams in a tangible fashion within the different spheres of activity in her life, our athlete was able to define her personal **vision** of her future. She gave herself specific strategic objectives to attain. It is within this context that her **mission** was able to ceaselessly inspire her to orient her decisions and daily choices and allow her to follow an optimal route toward the shore of her dreams.

My friend lived the same experience. By writing his **mission**, this husband, father and business executive was able to express his basic values and principles of life. After defining his mission, he then identified strategic goals that were the best concrete translation of his fundamental principles and desired results. He set the goal of greater personal involvement with his wife and more significant participation in the family life regarding his children's education. Concerning his work, his ambitions referred to a reduced level of production flaws and engaging his employees in the process of optimizing quality and service. For each sphere of activity in his life, my friend specified practical targets accordingly. Inspired by his mission and the dissatisfactions he wished to correct, he gave a tangible form to his personal **vision** of his future. In his case, he set a one-year deadline for attaining his strategic objectives, to revise his mission and readjust his objectives at the end of that year.

Rendering the ideal tangible therefore consists of clearly identifying the shore toward which we steer our ship. To **SEE THE DIRECTION** with lucidity means never losing sight of this shore thanks to the use of our compass. At present, we have equipped ourselves with such a compass by defining our personal **mission** from our strategic motives; this means our fundamental motivations and basic values. Now we need to tangibly define our dream, to give a precise form to the personal **vision** we have of our future. To arrive there, it is important we first set a deadline for ourselves. With athletes I often work within a four-year perspective, precisely a four-year Olympic cycle. In other domains, like with enterprises, we sometimes consider five-year cycles with annual revisions of strategic orientations. My friend, the businessman, opted for a one-year deadline. It's a matter of choosing a term you are comfortable with, remembering that you can readjust along the way. Personally, I consider planning more than four or five years ahead rather difficult, the more time passes, the more things change and the more our thinking may evolve, which risks rendering a vision, based on too long a period of time, obsolete.

Once our temporal frame has been defined, it is a matter of setting our strategic objectives, meaning how we picture our lives at the end of our deadline. The idea is to realistically express what we will attain in each sphere of activity of our life, if we have mended or overcome our actual dissatisfactions and respected our mission. What accomplishments, realizations, dreams, desires or wishes will we have actualized and materialized, if we have been able to correct our weaknesses and use our strengths and abilities to their maximum potential? To help us identify all our dreams and aspirations, it is relevant to refer ourselves to the fundamental motivations and basic values that constitute our new strategic motives. Re-reading our **mission** and trying to imagine how it might translate itself, from a practical standpoint, at the end of our deadline. Don't forget that the **ideal to attain** should help you nurture your satisfactions, this means permitting you to improve the strategic appraisal that you have drawn up at the end of the last two chapters. Re-read this appraisal, keeping in mind your dissatisfactions, flaws, weaknesses and resistances so you can define the shore of your dreams, a personal **vision** where all the sources of frustration and ineffectiveness would be eliminated or under control.

As you can see, all efforts of reflection realized at present are now useful for coherently and suitably defining the direction to follow. Keeping in mind your strategic motives and inspired by your **mission**, you make the most of the life force within you; you put into play all the positive dynamics that animate you and orient your mode of functioning. Relying on your strategic appraisal, you work to **change** your situation. At the same time, you stay vigilant and keep an eye on all your shackles, all the sources of inefficiency capable of undermining your mission and causing you to lose sight of the ideal that you wish to attain.

The same vigilance is essential for countries and nations. There will always be those individuals or groups that seek to change the rules of the game in order to satisfy their own personal interests. As wonderful and noble as the constitution may be, all sorts of tyrants will wish to profit and hinder the evolution of a nation who had but set for itself such proud beacons. All this is inevitable and a part of life. We must, at all times, remain conscious, lucid and keep one eye open. We must never forget that, even within ourselves, there exist inclinations or negative forces that ceaselessly attempt to hinder our progress and keep us from going all the way to our dreams.

Putting it into Action

1. Bearing in mind the results of your strategic appraisal (preceding chapter), identify as best you can the fundamental motivations and basic values that have guided your mode of functioning up until now.
2. Next define your strategic motives, meaning the motivations and values that should henceforth guide you and help you improve and correct your strategic appraisal. Do not hesitate to prioritize these motivations and values if needed.
3. From these strategic motives, define your personal **mission** gaining inspiration from the examples presented in the text.
4. Determine a temporal deadline for realizing your strategic plan.
5. For each sphere of activity of your life, tangibly identify the strategic objectives you wish to attain within your established deadline, keeping in mind your strategic motives, your **mission** and your strategic appraisal you wish to improve and correct.

Chapter 6

THE 4TH KEY:
GIVE YOURSELF A DIRECTIONAL MAP

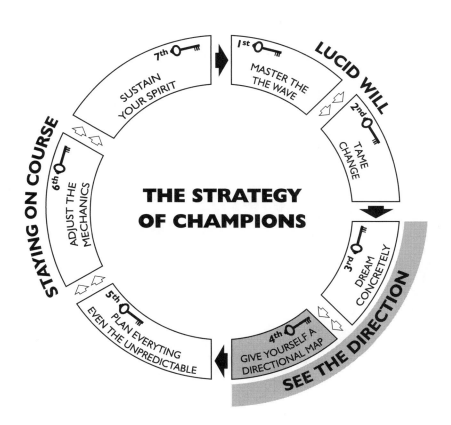

Each time as the year draws to an end, with the holiday seaon coming up, Ben gets back to life. As usual at this time of year, he feels dissatisfied with himself, disappointed in his achievements, in a poor state of health, depressed and exhausted. But, the perspective of a new year invigorates him, restores his self-confidence. This time will be different; things will change!

For several weeks he works on devising his plan. He straightens his spine and his smile returns. He already feels the pleasure he'll get from correcting his situation and re-taking control of his life. Through anticipation, he experiences the satisfaction of achievement and the objectives he will successfully attain. He readies himself and psychologically prepares for change. Hope returns and happiness begins to inhabit him once again as he carefully draws up his list of New Year's Resolutions!

All of Ben's good intentions are fine strategic objectives that he vows to accomplish during the upcoming year. His expectations are high, his need for achievement is huge and his appetite for renewal only grows as the deadline gradually approaches. His list of resolutions lengthens and no sphere within his life can escape the wind of change that whistles through the universe of his dreams of satisfaction and success.

Yes, this would be a good year. He would become closer to his wife, spend more time with her and help her out more. He would assist his children with their homework and follow their progress at school more closely. He would stick to a strict budget that would help him eliminate his debts and make a fresh start. He would finally take care of his health... no smoking, less alcohol, more physical exercise and better nutritional habits. There were training courses he'd wanted to take for a long time to improve his professional status. Not to be forgotten, more enjoyable and more frequent leisure activities. Without respite, he enthusiastically prepares himself and creates a feverish atmosphere around him, a little like the nervous energy that seizes a colony right before great migrations.

Then, the big day arrives where he drowns all of his dissatisfactions and inefficiencies in his last glass of champagne in celebration of the New Year. He would be able to focus on the task at hand and transform his life. In the following week, he registers for those training courses he's always wanted to take. He quits smoking, cuts down on his drinking, starts a physical fitness program and modifies his nutritional habits. He returns home early from work to help with the children. He cooks meals with his wife, helps her with household chores and together they make a daily assessment of family operations each night. He purchases a subscription to a series of concerts and plays to enrich his leisure activities and spends more time with his wife. Everything starts out magnificently. Ben isn't a daydreamer or a wishful idealist. Once he decides to change his life, he takes concrete measures to do so.

But then, there are problems. Each year the same story repeats itself. The initial momentum doesn't last. Ben always ends up running out of breath. By attacking all of his objectives at once, as if each was as crucial and critical as the next, he rapidly overloads himself and becomes worn out. At the beginning, everything goes well. Morale is high and nothing seems impossible. But, by over-exerting himself and self-imposing too many changes, Ben becomes exhausted. In a short while, the shock of reengineering his whole life begins to destabilize him and he is unable to keep up the pace. In relation to the immense effort he's made, the results are neither obvious nor as expected.

Like every year, Ben then begins to slow down his rhythm, shelving some of the projects he's started. Feelings of dissatisfaction, failure and disappointment resurface and drain his energy and motivation. Little by little, to offset his frustration, he returns to his old habits. He comes home later, spends less time with the children and gradually, to his wife's great disappointment, he drops his leisure activities. Then, as long as he is experiencing failure and not achieving his objectives, he starts smoking again, drinks more and turns to food in search of the satisfaction he can't find elsewhere.

The year ends, yet again, on a note of lost confidence and discouragement. He feels disappointed, physically exhausted and mentally fatigued. But, Ben is courageous. The holiday decorations awaken his hopes and spark his inner flame of renewal. Yet again, he will let his enthusiasm run wild. Like the phoenix, he'll rise once more from the ashes of defeat to reset his inner fire and unleash around him the commotion and feverishness of combat. Meanwhile, here's the problem. We can't freely repeat, year after year, the same pattern of failure without suffering the consequences. It's a bit like the story of the child that amused himself by crying, "Wolf!" One day, no one believed him and he was eaten. Ben will face the same reactions. Nobody around him will believe him anymore and they'll no longer wish to buy into his pipe dreams. In time, Ben will lose faith in himself. His confidence and self-esteem will diminish more and more, to the point where he'll drop everything and resign himself to finishing his life like too many people do, disappointed, dissatisfied, frustrated and worn out.

Many people experience the same difficulties. Lots of businesses and organizations let themselves fall into similar traps. They all have a clear enough vision of the shore they wish to reach. They all see, relatively well, the direction they must take. But, in the great majority of cases, people don't know how to optimize the path they will follow. We attack everything all at once, or almost everything. We emphasize projects that won't have any significant impact on the functioning we wish to improve. We stir things up, run out of breath and drown ourselves in a whirlwind of activity… this need for action at any price, without enough thinking before acting. All things considered, we manage to obtain very few real or tangible results to show for all the effort and time we have devoted. Doubt, discouragement and a drop in motivation resurface. One day we realize that we've returned to our old reflexes without having managed to improve anything or change the dissatisfactions that haunted our daily life.

One of the fundamental reasons behind the syndrome of "returning to old reflexes" is the fact that we lack a methodical and coherent directional map. We don't know how to define priorities. We are not skilled at identifying those stages, which are crucial and essential to our progress. We fail to give ourselves the adequate steps for efficiently climbing, bit by bit, the stairway that will take us toward satisfaction and success.

I repeatedly tell those I work with that confidence is built on success; one success calls for a second and, one thing leading to another our self-esteem develops. To get to that point, we need to properly gauge our objectives. We must learn to distinguish what is important from what isn't, what is urgent from what is less so, what will bring us more results and satisfaction from what will give us few outcomes for the effort put in. In other words, it is essential for us to set priorities to avoid undertaking everything, indiscriminately, all at once.

By using the third key of success, you have precisely defined the shore you wish to reach. **DREAMING CONCRETELY** enables you to translate your hopes for success in life into practical intentions. You have given yourself strategic objectives to strive for and a directional line to follow.

Now, you mustn't overlook the fact that captains rarely reach the end of a long voyage without making any stopovers or passing through intermediary ports, before finally setting anchor in the bay of their coveted paradise. It is the same with success. It is not achieved overnight. The satisfaction of realizing every one of your strategic objectives is the fruit of a gradual evolution, which allows you to meet each of them little by little and not all at once. In fact, your course will be marked out with successive ports and to optimize the route to follow, it is important to foresee before departing which ports will be most pertinent to pass through, establishing priorities and the preferable order for meeting each of them.

The topic of priorities inevitably leads to the application of the Pareto principle (see chapter four and footnote number seven): optimization with respect to the 80/20 rule. You will achieve 80% progress more rapidly, leading to a greater feeling of success, if you know how to target that 20% of your efforts or accomplishments, which would be the most pertinent sources of satisfaction and success within your life strategy. By starting with 20% of the most judicious adjustments or achievements, you are assuring yourself of the most efficient and effective method. By selecting those 20% key projects you will most effectively utilize the fifth golden rule of successful change: **don't tackle everything at once** (see chapter four).

How, from a practical standpoint, can we respect the Pareto principle? What is the best way to set priorities for achieving your goals? This is what the fourth key of success enables you to do. It helps you define a DIRECTIONAL MAP that will clearly identify the most important steps of your route and when it is preferable to cross them.

Concerning the strategies of businesses and organizations, we now come to the phase of "STRATEGIC PRIORITIES". This is when enterprises determine their key factors for success as well as their critical concerns. This is the time when they put their projects in order of importance and assign priorities to obtain, as quickly as possible, the 80% improvement that will guarantee their success and sometimes even their survival.

When athletes reach this stage, we establish strategic priorities for the different technical, tactical, physiological and psychological components of their training plan. Thanks to these priorities champions are able to rapidly correct their performance flaws and improve their weaknesses. By stressing the most pertinent factors, they successfully achieve their highest objectives in the shortest time and at the lowest energetic cost.

For psychological consultations with patients, this is the moment when I ask the question: WHAT DO YOU CHOOSE TO DO? This question pushes people to determine which factors are primarily most important and preferable to change or achieve in order to attain, as soon as possible, what they wish to become.

Determining strategic priorities is thus an essential step in any procedure for change. It's the key to the strategy of champions that enables you to equip yourself with a good DIRECTIONAL MAP. Thanks to this directional map, you can optimize the route to follow and achieve your most important and highest strategic objectives, in the shortest time and with maximum effectiveness.

The Key Factors of Success

This first step in establishing your priorities consists of revising your list of strategic objectives, referring to your dreams and potential achievements identified in the preceding chapter, to clearly discern true **wants** from mere **wishes**. A **want** is an objective you can distinctively see the demands for. You are conscious of the effort required to achieve it. You lucidly see the associated costs and risks. In no way do you hide the amplitude of work required, BUT you are prepared to do everything, with full knowledge of the facts, without giving up, in order to achieve it.

A **wish** is not as clear and precise in your mind. Or else, you see all the implications, risks and efforts required BUT you are not necessarily ready to undertake everything in order to accomplish it. You are not convinced that the price to pay is worth the expected results and you hesitate in committing yourself onto a path that is uncertain, insufficiently clear or maybe even risky.

First identify the **wants** and the **wishes** among your strategic objectives. Having done this, you filter and refine the direction to follow by focusing your energies toward what is most pertinent to you. Put aside the strategic objectives that are wishes. This doesn't mean you are indefinitely abandoning these dreams or "desirable" achievements. You are putting them on hold; waiting until they become more precise or more pertinent after you've attained your more fundamental objectives.

If you have retained a great number of **wants**, it is important to estimate, as best you can, their relative importance. The best way is to examine each of these wants under the light of your **strategic motives** and your **mission**. With your strategic motives and your mission, you have already specified the driving forces or elements that are most important to you. Now, it is a matter of becoming conscious of the existing relationship between these driving forces or elements and your objectives that are **wants**. You can assign a weight of importance to each of these wants based on a subjective evaluation scale where zero signifies an importance of almost nothing and ten, an utmost importance. By thus attributing a weight to each of your wants, you can more easily pull out those that are particularly significant to you and more clearly spot where your priorities lie.

After having gauged each of your wants in this way, retain the most significant ones, for example those you have attributed an importance of six or more. These are the wants that henceforth constitute your priority strategic objectives. These are the priority objectives that are best to attack first if you wish to rapidly achieve satisfaction and gradually construct significant achievement. This doesn't mean you give up all your other wants or objectives with lower levels of importance. You are putting them aside temporarily to reconsider them once you've obtained satisfactory results on your priority plan.

By identifying your most significant strategic objectives or wants, you have specified what we call the **key factors** to your success. These key factors constitute the most fundamental elements of your directional map. They represent the most important ports through which you must pass to reach the shore of your dreams. Now what must be determined is when you will set out to sea to reach each of these ports. To add precision to your directional map you can estimate in advance how long you need to methodically work on each of your priority objectives / wants. Try to establish, for each of your **key factors** of success, a starting date for putting it into action and a completion date for achieving your strategic objective. Be as specific as possible without forgetting that nothing is ever definitively written in stone; you are always free to make adjustments along the road. The basic principle here is to give yourself a more detailed idea of your achievement calendar for each of your priority strategic objectives within the global deadline you have set for your strategy in the preceding chapter.

The Critical Concerns

For a champion being **concrete** does not only mean setting precise objectives for obtaining well determined tangible results. Being **concrete** also requires knowing and foreseeing **what** needs to be done in order to achieve these results. The whole problematic is now situated on this level. What projects or concrete initiatives should you undertake to reach your ends? What is required to accomplish, realize or do from a practical viewpoint to obtain the expected results?

Identifying the most pertinent and efficient initiatives or projects toward attaining your objectives is not necessarily easy. Certain **key factors** of success are more easily accessible than others to simple pragmatism and operational management. For our athlete in the preceding chapter, the objective of winning a gold medal in her sport discipline could easily be linked to precise initiatives on the technical, tactical, physiological and psychological training plans. There exist well-established bodies of knowledge and expertise that enable us to define the way to follow. On the other hand, translating into projects or concrete initiatives, such objectives as "a greater personal commitment to my wife" or "a more significant involvement in my family life" or even "employee participation in the optimization process", represent a whole other degree of difficulty. At first glance these types of strategic objectives don't appear to translate as easily into pragmatic action. Contrarily to the gold medal, the concrete factors for attaining a desired level of excellence don't jump out as forcefully and are not related to any precise bodies of knowledge or established systematic expertise.

However, the procedure to follow is not that different. In sport, to meet objectives that are endlessly higher, we have defined, ever more precisely, the best things to do within the technical, tactical, physiological and psychological training plans. By focusing our efforts on concrete ways of acting, on modes of functioning specific to our training programs, we have determined a continually more refined path toward attaining optimal performance. For individuals, the procedure is essentially the same. Regardless of the targeted objective, it is important to ask ourselves what we should practically and concretely achieve in our daily lives. What should I do to "achieve" a greater personal partnership with my wife"? What can I change, improve or correct in my mode of functioning to take "a more active role in my family life"? What particular action would help us favor the "employee participation in the quality optimization process"?

To attain our personal strategic objectives, we must then, as champions do in all disciplines, find concrete ways to act in day-to-day life. If we have not made this effort, our greatest objectives will be merely wishful thinking and our desired shore will become nothing but a mirage on the horizon of our dreams.

All objectives can be translated into practical initiatives or concrete projects. We just have to observe our mode of functioning, our way of acting and ask ourselves what it is that we can adjust or improve in order to attain our targeted goals. It's a matter of lucidly and carefully examining reality to determine what can be done to reach the goals we have set. For example "greater partnership with my wife" could mean increasing time spent at home, improving my listening skills in our interpersonal exchanges or taking more initiative in planning our joint leisure activities. "Greater participation in family life" can involve devoting more time toward supervising the children's homework, sharing more of the housework or reducing my social activities at work. For achieving "employee participation in the optimization process" I should perhaps improve my analysis and understanding of the needs and aspirations of my personnel, outline with the help of certain directors and managers a quality optimization procedure or put in place a more effective delegating approach.

By taking the time to think about your situation and properly observing your mode of functioning and your reality you will be able to determine what you need to do to reach your priority strategic objectives. By identifying practical initiatives and specific projects you can pinpoint the **critical concerns** that will enable you to shape your **key factors** of success. There is no other way to lead your ship from one port to another all the way to the shore of your dreams.

In business, **critical concerns** correspond to the most important projects of change or improvement that we wish to put in place for shaping the organization's vision of the future and attaining their most important strategic objectives. Your **critical concerns** play the same role. They allow you to actualize your personal strategic vision. They are the practical vehicles of your progression towards achieving your priority objectives.

The projects or initiatives that you will define invariably belong to one of the following categories: elimination, modification, addition or maintenance of a way of behaving according to your mode of functioning or your reality. When you are dissatisfied with your personal achievement or well-being you can **eliminate** a reaction or a behavior that is preventing you from attaining your objectives. You can quit smoking, free yourself once and for all of an annoying stutter or a recurrent headache. You can rid yourself of your intolerance or never again let yourself manifest a reaction of extreme anger. It can also involve silencing the inner voice that continually criticizes you or putting aside your jealous nature or your tendency to procrastinate. In other words, **elimination** means once and for all erasing those reactions from your repertory of behaviors and your mode of functioning, which are no longer suitable and undermine your life strategy.

It could be that you simply want to **modify** certain behavioral components in order to adjust them better. This could translate into the desire to improve your physical fitness, lose weight, enhance your listening skills, increase time spent with your family, refine your concentration or your way of making decisions, build your confidence, use your time more methodically, spend less, etc. The notion of **modification** forces you to reconsider your habits or behaviors in order to adapt them better for optimizing your mode of functioning.

The concept of **addition** is the enrichment of your repertory of reactions and behaviors. You can decide to learn an efficient problem-solving technique, take up a new recreational activity or learn a second language. You can create a new product, implement a new way of doing something, invent a new work procedure, include daily life habits that are out of the ordinary for you, express those emotions you usually keep buried inside or henceforth seek help or support when you need it. **Addition** means innovating, expanding your horizons, enlarging your ability to adapt to reality by deepening and enriching your mode of functioning.

Finally, there are most certainly elements of your repertory of reactions or behaviors that are entirely satisfying and well adapted for helping you effectively attain certain strategic objectives. You will then decide to **maintain** these elements and to methodically utilize them in your optimization procedure. Thus, you may opt to maintain your daily walk toward attaining your objective of improving your health. For better contribution at home, you will keep those habits that already help you in this way. In aiming for greater efficiency at work, you will identify the strengths and abilities you already possess and continue using and exploiting them. It is important to specify, with regard to your different strategic objectives, those reactions and responses that are already satisfying in order to **maintain** them effectively and use them clearly within your new life strategy.

By specifying what you should maintain, eliminate, modify or add to your repertory of reactions and behaviors, you will establish your list of **critical concerns**. These concrete initiatives enable you to move from your actual state (your strategic assessment) to your ideal state (your personal strategic vision). They will define in a practical manner the way to follow, the ports to pass through, to transform your present dissatisfactions into satisfactions and successes. They will constitute all the specific projects to undertake for achieving your strategic priority objectives.

The Operational Priorities

At the beginning of this chapter we saw that one essential element of success which helps us to follow a strategy through, is to not undertake everything at once. You must know how to set priorities and be able to assign an order of importance to the different things you wish to achieve. The fundamental idea behind this is the selection of 20% of those most crucial projects, which will lead to an 80% improvement or increased satisfaction (Pareto Principle).

In determining, among your strategic objectives, which were **wants** of significant importance, you have begun to place priorities in your life. However, after having specified the diverse critical concerns associated with each of these wants, you can find yourself in a situation where you are threatened by the "New Year's Resolutions" syndrome. You can, like our friend Ben, succumb to the temptation of undertaking too many projects of unequal importance all at once.

If your most important wants are few and have generated only a small number of critical concerns or projects, it is easy to determine your priorities intuitively and to give yourself a strategic schedule that won't overload you. However, in many situations, this is not the case. Very often, due to the determination of your critical concerns, you find yourself with quite an imposing list of projects and initiatives for attaining your principal strategic objectives. If this is the case, you need to think again within the perspective of the Pareto Principle to give yourself operational priorities.

An effective method for determining these operational priorities is to evaluate each of your projects or initiatives from the point of view of their **impact** and **urgency**. The impact of a project refers to the consequences or repercussions it will have for you. It consists of estimating the amplitude of impact. The more a project can bring you well-being, benefits or positive repercussions – or the more it will help you avoid discomfort or negative consequences – the greater the amplitude of the **impact** and it will be more important for you to undertake it. You can evaluate the impact of each of your critical concerns in attributing a weight from zero to ten where zero is the lowest amplitude and ten is the utmost amplitude.

In addition to **impact**, it is also important to bear in mind the **urgency** of each of your projects. With equal impact, two initiatives don't necessarily need to be achieved as rapidly as one another. The positive consequences of quitting smoking and losing weight can seem equally important for your physical health; however if you are developing serious chronic bronchitis because of smoking it becomes more urgent to quit this habit than it is to watch what you eat. Eliminating your debts on one hand, and making certain investments for your future on the other, could have repercussions of equal impact for your financial situation; however the urgency of eliminating your debts could be that much greater if they are ruining your budget and keeping you from putting money aside. The notion of **urgency** adds nuance to the **impact** of a project. It especially enables you to more easily distinguish among initiatives that appear to have impacts of similar amplitude.

The **urgency** of your projects can be estimated by giving each of them one of the following attributions: very high, high, medium, low or very low urgency. Once each initiative or project has been evaluated in this way, it will be easier for you to determine its relative importance. The most important project will be the one with the greatest impact combined with the greatest urgency, and so forth. First of all keep in mind the impact of your different projects and next separate them according to their urgency as suggested by the sequence of priorities presented on the next page.

If more than one project is found on equal footing, then assign a more precise order by examining them more closely in relation to one another. The targeted goal is to determine which of your critical concerns you will attack first and which you will undertake a little later, in order to reach maximum achievement and satisfaction.

The **operational priorities** you have given yourself will orient the sequence of realization of your diverse practical projects or initiatives. They are essential if you want to avoid drowning yourself amidst a whirlwind of activity. To avoid falling into the same trap as Ben and end up, like him, discouraged and giving up on everything, make sure you undertake one thing at a time and stay away from overloading yourself. Take the time to establish your operational priorities so to be sure that you first of all shape the critical concerns that will guarantee you the most success in the shortest time. Don't forget that success is built on success! The faster you obtain significant satisfaction, the greater your motivation and persistence will be for going all the way with your strategic pursuit.

Amplitude of Impact	Degree of Urgency	Priorities
10	Very high	1
10	High	2
10	Medium	3
10	Low	4
10	Very low	5
9	Very high	6
9	High	7
9	Medium	8
9	Low	9
9	Very low	10
8	Very high	11
o	o	o
o	o	o
o	o	o
Etc.	Etc.	Etc.

Sequence of priorities as a function of **impact**
and **urgency** for your initiatives or projects.

The Strategic Schedule

In order to be concrete and methodical right to the end of the direction you want to follow, you now need to schedule on a timetable the diverse projects and initiatives you've decided to undertake. If you want to gradually and effectively pass from your strategic appraisal to your strategic vision of the future, respect the operational priorities you have established without however overloading yourself with work in your daily life. Estimate as best you can the quantity of efforts and the energetic costs required for each of your projects, each of your critical concerns. From these estimations, next specify the start dates and completion dates of each bearing in mind their order of priority. Try to establish, in weeks or months, the length of time demanded by each project, leaving room to readjust your predictions along the way. This forces you to keep a more realistic eye on your use of time and your deadlines.

In determining the time limits for each critical concern you aim to establish a logical, coherent and well-measured **strategic schedule** from the point of view of workload, effort and energetic costs. This first draft of the schedule is not definitively set in stone. You must give yourself time to try it out for a few weeks – even a few months – to appreciate how realistic your set limits are. If, after this period of time, you realize you had too great an appetite or, contrarily, everything is too easy and you're waiting for yourself, then nothing is stopping you from readjusting the weight of your workload. At this moment you establish a new schedule, better suited to the rhythm of your progression...but always remain well focused on the priorities you have given yourself!

Once the start date and completion date for each project has been determined, it is practical to regroup and design a comprehensive table to record all the deadlines you have to meet. This enables you to view, with a simple glance, the path you have to follow and all the steps you have to gradually cross toward reaching the shore of your dreams. With a synthesized summary such as this, you have in front of you a clear and methodical **DIRECTIONAL MAP** that will help you keep the direction to follow clearly in view at all times.

There are many ways to construct a synthesized table. Here are two examples frequently used by clients I've worked with. The first method, as illustrated in Table 1.1 (in the Annexes) consists of drawing up a list of your diverse projects by order of decreasing priority. Then, taking into consideration the time dimension (months and year; you can also utilize weekly subdivisions), you indicate the duration of each project with a continuous line.

Another way to proceed is to bear in mind both your **key factors** of success and your **critical concerns**, which are grouped under each of these key factors. Table 1.2 (in the Annexes) illustrates this method of creating a more precise view of the whole when many critical concerns are nested within an important number of key factors of success.

The following case illustrates the use of this second type of table. It concerns a young intern in clinical psychology who completed his residency in June of 1990. Dissatisfied with many things in his life, Sebastian wanted to readjust his mode of functioning to achieve a greater sense of well-being and satisfaction over the course of the next three years. In the autumn of 1989, we had worked at establishing a strategy of life that could effectively guide him along the road of success.

After having completed his strategic appraisal, Sebastian determined the direction he wanted to follow. His strategic vision of the future put into question many aspects of his way of acting in the different spheres of activity in his life. His revised strategic motives and his mission led him to set a great number of objectives. After having identified, among his objectives, his most significant wants, he defined for each, a group of projects and concrete initiatives that he counted on achieving in the months to come.

Sebastian's appetite was big and all his good intentions were equaled only by his youthful dynamism; he would have taken on everything at once. But, by witnessing the effort and energetic cost this demanded of him, he decided to set operational priorities. He therefore methodically evaluated the impact and urgency of each project in order to give himself a realistic and coherent directional map.

For the purposes of this example, we will consider his three most important key factors of success as well as the 10 priority critical concerns attached to these. His first most significant strategic objective concerned his physical sphere; within a period of two years he aimed to rediscover the state of health he'd enjoyed before starting university. To realize this want, he thought of undertaking four specific projects: quit smoking, control his eating habits, start a physical conditioning program and maintain his outdoor activities (hiking in the mountains).

His second key factor of success pertained to his material sphere. In three years he wanted to set up his future by providing himself with a solid financial structure. To achieve this, his critical concerns consisted of paying back his student loans, investing in a retirement savings plan and putting aside a portion of his salary for a down payment on a house.

His third most significant strategic objective concerned his professional sphere. He wanted, within three year's time, to become a respected and recognized professional. To achieve this want, he defined three precise projects: actively throwing himself into the political activities of his professional order, enrolling in the continued education training program offered by the order and making his point of view known by writing articles in professional journals.

Table 1.3 (in the Annexes) illustrates how Sebastian synthesized his strategic and operational priorities; we can see the time deadlines linked to each of his three most important **key factors** of success as well as the 10 **critical concerns** associated with these.

With his synthesized summary, Sebastian equipped himself with a precise **DIRECTIONAL MAP** to guide his ship towards the shore of his dreams. Without such a map, without well-defined strategic and operational priorities, it is very easy to lose yourself along the way. Like our friend Ben and his New Year's Resolutions we can quickly lose ourselves in the torment of action and rapidly run out of breath by dashing about to stamp out all sorts of small insignificant fires, without ever obtaining any satisfying results. Without priorities or a **DIRECTIONAL MAP**, the changes that bring satisfaction will wait, success will appear more and more distant and discouragement will cause us to lose sight of the direction we have taken such care to select.

Putting it into Action

1. Determine which of your strategic objectives, identified in the preceding chapter, are **wishes** and **wants**.
2. Specify the relative importance of each **want** in order to select the most significant ones. As suggested in the text, you can attribute an importance from zero to ten for each **want** and next keep those with a value of six or more. This will give you your **key factors** of success.
3. Determine the time deadlines for each of your **key factors** of success by specifying when you would start work on each and when you would like to reach each strategic objective.
4. Specify what you need to do to realize each of your **key factors** of success: identify your **critical concerns**; this refers to the initiatives or projects you have to achieve to realize your most significant strategic objectives.
5. Assign an order of **operational priority** to each of your **critical concerns**: consider the amplitude of the **impact** and the degree of **urgency** for each of the projects and initiatives you want to undertake and establish a priority sequence taking inspiration from the example presented in the Sequence of Priorities Table (page 191).
6. Establish your **strategic schedule** by determining a start date and completion date for each of your critical concerns; represent this schedule in the form of a **directional map** based on the examples illustrated in Tables 1.1 through 1.3 (see the Annexes).

PART 4

THE STRATEGY OF CHAMPIONS:
STAYING ON COURSE

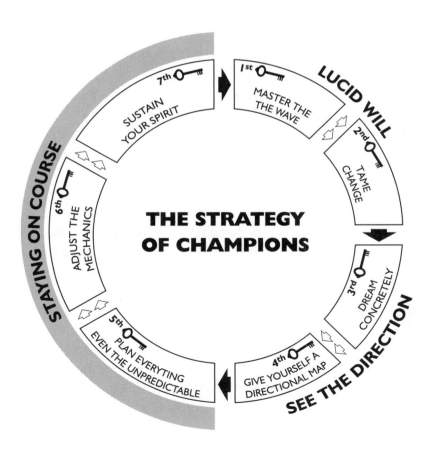

CLEARLY SEEING your direction and equipping yourself with a well-organized and methodical directional map are unavoidable basic conditions of a successful journey. Nevertheless, it is not enough for the captain to forestall the most important ports and set the course that will lead him without fail to the end of his journey.

As my grandfather stressed: "It's all fine and well to want something and to know what to do; but, if we don't use the proper means to get there, nothing will change. Everything will merely be wishful thinking and remain doomed from the start. If you don't properly plan how to do the things, if you don't give yourself the appropriate tools to obtain good concrete results, you will get nowhere. Without practical means and tangible results, without having precise goals to strive for day after day, you will need to be content with just dreaming, with your head in the clouds and your feet stuck in quicksand; you will never be able to STAY ON COURSE toward your destiny and will sink down, little by little, as most people do, into the sullenness of your daily life with, as a bonus, a mounting feeling of helplessness."

To stay on course, the captain carefully plans the details of how he'll get to each port. Every day, he takes his bearings and assures himself that he is truly on the right azimut and that he has reached his previously set goals. By being pragmatic and rigorous by planning how to navigate in the face of all types of circumstances and dangers, he will be able to maintain the course he's set for himself.

Just like a clever captain, we will now look into the most effective methods that will enable us to STAY ON COURSE towards the shore of our dreams and see HOW we will be able to successfully plan the route to follow for consolidating our strategy for success.

Chapter 7

THE 5TH KEY: PLAN EVERYTHING, EVEN THE UNPREDICTABLE

BERNARD was the fourth person entrusted with this particular task within the factory of over 5,000 employees that manufactured specialized machinery. The challenge was huge. The organization had clearly defined their strategic orientation at the upper management level. Their mission clearly stated that, from the start of the game, the enterprise intended to become the world's top manufacturer at the lowest cost, while supplying their customers with products of a constant quality, superior reliability and devoid of defects.

Within the context of this mission, one of the most important **key factors** of success was to completely eliminate useless costs related to the manufacturing defects of various products leaving the factory. One of the top priority **critical concerns** linked to this key factor was the aim to eliminate, in the course of production, all defects related to leaks in manufactured machines (for example: oil leaks in motors). The project was considerable and the repercussions were huge, because the rate of leaks observed by quality control was very high and cost the enterprise a small fortune in rejected materials, repairs and lost time.

Considering the importance of this problem, a manager was specifically assigned to oversee the project's execution for the whole factory. This individual had complete latitude for how he/she would achieve this and was personally accountable for the results obtained to the management group assigned to actualize the organization's mission.

The first project manager firmly believed in the virtues of training. If there were that many defects, it was because the employees were not suitably prepared to properly accomplish their jobs. In conjunction with the department of human resources, he set up a huge technical training program aimed at improving the knowledge and know-how of each and everyone. Over several months hundreds of groups of employees took all sorts of courses. The beehive was buzzing with activity. Full of good intentions, everyone bustled themselves to complete their training and attain a level of competence that, in the future, would change the portrait of production quality within the whole enterprise.

Time passed. Everyone had a nice little diploma pinned to his or her workstation. But after months of effort nothing had really changed. The leaks were still as numerous and employee enthusiasm had diminished. Management's patience had also thinned until the day one of the big bosses declared that if nothing had improved despite all the training, it was because the employees were being nonchalant, lazy and ineffective. More leadership was needed, someone of greater caliber to correct the situation. In other words, they needed muscle to master the troops.

Thus a new manager was assigned to the leak project. He was a true Mr. Hardliner. Each morning he gathered his immediate subordinates to push them and motivate them. It worked well at the beginning; enthusiasm was renewed wherever the subordinates went, in their turn, pushing every employee under their control. Be conscientious, pay attention, be responsible, these were the orders. But, what to do to concretely fix the problems on the assembly line... nobody talked about this! As, once again, no significant changes occurred, Mr. Hardliner lost patience. He himself went to thrash his troops more and more often. The words of encouragement and motivation were transformed into reproaches and reprimands. Blaming and punishments became more and more common and the work atmosphere rapidly degraded. Absenteeism went up, many subordinates no longer wanted to work with the project manager and, in addition, the rate of leak defects grew rather than diminish.

The situation needed to be urgently straightened out. The management offered Mr. Hardliner early retirement and entrusted the leak project to a new more humane individual who had worked for a long time in a large quality consulting firm. The new manager had the delicate task of restoring a positive atmosphere while reducing manufacturing defects. He asserted that this didn't worry him in the least because he knew the secrets of quality production. He gathered everyone and exposed his action plan where people finally became once again the system's valued gear wheels of efficiency. For him, each and everyone had the competence to fix the problems; they just simply needed to be given the opportunity and the time. He established quality circles where, in each section of the factory and in each department, groups of employees would meet to brainstorm about the leak problems and try to come up with solutions. The work atmosphere became more positive and a certain number of defects were corrected. Nevertheless, the efficiency of the quality circles rapidly hit a plateau. The major problems still subsisted and the costs of returns and rework didn't decrease significantly. People started to suggest that the time dedicated to quality circle meetings was more costly than the losses caused by this famous puzzle of leaks appearing in the course of production!

As it became more and more evident that the project was going nowhere, the management no longer knew which Saint they should pray to for resolving the problem. Once more, a manager change was needed. But, now who to appoint and above all, how to do it?

Bernard was not someone who spoke loudly. However, he had made very pertinent suggestions within the context of the quality circles and, very importantly, he seemed well respected and the people who worked for him listened to him. With no other alternative, management promoted the third project manager elsewhere and resolved to entrust Bernard with the delicate operation of eliminating leaks. They made him understand that they wanted concrete results and a significant reduction of the problem within one year.

It is within this context that I had the opportunity to meet Bernard and to appreciate his qualities and intelligence. After two weeks of thinking at the beginning of his tenure, he met with me to discuss the matter and compare his ideas.

"After all these failed attempts to eliminate the leakage problem, I believe, he said, that we don't know what we are attacking. No one has a precise idea of everything involved in this history of leaks and we are incapable of pinpointing most of the real causes of the difficulties we encounter.

"It is not that the employees are incompetent. On the contrary, technically they really know their jobs and they all have the necessary experience. They clearly see what is happening in the field and they truly want to change the situation. The difficulty is that they don't know exactly what to do to effectively solve the problems. When something doesn't go well, when leaks appear, for example, they are not able to retrace the cause. In the heat of action, they are unable to coldly analyze the problems and find effective solutions that will give concrete and definitive results.

"The more I turn this situation over in my head, the more I am convinced that we are not going about this in a sufficiently methodical manner to get to the bottom of this problem. We attack everything at once. More often than not we are only putting out fires without improving anything.

"I believe there was good in the other attempts we made. Employee involvement is essential, because they really know what happens in the field; they possess pertinent information that will enable us to resolve our problems. On the other hand, they don't always know how to analyze or effectively attack these problems. It is more this that they need to learn in training. Not training for the sake of training...not courses to clear our conscience...but rather something that can be directly adapted to their needs and to the problems they need to solve.

"We know maybe **what** to correct, but we don't know **how** to do this. We need to give ourselves a more methodical action plan and properly specify our problem from the start, in order to attack one difficulty at a time. It also means we need to use good tools that will enable us to get at the source of each of these difficulties to eliminate them and obtain concrete and long lasting results. If we take the time and care to do this, we will fix our problems and obtain all the success we desire." With a methodical and intelligent action plan, we were able to rectify the situation. Within one year, thanks to meticulous and structured work, the rate of leaks diminished by more than 75%. This was translated into a savings of hundreds of thousands of dollars for the enterprise all while creating a climate of dynamism where the employees were given a sense of "empowerment" which still has positive repercussions to this day.

What Bernard achieved within a business context, we can all do at the individual level. We have arrived at this point: the fifth key of success. Once we've specified our **critical concerns** and our **directional map** we have identified **what** to do to succeed. We now need to determine **how** to do this for each of these **whats**.

We reached the action plan phase where it is important to **PLAN EVERYTHING, EVEN THE UNPREDICTABLE**. Within the context of a business strategy, this corresponds to the phase of **STRATEGIC DEPLOYMENT** where the plan of attack for each critical concern is "deployed" concretely as a function of the field demands. For individual therapy, this is the time to ask the question: **HOW WILL YOU DO THIS?** which follows the preceding question: **WHAT DO YOU CHOOSE TO DO?** It is at this moment that people put a detailed treatment plan in place to assure themselves that they will concretely resolve any difficulties they could face.

Without methodically planning **how** to do it, all great projects put forward would be merely utopias of reassuring illusions. To lead each of your **hows** to term, you must give yourself logical and precise action plans. This also requires that you use, in these plans, practical and operational methods that will enable you to obtain concrete, satisfying and long-lasting results. But first before starting, it is essential, in order to be successful, that you carefully define each of the projects you wish to undertake or each of the problems you want to resolve.

Carefully Define Each Critical Concern

By making an appraisal of the complex attempts to resolve the leak problems, Bernard learned one fundamental lesson from all these fruitless experiences: we don't plunge headfirst into the battle unless we truly know our adversary. It is extremely easy to fall into this trap, in too much of a hurry to get moving towards our goals. Many people get discouraged and give up because they have taken on too much or been too imprecise from the start.

To successfully take your projects to term, you must assure yourself that each of your **critical concerns**, each of your **whats**, are well defined and differentiated. It is important to examine each project to clearly see all that is implicated and all the different components that could be involved. In other words, this means analyzing the opponents before jumping into the action and tackling them.

Bernard had a good sense of the far-reaching effects of this fundamental principle. Before establishing a plan of action as it was, he took the time to really define his project. To obtain success, he needed to stop himself from naively allowing the vague and gigantic leak problem to overtake him. To create an efficient action plan he had to first off identify each of the varieties of leaks that arose during the course of production, and then methodically and orderly tackle them one by one, just until the problem was completely eliminated.

This approach respects the fifth golden rule of successful change: **don't tackle everything at once** (chapter 4). In the manner of champions, Bernard showed he could be **methodical, concrete** and **patient**. He transformed a project that was too vast and poorly defined – "elimination of leaks in manufactured machines" – into a group of smaller, more specific projects that could be concretely handled. To reach that point, Bernard carefully identified each term involved in the reality of production, that had been too vague and too general in defining the problem: what does the word leak mean and what does the expression machine refer to? Each time the definition of a critical concern, a project or a problem involves words of a general, ambiguous or imprecise nature, you risk bogging yourself down in artistic fuzziness and inefficiency. To avoid this trap, spare no trouble in fully examining what the different terms used in defining your projects or problems to resolve actually signify in reality.

To specify your thoughts ask yourself practical and precise questions that force you to make each word operational and explicit. Here are some examples of specific questions Bernard raised to help improve his definition of the leak problems he faced:

- ° what do you mean by... "leaks"..."machines"?
- ° can you give me concrete examples of...leaks...machines?
- ° can you be more precise when you refer to...leaks...machines?
- ° is it possible to improve upon your description of...leaks...machines...?
- ° can you be more specific and practical when you talk about...leaks...machines?

These questions helped uncover the fact that we needed to differentiate between the two types of machines, the trucks and the excavation machinery, and that each type had three different models. We also noted that we had three major varieties of leaks: oil leaks, air leaks and water leaks. Each leak variety could then be subdivided into more specific components like the oil leaks in motors, breaks, transmissions...or even the air leaks in gear cylinders, in compressors... and so forth.

We continued asking questions just until we had successfully fragmented the colossal and overly vague critical concern we'd started with, the original gigantic **WHAT**, into a group of small very precise projects that targeted each particular type of leak for each distinct type of engine. Thanks to our analysis, we identified all the small battles we needed to wage on the field in order to win the war against manufactured engine leaks. We knew henceforth that we should solve the sealant joint oil leak problem of the type X motor for truck model Y… or we needed to focus on the evacuation pipe water leak of the cooling tank of model Z excavators … and so on. Each of these specific projects, each of these small **whats** belonging to the initial gigantic **WHAT**, was defined in an equally practical and precise manner. This enabled us to assign a priority order to all these small **whats** and tackle them one by one, while establishing a methodical action plan for each of them. By focusing on completing an analysis and careful definition, the initial huge concern was gradually transformed into a remarkable success for the whole enterprise.

The basic idea is to properly define the operational grounds before undertaking the campaign for change. The more we deploy our dreams into everyday reality, the more we must ensure that we specifically target what we need to do. The more we engage ourselves in the action, the more our operations need to address very precise things, very specific elements of functioning that we could tackle separately and individually.

Consider the case of athletes whose major concern is improving their control over competition anxiety. Many lose their way when attacking such a project. Without adequately defining the problem, they will achieve nothing and will develop a feeling of helplessness that will further increase the stress they'd wanted to be liberated from. To effectively tackle this type of concern you must really zero in on it and define it well. By asking the same type of practical questions used in the case of engine leaks, we must specify what we mean by the terms anxiety, competition and control. By asking athletes to be more precise and concrete, we can identify distinct intervention targets like reducing their activation level during pre-event waiting periods, eliminating their doubts and anxieties right before the start of a race or focusing on the technical execution of a certain movement during a specific point of the event.

If, for example, one of your top priority critical concerns is to lose weight, ask yourselves first off what this means from an operational point of view. Before embarking on your miracle diet, which, more often than not, will never help you definitively eliminate your tendency to put on weight, ask yourselves what you realistically mean by weight control. You must realize there are two fundamental components to consider: reducing your caloric INPUT and increasing your OUTPUT through energy expenditure. By pursuing your practical interrogation, you will discover that maybe, in your case, reducing your INPUT means correcting certain bad nutritional habits, that, in turn, means reducing the amount of food you consume, eating less fattening food or eating at more regular hours. Increasing your OUPUT can mean taking up an outdoor recreational activity on weekends, regularly participating in a sport or incorporating physical activity into your daily lives.

Too often our critical concerns resemble Bernard's leak problem or an athlete's competition anxiety problem. We are not accustomed to thinking in concrete and operational terms. We don't take the time or the trouble to carefully define and properly subdivide our big projects or overly vast and ambiguous problems. However, if we make the effort to do this, we gain tremendously in terms of effectiveness.

When your **critical concerns** refer to the following types of problems to resolve or projects to realize: enhance your professional competence, improve your family life, be more attentive to your wife/husband, stop putting things off until tomorrow, have more confidence in yourself, stop worrying about everything, overcome your depression, conquer your burnout, renovate your home, prepare for your retirement, etc., you are thus attacking something that is too huge, too general and too vague. All these types of problems or projects demand being carefully defined before being tackled. By making the effort to specify them in practical and realistic terms, by dividing them into groups of well differentiated initiatives, it will be easier for you to establish methodical actions, to focus on the **how** that will enable you to realize each of the **whats** of your life strategy.

Grasp the Root Causes of Each Problem

Another major reason why action plans are not fruitful and don't enable us to realize our dreams is the fact that we don't bother to grasp the root causes of our problems. The methods we then choose for correcting the situation continue to be ineffective and fail to lead to any notable progress or lasting changes; they fail to neutralize the influence of the deep roots of our difficulties.

Each time one of our critical concerns refers to a dissatisfaction to correct, a frustration to eliminate or a problem to resolve, we must **identify the real causes** in order to provoke significant and permanent improvement. To forget this fundamental principle is to neglect the sixth golden rule of successful change (chapter four). Ignoring this rule leaves the causes of your dissatisfactions and problems the complete freedom to control you and to hold up your progress, despite all efforts put into improving your situation.

To solve his problem, Bernard was perfectly aware that they needed to correct or eliminate the root of each cause for each type of leak identified on the production process plan. Controlling anxiety requires, for athletes as well as for all stressed individuals, that you identify and muzzle the causes responsible for each stress or anxiety reaction. To correct such bad nutritional habits we're obliged to ask ourselves why we developed them and what factors helped maintain them. Grasping the root of our dissatisfaction or problems is the only definite way for us to take the adequate methods for controlling them and once and for all eliminating them.

When we think about a "source" or a "cause", we usually refer to what provoked or was responsible for a phenomenon. We say: such a remark provoked someone's anger or the icy road was responsible for this accident and also, this governmental policy instigated social dissension. In each case we try to explain, to understand the **why** of what has occurred. If we understand **why**, we can more easily prevent or correct the phenomenon, by eliminating or better controlling the cause responsible for it.

Here is the general idea… grasp the root for a better understanding, for mastering the situation and making pertinent adjustments. However, this is not so easy in reality. A phenomenon can appear to be provoked by a particular cause on the one hand, but with a closer look, we can often see the influence of still other factors that facilitate or sustain the problematic situation. Even if the ice directly provoked the accident, the car's speed, a sharp curve in the road or the vehicle's poor condition could also have played roles in the fatal event. A remark can incite someone's anger, but that individual's state of intoxication or the stress of that particular situation could also be factors. The governmental policy could be merely the last drop that causes a vase to overflow within a difficult socio-economic context.

Retracing the roots of a problem in order to definitively correct it is not necessarily easy. Reality often hides a number of less evident **whys** that are equally important to consider. The more complex a problematic situation is, the more numerous the roots and the more intermingled they are in a correspondingly complex manner. We then face a network of roots that must be properly identified and untangled if we wish to make it out and clearly see what's happening. Moreover, all the sources of a problem are not necessarily equally important or each as fundamental as the other. It is thus also necessary to clarify this network of roots to give them order and extract the essentials if we truly want to rectify the situation for good.

Bruno's example illustrates well how a complex cause network can stimulate and maintain a difficulty of functioning. One of the critical concerns of his strategy of life was to lose weight. A more meticulous and concrete definition of this concern brought out that he should, among other things, reduce the amount of food he ate. To once and for all solve this particular problem, Bruno decided to retrace its diverse causes. By asking himself **why** he ate too much, he realized his difficulty occurred at particular places and during particular moments, in precise circumstances and in the presence of specific people. He didn't always overeat and he needed to fully target what, in certain occasions and not others, pushed him to overeat, in order to correct the situation for good. The most important roots that surfaced from Bruno's internal interrogation were:

- ° having lunch with colleagues in an atmosphere of work and pressure;
- ° the type of restaurant picked for his lunches;
- ° eating too fast without giving his stomach enough time to feel full;
- ° ineffectiveness of his time management and organization at work; this would lead to an overload that worried him and caused him to eat;
- ° his way of thinking, his need to always be perfect and his fear of not doing an efficient job;
- ° his idleness on Sundays which gave him too much time to worry about work and drove him to eat;
- ° his wife that talked to him incessantly about family problems, at night during dinner;
- ° the pressure exerted on him by certain colleagues at work;
- ° having learned at a young age, through the example set by his parents, to compensate his dissatisfactions and helplessness by eating too much;
- ° his work responsibilities demanding more of his time and energy.

The numerous causes identified by Bruno were not all of equal importance. They were not all situated on equal footing. As I mentioned in the fourth chapter (the sixth golden rule of successful change), the level of control you have over a specific cause can vary. Your reactions, behaviors, beliefs, shackles, values and way of thinking are under your total or direct hold. The reactions of others are only partially under your control, according to the attitude you've adopted. Events in your past cannot be changed and many elements of your external reality totally escape your control.

To successfully, effectively and rapidly correct a dissatisfaction or problem, it is best to first attack everything that falls under your total or direct control. For this reason, Bruno decided to break up his network of causes by tackling, as a priority, the first six sources that entailed his difficulty with overeating. It is with regard to these precise **targets** that he elaborated action plans aimed to improve his situation.

Another important factor of success fundamental for identifying and correcting the networks of causes that drive your dissatisfactions and problems, is to know when to stop. It is important to question yourself to uncover all the roots of a problem, but at a given moment, you must put the breaks on this questioning and get into action. Bruno could have continued asking himself why, for example, did he always want to be perfect, how had he acquired his fear of not doing an efficient job or why had his parents influenced his way of acting. Are more precise answers to these questions necessary, at this stage, for helping him concretely and immediately change the behavior that is harmful to his health? Would they add essential and significant information without which he would not be able to undertake the task of actually correcting his bad habit? Aware of these considerations, Bruno had instead arrived at a stage where he needed to get into action and face the music.

There comes a point where it is time to put your questions aside and undertake adequate methods for attacking the sources of your dissatisfactions. You need to be aware of the fact that you can dig endlessly through your past in an attempt to understand all its twists and turns and your psychological functioning. You would probably not have enough time your whole life to untangle the maze of your inner complexity. It is easy to turn in circles and lose yourself (or enjoy yourself) inside the incredible entanglement of your psychodynamic. But, during this time, the change is being delayed and above all, for many people, no effort will be needed to correct their situation and adapt themselves.

Knowing where and when to put aside your questioning is, in the manner of champions, learning to be **optimal**. Seek out what is needed for beginning your process of change and do this to the best of your knowledge. Don't be paralyzed by excessive analysis. When we learn to use a computer, we don't read the whole instruction manual before doing some practice exercises. We try to understand a few basic steps and practice to verify our comprehension and mastery. Then we return to our reflections and our study to prepare ourselves for subsequent exercises. We don't learn to master a new sport by spending months reading about it, watching videotapes and observing experts. We must dive into action in order to learn, progress and change. Why then is it not the same for all aspects of our mode of functioning as well as for our problems and dissatisfactions?

Establish Action Plans

Once your critical concerns have been carefully defined and the root causes of your dissatisfactions or problems fully identified, it is time to dive into action yet without charging along head down into the first obstacle sitting on your path.

Once the captain raises the anchor the morning of departure, he is not content to simply hope to reach the end of his voyage without incident. He has determined his destination. He has set the course to follow, outlined with the ports and steps he has to go through. He has given himself a directional map to guide him throughout his whole trip. But, this is not sufficient. The experienced captain knows that once at sea, there is a lot at risk. He doesn't want to leave anything to chance. He cannot allow himself to be tossed about at the mercy of the winds and tides. He wants to give as little power as possible to the unexpected that lies in wait.

For each day of navigation at each stage of the voyage, he takes the effort to plan. He sets positions to reach and gives himself precise tracks to follow. He foresees all the ways for staying on course and adjusting himself in case conditions change. He bears in mind all the necessary factors for assuring an effective and safe daily progression.

Your course of conduct is shaped on the captain's example. You have determined your destination based on your strategic appraisal. You have given yourself a dream to realize and a compass to orient yourself. With your key factors of success and your critical concerns, you have defined a precise course to follow and equipped yourself with a directional map to guide you. You must now precisely plan the details of your itinerary for assuring your navigation in daily life.

In the manner of a captain, it is important to leave nothing to chance. For each specific project as for each root cause of your dissatisfactions or problems, you must set the positions to attain, this means giving yourself concrete results to achieve throughout the course of your progression. You must also choose the appropriate means for reaching these results and make all the necessary arrangements to effectively use these means. Stated another way, it is time to specify the **how** of your progression toward realizing each of your dreams.

Figure 2 illustrates the process we followed up to now and the course that will lead you to the end in a profitable and effective manner. **The ideal** to attain, the shore of your dreams, is situated at the top of the pyramid. It is accessible thanks to your **key factors** of success (your most significant strategic objectives) that, for their part, are actualized through each of your **critical concerns**, meaning your big projects or big **whats**. These **critical concerns** will be, when required, divided into more precise **components** (your small **whats**), meaning more specific and practical projects or problems. Finally getting to the particular **targets** of each of your specific projects and the **root causes** you have chosen to attack for correcting each of your problems. To actualize your strategic procedure, in order to pass from dream to reality, what remains to be done is to put your methodical and operational **action plans** into action.

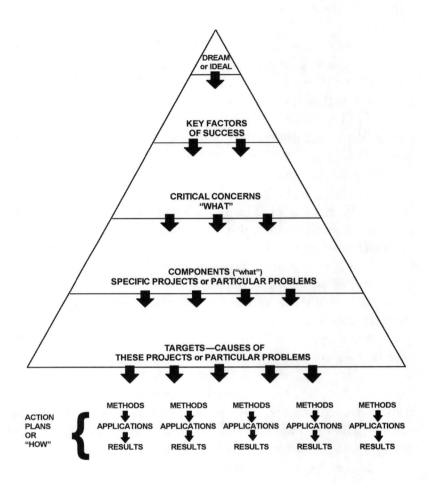

Figure 2
Procedure for the focus of the strategy of champions:
from dream to reality

For Bruno, one of the key factors at the base of his ideal of life was to improve his state of health. One of his critical concerns linked to this key factor aimed at losing weight. By dividing up this big what, Bruno became aware that one important component was that he needed to correct his bad habit of eating too much. Analysis of this behavior revealed the network of causes that maintained it and this brought him to target the most important and controllable sources of his problem. For each of these targets, he then had to establish precise action plans for obtaining concrete results, while determining the appropriate methods for attaining them.

Bruno's procedure illustrates well the different steps that can outline, according to your needs, the focus of your strategy for success. This procedure is applicable to all types of situations. One of the key factors of success of your dream ideal might consist of improving the material side of your life. This could include, among your critical concerns, renovating your home. This huge project is in turn divided into many components like, among other things, improving the windows of your home. The targets for desired change on this level will thus correspond to the size of the windows, their gradient of thermal insulation or their security aspect.

One of the most important factors for your strategy's success is to properly subdivide your ideal to make it attainable and feasible. The more you go towards the base of the pyramid of figure 2, the more you unfold your dream, the more specific you become and are able to give it life[11]. Now you must complete this deployment while thinking of concrete results and practical methods, in order to establish a logical and effective operation plan for each of your projects and **targets**.

Aim for Tangible Results

Setting concrete results to attain is the only way to avoid dreaming with eyes shut. Without observable results, the aimed for ideal, your key factors of success, your critical concerns and your specific projects will be mere utopias. If there is nothing to confront you, to render you aware of what you have or have not attained, you will long delude yourself about the tangible progress you have really accomplished.

Aiming for concrete results is what the seventh golden rule of successful change (chapter four) is about. If you don't know how to provide yourself with practical objectives expressed as perceptible and tangible realizations, the change will mean nothing. You must define observable and, if possible, quantifiable indicators so that you can unmistakably witness the progress you achieve. Short of indicators, without measures of your progress, how will you know if the methods used in your action plans are effective? How can you determine if you have evolved and really changed? How will you be able to say that you have attained your desired goal?

Reaching for concrete results is an unavoidable condition of success. It requires that for each of your projects, for each of the specific targets you want to attack, you must specify what you are aiming for in terms of measurable indicators. Before beginning a project, ask yourself what will be the indices or measurements that will indicate if you have progressed and succeeded. In Bernard's case, the critical concern of eliminating leak defects was monitored by a variety of indicators for the number of leaks: the total within the whole factory, the number according to the type of leak and by the type of engine. Each component of this critical concern also had its own particular indicator like the number of oil leaks in type X engine sealant joints. Once the causes of this problem had been well identified, the target for solving it focused on the necessity to standardize the procedure for bolt tightening of the motor head for all employees. The progress indicator relative to this aim was the actual percentage of the gradual use of the new tightening procedure.

Without these measurable indicators, it would have been impossible to follow the evolution of our progress. We could have long deluded ourselves with illusions of our efficiency, like the great majority of individuals who attempt to change without ever taking the time to lucidly and honestly verify the course of their progress.

You can give yourselves measurable indicators right from the start when working out the details of your strategy of champions. In the case of Bernard's enterprise, the defined measurements on all the strategic levels enabled them to trace the impact of each base operation on the strategic objectives and the organization's desired ideal performance. This is what I call the cycle of a realized dream as illustrated in figure 3.

In this cycle, the measurable indicators defined at the different stages of the strategy's implementation enables you to gradually transform your **strategic objectives** into **operational objectives**, meaning concrete results attained through practical operations within the framework of methodical action plans. Then, from the obtained results and thanks to your **operational objectives** and your measurable indicators, you can climb back up the strategy's course to verify the effectiveness and witness whether, in reality, you draw nearer to your dreams and **strategic objectives**.

The procedure illustrated in figure 3 represents the ideal complete cycle of your realized dream. Many people often ask me if it is absolutely essential to always have clear and precise objectives and if we must strive to measure everything.

There are no magic recipes for answering these questions. Giving yourself targets to reach is, just like champions, taking **responsibility** for your destiny. Like them, you must know how to be **methodical** and **concrete** in your progression toward success all while being **optimal** in your procedure. You must not become obsessed with setting objectives and thus provoking paralysis by analysis. Do just what is required, according to your needs, without overdoing things, that's the secret. You must try, learn and correct to find the accurate and effective dose. However, without personal objectives, you risk letting life and others take charge for establishing them for you; or you let your own shackles set your objectives and lead you by the tip of your nose.

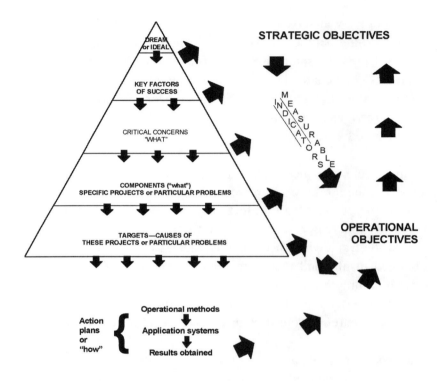

Figure 3
Implementation procedure of the strategy of champions: the cycle of your realized dream

A patient of mine was complaining of fatigue and of overexertion. She didn't have all the control she desired over her life and, most of all, didn't clearly see her own definitions and limits. On the professional level, she worked tirelessly and when she allowed herself leisure time, she tried constantly to push herself to be the best. She never had enough time to do everything and was but very rarely satisfied with her realizations. Now, at work, she never established what she meant by a job well done. What she wanted to attain wasn't clear and her learned irrational shackles told her she should be perfect in everything and please everyone. These same shackles pushed her to exhaust herself in sport, always striving for perfection and the image of being the best. Her self-definition relied largely on the perception others had of her and she thus found herself tossed about by the judgments of others. Without conscious and lucid personal objectives, she didn't know where to stop and set her limits. The demands of others as well as her own shackles shaped her objectives and oriented a very huge portion of her strategy of life. From the moment she learned to set clear, precise and concrete objectives, in accordance with her strategic orientation, her life changed. She realized and understood that she should first of all define her own limits to retake control and get away, once and for all, from her tendency toward exhaustion.

As for knowing if you should and could specify measurable indicators for all the objectives you've set, the answer, here also, doesn't rely on any magic recipes. Without measures, it is more difficult to find out what your real progress is and to assure yourself that your tools of change are effective. On the other hand, spending most of your time observing and measuring yourself can lead to obsession and become totally counter-productive; knowing how to be **optimal**, this is the secret. You must respond to your needs and give yourselves simple progress indicators that are easy to observe, cost little and require very little time for measuring and following them.

But, is this always possible and realistic? How, for example, do you measure the improvement of the image of a business? How do you evaluate the competition anxiety of athletes or their degree of muscular tension or their activation level? By what indicators could Bruno specify the effectiveness of his use of time or the improvement of his way of thinking regarding his quest to always be perfect? With a bit of ingenuity and, above all, in properly defining what your words or concepts mean, you can give yourself measurable indicators that are both simple and easy to follow. In the case of the business, they must specify what is meant by "image". For a petrochemical industry, image is linked to people's reactions, within the company's vicinity, to unpleasant odors and related pollution emitted into the atmosphere. The progress indicators, related to the organization's efforts to correct its odor problem or to improve its image, have thus taken into account measures like: the number of weekly complaints coming from neighboring residents, the results of a small telephone survey conducted among the adjacent population before and after the corrective actions and a technical measure of pollutants emitted from the factory. By taking into account these three types of indices we have an idea of people's perceptions relative to the effectiveness of our adjustments and at the same time, of the image projected within the community.

In the case of competition anxiety, it is not easy to objectively measure all the responses athletes experience on the field. Psychological reactions are not easily measured with technical instruments. In these cases, I simply use subjective measures of progress. An athlete's general reaction of anxiety can be evaluated by a subjective percentage on a scale from zero to 100: zero is no anxiety and 100 signifies the maximum anxiety the athlete could experience. Such subjective percentages are extremely valuable indicators because athletes can assess where they stand in relation to themselves and follow their own progress. We can use analogous scales for the degree of muscular tension and the activation level. In this way, if we turn to techniques of relaxation and activation control at various crucial moments during competition, we are able to verify their impact on the athletes' physical responses as well as on their more general psychological indicator of anxiety.

Bruno had defined his effectiveness for his use of time as follows:
a. the number of effective hours spent at the office, door closed, sheltered from the distractions and inconveniences of his colleagues,
b. working on the tasks as defined in his daily agenda,
c. as a function of his weekly and monthly objectives.

His measurable indicators were related to the number of effective work hours, the percentage of planned activities achieved throughout the course of a day and a subjective weekly indication of his satisfaction evaluated on a scale of 10 (0 being total dissatisfaction and 10 total satisfaction).

With such indicators, Bruno gave himself the objectives of progressively increasing his actual daily hours of work from 4,5 to 7,5 throughout one month, of augmenting his daily activity achievement rate from 50% to more than 90% and of increasing his subjective degree of weekly satisfaction from 3/10 to 8/10. Thanks to these measures, Bruno was able to follow his progression and verify whether the planned methods of his action plan were truly pertinent and effective.

As for improving his way of thinking, on the first hand, we identified the different types of thoughts or ideas that passed through his head whenever he wanted to be perfect. Because the influence of these ideas arose on numerous occasions throughout each day, the measurable indicator became the total number of ineffective thoughts within 24 hours. To measure this number, Bruno kept a stash of paper clips in the left pocket of his vest and each time an idea of perfection bothered him, he transferred one of these paper clips to his right pocket. This became, by the very act itself, a trigger for using his technique for restructuring ineffective thoughts each day.

Thanks to this simple measure, it was easy for us to follow the evolution of Bruno's way of thinking and to verify, at the same time, the impact of our corrective tools. The targeted goal was to go from an average of more than 30 ineffective thoughts per day to less than 10 within a period of six weeks.

As you can see, with a little imagination and ingenuity, we can easily define simple measurable indicators that are not costly and easy to follow. Such indicators are extremely important, as they are the only true tests of the effectiveness of your action plans and tools for change. They are, in some way, the guardrails of the cycle of your realized dream as illustrated in figure 3.

Select the Appropriate Means

The selection of appropriate means is to choose suitable tools for giving a concrete form to your life strategy in day-to-day reality. After having determined your strategy's precise targets and desired results, you need to consider how to proceed. You have now arrived at the phase of practical operations and field applications that will daily transform your dream into success.

Selecting the appropriate means is to set up the backbone for each of your action plans. Around this central framework are structured all the practical applications necessary for realizing these plans. Between becoming aware that something needs to be changed or done and the actual change itself, a ditch must be crossed. Becoming aware of your technical fault during the execution of a golf drive or tennis serve won't automatically fix the problem. You must return to corrective exercises, meaning concrete and effective methods for use in daily practice to correct the fault that undermines your efficiency.

Such truth is very evident in reference to examples like tennis and golf. Unfortunately, we have the tendency to forget this in the reality of life. We too easily have the impression that it is enough to understand our failings, to become conscious of our problems and to wish ardently for change in order for it to arise. Don't forget that the technical flaw in sport was "practiced" often and maintained over a long period of time. A bad habit is anchored in your memory and motor reflexes and, to undo it or replace it, you must physically work hard and sometimes even for a long time.

It is the same for all other aspects of your life. Becoming aware that you must change your attitude within your relationship or be more attentive to your children or further still, become more efficient and stop always putting things off until tomorrow... is very praiseworthy but totally insufficient. If you don't take adequate practical means, if you don't know how to use the methods or suitable operations, nothing will be produced or changed. This is a fundamental element of the eighth golden rule of successful change (chapter four): you must **deliver the goods**, which demands using appropriate means.

For all the clients I've worked with, there is always homework to do. I never end an interview with a simple good-bye. Once my clients leave my office, they leave with suggestions for practical exercises to do during the following week. We define these exercises together and in agreement. In this way, clients have the possibility of working on their mode of functioning and to concretely progress from one meeting to the next. They then have the feeling of taking charge of themselves; they more easily rediscover their hope, confidence and control over their lives. At the same time, the therapeutic process is more rapid, more effective and also less costly.

These are the basic principles. But, what is an appropriate and effective means? In the practical reality of your life strategy, it concerns a means that: (1) requires you to accomplish an action, behavior or operation, (2) that is to be executed in a methodical and concrete way, (3) which will help you get nearer to your operational objectives, (4) in having your measurable indicators progress toward the desired direction, (5) as rapidly as possible (6) and at the lowest monetary and energetic cost.

An adequate and effective means is not thus a magic pill. It is chosen with care, as a function of your aims and objectives. It requires daily concrete work and must produce positive repercussions within a reasonable delay, without exhausting or ruining you.

At this actual time, with our knowledge of how human beings function, we possess a range of intervention tools and techniques that enable us to respond to all types and varieties of needs. Whether it concerns correcting problems, improving our well-being, increasing our effectiveness or optimizing our performance, we have many more effective methods available to us than we suspect. More often than not, the difficulties we encounter in our search to improve our fate and change, don't usually correspond to an absence of adequate means. They more often depend on our ignorance or incorrect use of these means: whether we fail to choose the right tools, whether we employ them improperly or whether we lack the tenacity to go all the way with what we have started to do or change.

If we take the trouble to properly identify our needs, we can correct and adjust our way of acting and our dynamic of functioning simply as we please. If we want to truly change and optimize our performance or our well-being, we can rely on techniques and methods that enable us to do this.

We can adjust our physiological reactions in a very precise fashion through diverse intervention techniques of relaxation or efficient breathing; for athletes, it is possible to modulate their activation levels to attain exactly the degree of arousal or relaxation required for the optimal execution of a task. We now have a much better understanding of exercise physiology, the biomechanics of movement and nutritional guidelines, so that we are able to maximally profit from our human machinery.

Concerning our behaviors, it is possible to adjust and correct our attitude and our way of being with respect to our needs and the circumstances we have encountered. Control methods and behavior modification enable us, in many cases, to remake a political leader's image, to teach athletes to develop the attitude of a champion or to help individuals master their disruptive or ineffective behaviors.

When it concerns harmonizing our emotional reactions, we can work on our capacity to systematically modulate our emotional registers. It is equally possible for us to work on the thought systems and beliefs that cause and support our emotions so that we may understand them better, live through them or harmonize them as needed.

If we wish to optimize our way of thinking or processing information, there is a wide range of tools that are as diversified as they are effective. We can rely on specific methods for improving our attention and concentration. It is possible to learn how to talk positively to ourselves or use our capacity for visualization in an effective way. Our negative thoughts can be detected, corrected and restructured into positive and dynamic thoughts. We can learn to analyze and solve our problems in a methodical manner, to make decisions and choices in an optimal way, etc.

As you can see, we do not lack resources. Our toolbox is very well equipped and it enables us to control at will our way of acting and behaving[12]. It is equally feasible to go even further and deal with the contents of our memories. We could, if we wanted to, examine the different psychodynamic aspects of our development and question our fundamental representations of the world, our beliefs and our values. If we so desired, it would be possible to gradually restructure these worldviews as well as smashing the shackles of inefficiency that poison our internal universes. Nevertheless, as I've already mentioned, we must be careful not to lose ourselves in the twists and turns of our immense complexities and end up perpetually turning in circles, never changing anything that dissatisfies us in the here and now.

Finally, when necessary, we have the freedom to do what we must to modify and adjust the various controllable elements of our external reality. This requires that we methodically define all the actions and operations relevant to effectively act upon our environment and thus change the situation that undermines our efficiency or well-being.

If you truly want to change, progress and take your strategy of life to term, it is possible to do something on all these different levels of your dynamic of functioning. An expansive range of means is accessible to you and it's up to you to choose the tools and operations needed for reaching your targets and meeting your objectives. These means and these tools will constitute the central framework for each of your action plans.

Methodically Assemble Each Action Plan

You have identified those components – specific projects or particular problems – that are the most fundamental of your top priority critical concerns. You have methodically determined the causes of these problems and the targets of these projects you want to work on. For each one, you have given yourself measurable indicators and operational objectives to reach. You have carefully selected the means, techniques, tools or operations that will enable you to achieve these objectives. Now, from these diverse elements of information, you must assemble a coherent whole to create action plans that are practical, methodical and effective.

Table 2.1 (Annex) suggests a simple and practical way to assemble each of your action plans. The critical concern and its component (where this is the case) are identified at the top of the table; the objectives linked to them can also be indicated. Next, for each target or pinpointed cause, the operational objectives are specified as well as the technique (means, tools, actions or operations) for achieving them. The application procedures – where and when to act, who is involved, which material, technical, human or financial resources are required and what the cost will be – are concurrently planned whenever pertinent and necessary. The sought after results, as well as those already obtained with respect to your different actions or operations, could also be taken into consideration.

Attempting to **PLAN EVERYTHING, EVEN THE UNPREDICTABLE**, is proper to those that are able to see far into the future. By referring to a synthesis table for methodically assembling and fully describing each of your action plans, you simplify things for yourself and make better use of the fifth key of the strategy of champions. No matter what method you choose to proceed with, always have a global view of what you need to accomplish for each of your projects. Like the captain, don't leave anything to chance and meticulously plan out your navigation. Even if you don't make use of a table similar to the one suggested, make sure you complete a global and methodical description of each of your plans so you don't forget anything nor take the wrong road once thrust into the heat of action.

Tables 2.2, 2.3 and 2.4 (Annex) illustrate three different examples for using the proposed planning table. The first example involves the case of the leaks our friend Bernard had to face within his enterprise. Only the problematic situation of oil leaks at the sealant joint for type X motors is considered. The second example is the treatment for control of competition anxiety for an elite athlete. The third case is that of Bruno and his difficulty controlling his weight.

As you can see (Table 2.2), Bernard has carefully established his action plan and the results didn't take long to appear. He could eliminate the sealant joint oil leaks of type X motors more rapidly than expected. It was the same for all his projects, such that within one year he had largely accomplished all his objectives, earning himself one of the most enviable reputations within the whole organization.

Concerning the action plans of the elite athlete who wanted to improve his control over anxiety (Table 2.3), one of the fundamental components was reducing his activation level during the long waiting periods preceding each competitive event. We decided to work on three targets during these waiting periods:

the excessive muscular tension he felt, the fact that watching other participants raised his anxiety/activation and, finally, the negative thoughts that beset him throughout these periods of time. Taking each target into account, we set precise operational objectives and identified the psychological control techniques he would use to attain them. For each technique, the athlete then determined the specific operations he needed to accomplish to effectively master them; he also specified the application procedures of these diverse operations so he would benefit from a methodical and realistic mental preparation plan. The expected results from each operation as well as what had been already achieved following the implementation of the plan is briefly presented. The athlete added a heading titled "general" to his synthesis table for linking his results to the particular objectives of his critical concern and its component. In each case, all the targeted goals were attained and he was able to control his competition anxiety even better than he'd hoped after just six weeks of implementing his action plan.

The third example (Table 2.4) presents a part of the action plan designed by Bruno to correct his bad habit of overeating and lose excess weight. I only take into account here the first three targets previously identified for this specific case. For each target, the operational objectives were precisely determined. The operations described in relation with the third target incorporate a behavior modification technique into the planned means for attaining the targeted objectives. The desired results as well as those that had been obtained following the implementation of his plan are taken into consideration as a function of each of the realized operations.

Bruno proceeded similarly for each of the other targets we identified. After only two months, his weight dropped from 90 to 82 kilos and this, without following any miracle diet. Each month, we did an evaluation test of the average number of calories per day over a period of three days. Without directly fixating on this factor every day of the month, Bruno was able to reduce his dietary input to 2,400 calories/day after eight weeks. Without turning to any magic pill, he had decided to attack his problem at the root, meaning the network of causes that maintained his ineffective life habits. Thanks to an action plan that was global, methodical and meticulous, he was finally able to achieve the very objectives he'd unsuccessfully coveted for so long.

Before concluding this section on establishing action plans, I suggest you don't develop specific plans for all of your critical concerns identified in the preceding chapter and incorporated into your directional map. Only plan a small number of projects in detail, for example those that need to start within the first three months of implementing your strategy of success. Planning too much detail, too far in advance is not ideal. Many things can change along the route and force you to adjust according to circumstances, your evolution and the results obtained beforehand. The captain does not plan all the particulars of his navigation for the ports to come later. He first plans and realizes a bit of the way before specifically thinking about the steps that will come later.

Tame the Unpredictable

How many times have I heard: "it never works out as I planned" or "there is always something that doesn't go right, that doesn't go the way I'd like". Certain people are easily discouraged when faced with the unexpected. Each event, each circumstance that thwarts their projects cuts their legs out from under them or easily throws them. As a result they fail to use their practical means or their tools, gradually letting go of their action plans, abandoning their quest for change and improvement and letting themselves down.

Unpredictability is part of life. It can never be perfectly anticipated or totally eliminated. Meanwhile, we can prepare ourselves for facing it. It is always possible to react positively and to pull out the best from it. It is written nowhere that the unpredicted must undermine us and consequently lead us to failure.

The idea is to develop adaptation flexibility and learn to quickly recover your balance, regardless of what's happened. To do this, you must keep an open mind. You must accept that the unexpected, setbacks or undesirable events can happen. But beware, accepting the unpredictable in this way doesn't mean submitting to it and letting yourself be tossed about by it. On the contrary, accepting the unpredictable is receiving it like a challenge that can take you even further. This is looking ahead with the eyes of someone that has the firm conviction that nothing will stop him or her along his/her way to success.

Such a mentality relates to the great quality of **optimism** that characterizes all champions. This quality is not innate. It is developed and learned through experience, through the use of proper means. One way to cultivate it is to specifically tame the unexpected, visualizing the unpredictable to adapt to it better in a positive and dynamic fashion.

All the athletes I work with design alternative plans so they aren't caught off guard by unpredictable events during a competition. A study demonstrates that the best Olympic athletes are precisely those that, among other things, prepare alternative solutions to face the unexpected[13]. Rather than wait to be tossed about by setbacks, they take the initiative. Without fear, they foresee in advance all the situations that could arise and hurt their performance. At the same time, they anticipate how to effectively react to these events to overcome them and even try to prevent them if possible. Thus, athletes may ask themselves how to avoid waking up late the morning of an event or how not to be caught off guard due to a broken piece of equipment or even, how to ward off a huge rise in anxiety during the days preceding competitions. They will also mentally prepare how to react well if the start of an event is delayed, if there is a false start or if the opponent cheats, or is not sportsmanlike… and so forth.

Planning preventive procedures and alternative solutions in advance is one of the best ways to cultivate and prepare your adaptation flexibility. However it doesn't mean restricting yourselves to rigid scenarios and to absolutely and infallibly anticipate everything. In the way of champions, being **optimal** is foreseeing as much as possible without making yourself sick and sinking into obsession. If you know how to tame the unpredictable, very little can unseat you in life and if ever you are momentarily thrown to the ground, you won't take too long to get back on your feet.

In business, we adopt the same outlook. We examine the diverse operations of an action plan and try to predict everything that can undermine us or go wrong. This often leads us to define additional preventive operations that are very useful and are included in our original action plan before beginning our work. We also hold in reserve corrective operations if and when, despite all our efforts, certain difficulties arise. This thus enables the organization to rapidly adapt with minimum loss and maximum efficiency.

To develop your adaptation flexibility, it is possible to do the same thing with your personal action plans. Ask yourself about the potential difficulties liable to undermine the achievement or success of each of your planned operations. Think about how you can prevent these difficulties and, if they ever appear, how to correct them and rectify the situation. Prevention is an action we take in advance to neutralize and stop a problem from eventually occurring. For instance, we use fireproofing materials and prohibit people from smoking in a high-risk area to prevent a potential fire. Nevertheless, in the eventuality of a fire even then, we are prepared with water sprinklers, fire extinguishers and a fire service; in this case, we fall back on the corrective actions once the difficulty has manifested itself.

By making the effort to anticipate, as lucidly as possible, the traps, difficulties or problems capable of hindering you from attaining your objectives, you are better able to ward them off and plan how to remedy them if they occur even despite everything. You become proactive and help yourself feel better prepared to face whatever can happen, in a positive and dynamic fashion. You develop your adaptation flexibility and enhance your capacity for optimizing while giving yourself the necessary resources to go all the way with your life strategy.

Putting it into Action

1. Verify if you need to define each of your top priority **critical concerns** more carefully: is it possible to subdivide them into more specific projects or to pinpoint some particular problems? Don't examine all the **concerns** written on your directional map at the same time; begin your detailed strategic planning with the most urgent ones.
2. If you have pinpointed dissatisfactions or particular problems, clearly retrace the network of their causes. Establish priorities when a network is composed of many causes.
3. For each specific project and each particular problem – or for the critical concern itself if you haven't subdivided it – determine the precise targets you want to tackle within each of your action plans.
4. Identify, for each target, the measurable indicators you will use for following your progress and set operational objectives for each as a function of these measurable indicators.
5. Specify the means or tools you will use as well as the actions and operations you need to accomplish for achieving the operational objectives of each of your targets.
6. Next, put together your action plans. For each component (specific project or particular problem) of your top priority **critical concerns**, specify the application procedures (where and when to act, who is involved, what material, human, technical or financial resources will be required and at what cost) of the diverse operations planned for enabling you to meet your operational objectives. Determine, wherever possible, the expected results of each of these operations.
7. Tame the unpredictable by asking yourself what potential difficulties could arise during the implementation of each of your action plans. Try to discover the means to prevent these difficulties and identify alternative solutions in case they arise despite everything.

Chapter 8

THE 6TH KEY:
ADJUST THE MECHANICS

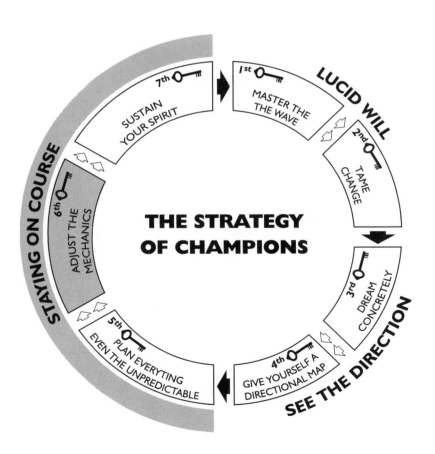

From now on your most cherished dreams are within reach. You have equipped yourself with a methodical life strategy grounded on a solid and concrete ideal. Now you must respect the eighth golden rule of successful change, this means **delivering the goods**, and doing so fully right up to the end.

The only effective way to meet such a challenge is by guaranteeing a methodical and coherent follow-up of your global operations in everyday life. There is a lot to accomplish and it must all be properly coordinated. Each day you will be able to make progress as long as you have correctly integrated all your plans within the framework of your everyday activities.

Proper organization of your operational follow-up is the key to successfully ensuring yourself of a constant and harmonious progression. Strategic living means thinking in a global manner while taking action in day-to-day reality. This is moving forward in a constant and progressive fashion while balancing your efforts without nevertheless overloading yourself. It is gradually adapting your way of doing things, bearing in mind the results obtained and the constraints encountered.

To accomplish this feat of power, you must be cautious. For businesses, this dimension of the strategic process is given great attention. This is what we call the **STRATEGIC FOLLOW-UP** stage. In therapy, this is the moment for asking the question: **WILL YOU GO ALL THE WAY?** In every case, it involves the same preoccupation: take the change to term by adapting it to everyday life.

Defining a methodical and coherent **follow-up** for the whole of your operations enables you to translate your strategic approach onto the same level as your regular activities and current concerns.

You thus learn to transform your present situation to gradually tame change and achieve success. To put an efficient **follow-up** in place, you must respect five basic principles that constitute the foundation of the sixth key of the success of champions: **ADJUST THE MECHANICS**.

Principle #1 – Don't Overdo the Planning

One of the great temptations arising the moment we put our action plans into gear, is the desire to progress more rapidly by taking double mouthfuls. At this stage, we are wrapped up in the new perspectives offered us and are impatient to experience progress and success. We thus have the tendency to overload our present situation leading to the following results: rapid breathlessness, difficulties, doubts, loss of confidence and quitting.

One of the secrets of success at this stage is knowing how to properly benefit from your efforts. You have given yourself clear and precise priorities. You have, to the best of your knowledge, identified 20% of the projects and operations likely to lead to 80% improvement and increased life satisfaction. You have all it takes to tame change and bring about success. This means not spoiling the sauce by sinking into blind haste, causing you to lose sight of your fundamental objectives.

When we work with high-level athletes, we take care to properly balance the volume and intensity of their training in order to guarantee an optimal performance progression throughout the entire year. By meticulously gauging our efforts, we can even favor a performance peak during the season's most important competitions. From the beginning of the year, we already know what the athletes need to achieve in order to meet their objectives. Meanwhile, we do not leave the starting blocks at full speed, working on all components of the technical, tactical, physiological and psychological preparation training plans all at once, right from the very first month of the annual cycle. Keeping our priorities in mind, we establish gradual, daily progressions of the efforts need-ed to achieve our goals while taking care not to overload the ath-lete or provoke short-term exhaustion. We also plan periods of rest and transition to promote recharging the system. With this approach, we aim to develop the athlete's intrinsic motivation and feelings of competence. A judicious and correctly gauged progres-sion leads to positive results, which in turn builds self-confidence, feelings of success and the desire to continue their efforts right to the end. In this sense, we should never forget that success is built on success and an accumulation of the opposite nourishes feelings of failure, powerlessness and quitting.

If you adapt this within the context of your life strategy, it is thus important to respect your priorities and not undertake too much right from the start. You need to find a way to progressively real-ize what you have planned, otherwise a mounting feeling of fail-ure and helplessness will weaken your motivation and spirit. You should also sometimes release ballast and reduce the workload if it ever becomes too heavy. It's better to slow the rhythm down and take a break rather than bring yourself to the point where your ideas are no longer clear and fatigue and discouragement threaten to win you over.

But how can you stay wise and properly gauge your efforts? There is no magic recipe for answering this question. The best way is to consider the diverse operations of your designed action plans under the light of your current everyday activities. These opera-tions should be able to insert themselves into your timetable with-out provoking major overload or undue stress on your way of functioning. If a possibility of overload or stress exists, you should then take smaller mouthfuls, whether this means reorganizing your schedule or your regular concerns to harmonize your rhythm of life and your will to change.

We shall see, with the following two basic principles, how to judi-ciously develop your timetable in order to avoid overload. The other danger that certain people need to watch out for during the elaboration of their success strategy is an obsession with planning. According to the type of projects to be undertaken and your characteristic mode of functioning, some will feel the need to plan each and every operation down to the most minute detail whereas others will favor a less formal and more flexible structure. Within this perspective, there is no absolute rule for guiding your procedure. It is important to respect your preferences and natural tendencies in this domain without ever forgetting that being **optimal** is a fundamental quality of all champions.

Another aspect of excessive planning is the desire to specify the action plans of too great a number of critical concerns – or of their components – which would only have to be undertaken later on. Even if we globally recognize all that our athletes should work on during the coming year, I very rarely plan the details of the diverse components of their training for more than one month at a time. Experience has taught me that planning too far in advance is, more often than not, a waste of time and energy. In realizing your first projects, the progress and change initiated will, in their own way, shape events. They will influence your mode of functioning and your vision of reality. They will inspire you to add nuances to your planning which you could have never imagined nor anticipated any other way. Based on acquired experience, you will be better able to optimally identify and adjust the specific action plans of your diverse critical concerns when these have to be gradually incorporated into your everyday life. This is the reason why I suggested, in the preceding chapter, to only develop your plans for those projects to be implemented in the first month of your success strategy.

Principle #2 – Go Step by Step

Being cautious not to plan everything too far in advance doesn't mean you don't still carefully establish the major lines of the path you will follow. A captain on a long journey clearly identifies, before ever raising anchor, the predestined shore, the steps to cross and the stopover ports. He then determines, at the opportune time, detailed navigation plans that will enable him to complete each stage of his itinerary, bearing in mind the evolution of events, the voyage's progress and circumstantial constraints, which he must confront.

The captain will adapt his practical decisions and concrete operations to his daily needs, while constantly situating himself within the global and coherent vision of the undertaken journey. The approach is the same when implementing operational structure and action plans within the context of a business strategy. The global vision, the organization's strategic objectives and the major lines of the route to follow are determined within a time frame of three, four or five years in advance. Within this more general perspective reside the specific objectives of the current year as well as the precise projects we need to realize for attaining them. The action plans for these projects will then be determined to help guide the evolution of operations on a monthly or weekly basis, according to the business needs. The whole constitutes a well-articulated process where the steps interlock with one another, centered on a strategic line of conduct and a coherent and homogenous global vision.

Going step by step, within global and coherent strategic planning, is the surest way to attain your ends without losing yourself, becoming discouraged or wearing yourself out. This principle is carefully respected when it comes to implementing the detailed preparation plans of elite athletes. As a general rule, we work on a comprehensive four-year Olympic cycle. Considering the performance results the athletes wish to obtain at the next Olympic games, we determine the level they need to attain for each parameter of training. With our future reference point so specified, we establish a gradual progression for each year with specific objectives to meet for each major international competition or world championships.

Within each annual cycle, we further outline phases of work (for example: periods of general preparation, specific preparation, pre-competition, competition, etc.) as well as training/preparation macrocycles within each work phase. Each macrocycle lasts from three to six weeks, according to an athlete's needs, and includes his/her own unique objectives. It is only within these macrocycles that we define in advance the details of those action plans that will guide the specific structure of our athlete's training program. We put these details in place, one macrocycle at a time, so as to properly verify the athlete's progress at the completion of each stage. In accordance with the obtained results, we will thus prepare and adjust the detailed training plans for the following macrocycle.

These training plans will, for their part, guide us in setting weekly operational objectives for the various components of each athlete's preparation. This weekly phase constitutes a training microcycle. Inside one microcycle is the daily content of each training session, which translates the entire complexity of a champion's preparation into everyday reality.

By proceeding in this way, the training plans of athletes will be progressive, coherent and constantly aligned with the ultimate strategic objectives of their Olympic cycles. When remaining conscious of their global strategy, champions know, each and every day, why they're at the gym, pool or rink. They always have a clear idea in mind of the aims they pursue; each daily training session includes precise goals for helping them progress and draw nearer to the dream they wish to realize.

What enterprises or athletes do could also be aptly applied within the context of your own life strategy. If you proceed by taking precise and well-defined steps, you greatly increase your chances of going all the way toward your dream and leading your change process to term. You will guarantee a methodical follow-up of your strategic planning and also gradually **adjust the mechanics** for deployment of your action plans.

From the work completed up to this point, it is easy for you to define, in the way of a champion, a progressive, step-by-step evolution. Your life ideal has been translated into strategic objectives to attain (chapter 5), in a manner analogous to elite athletes and their Olympic cycles. The fourth key of success (chapter 6) has enabled you to specify what to do for achieving these important objectives; you have prioritized your key factors of success and your critical concerns in the form of a directional map for guiding your process. In examining this directional map, determine your yearly objectives as a function of the major projects you wish to realize in making your dream tangible.

Within your annual cycle, you can delimit monthly macrocycles in order to methodically follow your progression. From the action plans you defined using the fifth key of success (chapter 7), next identify your operational objectives for each month of the current year. Don't take mouthfuls that are too big; proceed one month at a time, as suggested in the preceding section.

Keeping your monthly objectives in mind, subsequently subdivide your progress into successive weekly microcycles within which you will schedule tasks or operations for assuring that each of your action plans progresses. These are the tasks and operations you spread out in your agenda for each day of the current week.

By proceeding in this way, using successive steps within the framework of a global and coherent strategy, you will ground your success within the present. Each day will have its own importance and its own meaning because it will be a logical, useful and essential link of the long chain in realizations along the way to your success.

Principle #3 – Act on a Daily Basis

By unfolding your strategy for success in stages, you have progressively transformed your reality to make it more interesting and satisfying. You have translated your global vision and life ideal into **daily**

actions, which are focused on a lucid and consistent line of conduct. So as to take on their full significance, these daily actions should be listed in your agenda each and every day without, nonetheless, provoking undue stress on your mode of functioning. You must still take into account your normal habits and natural rhythm of life.

In order to facilitate this task accordingly, many athletes and champions of all types chose the logbook formula. In this journal they write down all pertinent and useful information that will enable them to actualize their strategy in day-to-day life. As a general rule, the logbook covers a period of one year. To start off, the objectives for the annual cycle are clearly identified. Separate sections are then reserved for each macrocycle or each month of the coming year.

Keeping the existing projects in mind, we determine the operational objectives to be accomplished from the start of each macrocycle or month. Next, the list of tasks and operations to complete during the course of each coming week is established from each project's actions. To this list we also add the activities and habitual behaviors that need to be considered during that same period of time.

By having all that needs to be done during the week clearly in view, it will become much easier to evaluate how realistic the situation is and to consequently adjust the work load. Certain operations might sometimes need to be rescheduled and the launch of certain projects may even be delayed. Your weekly to-do-list also enables you to become aware whether you're truly ready to face change in your daily life. If you come to realize that habitual activities force you to postpone too often or to overly stall the completion of your projects, it would be helpful to reexamine the rationale of your life strategy. The more you defer and put aside diverse elements of your strategy, the more your motivation will drop and your dissatisfaction will grow. A quitter's perspective will rapidly appear on the horizon with, in its wake, feelings of failure or powerlessness, which are not always easy to digest.

The weekly to-do-list is an excellent preventive method for avoiding this trap of overload that leads to quitting. It can also provide you with the opportunity to establish priorities for your timetable. One simple and practical method is to determine which elements on your list are imperative and must absolutely be completed over the course of the next few days and which are desirable but could be delayed or rescheduled for later. By specifying your priorities in this way, you give yourself a margin for maneuvering when faced with the unpredicted. You insert buffer zones into your timetable; if an unexpected commitment does arise, you then have the opportunity to absorb it by rescheduling certain less essential activities to improve your efficiency. If you have not saved such openings, if you have no potential for flexibility, then all surprises will be considerable headaches causing stress on your mode of functioning. When stress, fatigue and tension accumulate, it is more difficult to remain **optimal** and effective while continuing to be **optimistic**. The price to pay can be enormous if the pressure forces you to the brink of exhaustion.

Once the priorities for your weekly to-do-list have been set, there's nothing left to do but distribute all your activities, tasks and operations onto the schedule grid for each day of the week. By proceeding in this way, you establish your daily timetable without ever losing sight of your major strategic objectives. Your life becomes more harmonious because your direction will be clear and each day's efforts will be centered on a coherent line of conduct.

The daily planner included within your logbook can have different forms according to the tastes and needs of those who use it. Some like to save a page for each weekday while others prefer using a unique seven-day schedule in a big table. Some people choose to divide each day into blocks of 30 or 60 minutes while still others, more comfortable with larger blocks of time, divide their day into morning, afternoon and night. Regardless of the modality used, it is fundamentally important to never lose sight of your imperatives and desires once you've translated your weekly to-do-list into your daily planner. I often suggest that my clients use two different types of notation to clearly distinguish between these two categories of activity. For example, if you pencil in your notations for your desirables, you could then easily erase certain actions and move them around to make room for unexpected operations of a more imperative nature. Thus, the medium favors adaptation in leaving the door open for potential changes in your timetable.

Principle #4 – Fine Tune Your Progression

A logbook doesn't just serve to plan and orchestrate the evolution of your life strategy into stages. It also enables you to verify and control the rhythm of your progress in order to make necessary adjustments as the need arises. By working in stages, by dividing your development into cycles, you define reference points in time, which enable you to follow your own evolution.

Thanks to the operational objectives and measurable indicators of your action plans, each stage of your process includes concrete results to achieve. To evaluate your progress within each macrocycle or each month of your year, you simply have to return to the objectives and indicators of your diverse projects in progress. Don't move on to the next month or macrocycle without first verifying if you have effectively attained the intended results. If you are not satisfied, take the time to adjust your course.

The end of a macrocycle should be the occasion to briefly check on things before moving on. When I work with athletes, we rely on measurable indicators for the many diverse components of training we work on. At the end of each stage, we assess our progress before moving on to the next cycle. We examine the results obtained for each indicator the athletes have tracked in their logbooks. We can also plan more specific tests, simulations or real competitive situations for assessing if certain targeted objectives were attained. Thanks to these evaluations, we are prepared to make insightful decisions for our training during the course of the next macrocycle. We can correct certain approaches, increase or decrease the volume or intensity of work, add certain components or drop others according to the results achieved. Our methodical evaluation thus enables us to **ADJUST THE MECHANICS** and precisely set the objectives for the next stage.

The procedure is similar for following the implementation of an organizational strategy. The process adopted in Bernard's case aptly reflects how a step-by-step progression with periodic adjustments favors the methodical tracking of a procedure of change. Each specific project linked to the critical concern of eliminating leaks had its own operational objectives and measures. These objectives and measures enabled us to establish a monthly progression that Bernard's group could keep clearly in mind. At the end of each month, the progress achieved for each project underway was evaluated and the objectives for the following month were then defined. We decided at this moment if it was possible to start new projects; we adjusted our path according to the evolution of circumstances and the difficulties or constraints encountered. Owing to this approach, we gradually evolved, slowly but surely, toward the annual strategic objectives the organization had set.

A similar follow-up process also guided Bruno in his procedure to lose weight and improve his health. Bruno had six targets to attack and many action plans to realize. Each target had its own measurable indicators and operational objectives. From these, Bruno determined the monthly results he wished to obtain as well as more specific weekly goals (Table 2.4). The follow-up of these measures enabled him to regularly adjust his procedure throughout the weeks and months that flowed by.

A periodic evaluation of each month or macrocycle is not the only useful method for assuring a methodical and effective follow-up of your life strategy. Like Bruno, you can also verify, on a weekly basis, the evolution of your progress. You do not need to become bogged down, seized by excessive measures and spending all your time compiling tables of endless data. Learn again how to be **optimal**. When it comes to a business organization, when defects of production and lost time are observable on a daily basis, the evolution of measures and progress has to be followed very closely. In certain cases we will compile data each day and even for each quarter of work, as a function of the projects and action plans under way.

The same need for precision can be true for elite athletes. To illustrate this point, I once worked with a rider that had developed significant symptoms of anxiety and a phobic reaction after falling from a horse. She wasn't able to mount her horse and even lost her technical ability for working with even the most docile horses in the training center. After a meticulous analysis of her mode of functioning, we targeted a certain number of technical, physiological and psychological elements to correct and master her reactions and behaviors. Each target became the object of an action plan, which consisted of operational objectives and precise exercises to execute, both at home as well as on the practice field. The collection of exercises for the diverse action plans was then gradually spread out over time. Keeping the planned progression in mind, we had results to achieve each week and very precise goals to meet at each training session. For each day and each practice, there was a concrete element to work on and improve; at each training the rider had the impression of climbing the ladder of her global strategy toward rediscovering the level of performance she was truly capable of.

To track her evolution, she used a logbook in which she wrote her action plans, daily objectives and exercises. Each time she rode, she marked down, after training, the percentage of ease she felt at the beginning and end of practice. She equally kept in mind other measures relative to the evolution of the diverse technical and psychological aspects she needed to work on. In this way, when we met at the end of each week, we could evaluate the true state of her progress and **adjust** the exercises of the different action plans for the next weekly stage. By proceeding in this fashion, it didn't take long to correct the situation and reestablish the performance level the rider was accustomed to. The methodical aspect of her strategic follow-up favored a rapid and effective recuperation all while serving her, consequently, as the working framework for facilitating her training optimization.

Even if you don't have to compile such a detailed list of precise measurements within a journal, it is useful and beneficial to follow the evolution of your progress from day to day, week after week. If you make a habit of developing a weekly to-do-list and if you translate this list in the form of a daily agenda, it becomes extremely easy to regularly evaluate your evolution and the development of your change process. By properly planning each day around a clear and coherent strategic line of conduct, it is enough for you to take a few minutes to make an appraisal at the end of each day. At the same time, you can adjust and adapt your schedule for the next day with respect to the outcome of your assessment.

Certain people prefer to revise their plan for the coming day in the morning, to assure they won't forget anything and help prepare them mentally to face the diverse tasks and operations awaiting them. For these people, this is a chance to start off on the right foot and properly focus their energy before diving into the heat of action.

This same type of evaluation can be realized at the end of each week. You need a few minutes for reviewing your to-do-list. You can thus see clearly what was accomplished and what remains pending. This will guide you toward adjusting or rescheduling certain operations as well as occasionally modifying the structure of certain action plans. At the same time, you can profit by determining the to-do-list for the upcoming week and establishing your timetable within your agenda. By proceeding in this way, you will be a lot more conscious of your evolution and won't delude your-self with illusions of good intentions that won't go anywhere. Thus, at the end of each month or macrocycle, you will end up, in hand, with all the data and pertinent elements needed for making a judicious, useful and effective evaluation of that stage.

With a well-measured progression, a continuous follow-up and appropriate measurements, you wind up by achieving, step by step, from one macrocycle to another, the diverse objectives set for each annual cycle. Thus the only thing left for you to do is to make an appraisal at the end of the year for verifying where you have arrived regarding all projects and action plans you planned on tackling and achieving during the course of the last twelve months. Keeping in mind the level attained for your annual objectives and the state of advancement of your projects, you will be prepared to adapt your progression and follow-up for the coming year. You will return to your global directional map (chapter 6) to **adjust your expectations**. Thanks to a methodical and progressive fol-low-up you will turn, little by little, step by step, all the strategic objectives of your life ideal into reality.

Principle #5 – Coaching the Follow-up

The preceding principles have presented many suggestions for helping you lead your strategy for success to term. All these sug-gestions target one fundamental goal: achieving your dreams by harmoniously coordinating the execution of all projects and action plans you hold dear to your heart.

It is not necessarily easy or evident to effectively coordinate all our activities and concerns. It's especially simple to fall back on our more or less satisfying old habits and lose sight of, in the buzz of everyday life, our new rules of conduct. To keep from sinking into this natural return of order and avoid being dominated by the force of inertia that chains us to our sources of ineffectiveness, we must play smart and remain vigilant. We must use concrete methods to make sure we remain, never quitting as the days go by, on the way to success.

While helping you define a follow-up process, the sixth key of success maximizes your chances for going all the way with your life strategy. By dividing your progression into stages, by judiciously measuring out your efforts and regularly evaluating your progress, you proceed in the best manner there is for turning all your strategic objectives into reality. You have given yourself all the necessary tools for **ADJUSTING THE MECHANICS** along the way. You learn to become the real coach of your change process. As I explained in presenting the tenth golden rule of successful change (chapter 4), you fully and wholly **assume leadership** of your life.

For certain people, coaching themselves and assuming personal leadership are well-integrated abilities in their mode of functioning. This is not always the case for the great majority of people who are bogged down by their difficulties, their dissatisfactions and their ineffective habits learned long ago. Despite all your good intentions and in spite of all the methods and suggestions at your disposal, it is possible for you to feel overwhelmed by your personal situation. It's possible that it seems like Mount Everest standing in your way. You want to change, you hope to be happier, but the mountain you need to climb seems so high that your energy appears to evaporate and your courage has deserted you before you've even begun.

If you experience such a reaction, don't needlessly put yourself down and accept this situation. Don't belittle yourself in advance and allow that feeling of powerlessness. Stop flogging yourself with your regrets and reproaches. Your reaction is not atypical. In order to safeguard the integrity of our system, we have a natural tendency to resist change. We find the energetic expense associated with this change, costly and we react spontaneously to try and avoid it. Moreover, embedded within our vision of the world is our system of values and beliefs, which drags us down with our own shackles and sources of ineffectiveness likely to slow down, and even dramatically reduce, all our efforts for improvement and progress.

We are marvelous machines capable of the highest achievements and with the promise of greater successes. Nonetheless, despite all these positives, every one of us carries within the seed of our powerlessness. If we are not careful, if we fail to take the appropriate measures, we quickly reach our own level of incompetence, enclosing us within our own limits. We create our very own prison, cry over our misfortune and set aside the dreams that had so rightfully sparkled and cheered us up.

If you feel this tendency toward inertia, if weariness or immobility overwhelms you, don't give in. If you have dreams and want to change your life, tell yourself that it's written nowhere that human beings are condemned to unhappiness and failure. If coaching your own change process seems like a mountain or something too difficult to do, don't give up on reviving the flame that slumbers within. Don't ever lose sight of the fact that it's not common for a system – whether it is a human, a community, an organization or an enterprise – to accept and be capable of changing itself from the inside. This doesn't mean that change is impossible and that you're condemned to die, suffocated between the walls of your own prison. On the contrary, all hopes are permitted. However, to escape your paralyzing inertia and break your chains of powerlessness, you must sometimes accept the need for outside help. You must be wise enough to recognize your limits or weaknesses and force your system onto the way of change by getting the appropriate help.

Turning to an outside resource doesn't mean you give up your autonomy, show weakness or surrender leadership of your life. On the contrary, you are behaving with wisdom and clarity. You possess the intelligence and courage to recognize the strengths and weaknesses of your mode of functioning, helping yourself adapt, learn and get the most from your capabilities. Foremost, you are not abandoning the dreams that live within you.

Certainly, as I mentioned in chapter 4 (see the section: **Carefully Select Your Allies**), getting help and support can be risky.

Unfortunately there are too many incompetents, vultures and parasites in the domain of psychotherapy, coaching, consulting for enterprises or expert-consultants of all kinds.

I have too often worked with patients who had spent years in therapy, turning in circles, wasting their money and wrapped up in themselves. They came out of it even more lost and despaired than beforehand. The "Psy" or therapists of all kinds had forced them to immerse themselves within the twists and turns of their complexity, leaving them to drown, to then offer them the buoy that sealed their everlasting dependence. They had learned their consultant's language, knew their concepts and lived their theories. But regarding their own mode of functioning, they had come to understand nothing nor fix anything. They held onto the magical thinking that all they needed to do to fix all their problems was simply discover the mysterious and unknown causes of their dissatisfactions.

I have seen coaches live their fantasies of domination and power by using their athletes as pawns or convenient instruments enabling them to satisfy their own dreams of glory. Many youngsters full of promise have wasted their talents and burned themselves out by turning to incompetent adults who were only thinking of their own image and fame. These athletes were exploited, pressured and abused, with no consideration for their own mode of functioning or dreams and finally shoved aside when they didn't serve their users' aims well enough.

In the world of businesses and organizations, I have known all sorts of consultants that sell pipe dreams and mirages to their clients. There are gifted "snake oil salesmen" who, as in the old days of the Wild West, know how to make people buy their magic elixir capable of healing, in no time at all and without any effort, all the problems of the organization in trouble. The only concern of some is to sell off their product, their colored pedagogical books or expensive videotapes indispensable to the learning of new skills that, in the end, won't change anything relating to the problems of the enterprise. Very often, the nicer the material, the more it costs and the less effective it is. Other consultants are very skilled in selling, but flee with the wind when real problems surface. Certain people specialize in "activitis": they bring the organization to a level (and necessity!) of training activities second to none, but lose sight of the enterprise's real needs and the concrete results that should be obtained. Finally, still others are experts in flat calm. They attempt to profit from their client by first and foremost avoiding the creation of waves. They never give the full story or paint the whole picture, always go in the direction of the wave and extract a maximum amount of money without ever changing anything or improving the difficulties of the organization they work for.

Turning to an external resource for help is, in many cases, necessary and useful. When you're not able to break your cycle of ineffectiveness or the perceived difficulty of changing appears too great to overcome, you have no other alternative. Nonetheless, as I've just illustrated, this choice inevitably comes with risks. There will always be exploiters and parasites to take advantage and profit from the situation. For this reason, you must be prudent in selecting support. First of all have a clear idea of what you want from the external resource you consult. Don't choose the first person to come your way; inform yourself of the individual or organization's effectiveness and competence. Clearly express your expectations in order to witness their reactions and verify if they listen to you and understand your needs. Don't be shy to ask for bits of information so you may adequately understand the mode of functioning of the person or persons with whom you wish to work. Take the time to digest the information and compare other potential resources. Finally, never commit for an unspecified length of time; set a trial period for yourself, a length of time at the end of which you can verify if the obtained results correspond with your expectations and objectives.

The most important thing in all of this is to never lose sight of the fact that you are not seeking a guru, a magician or a mentor who will think for you in your place. You want to remain the master of your own life. You are now a lot more conscious of your mode of functioning and are better acquainted with the limits likely to undermine you. Thus what you really need, is a coach, a resource that can support you throughout the length of your change process. Never lose sight that, whether in sport, in business or in private life, **coaching** signifies:

the art of helping individuals, groups or organizations attain their objectives by teaching them to manage, as effectively as possible, their evolution, their adaptation and their change.

To truly help you, good coaches should first of all know how to listen to you so as to properly grasp your mode of functioning and understand your needs. They shouldn't get stuck in irrelevant details but rather attempt to develop a vision or **global** diagnostic of your situation. If they are competent and skillfully master their domain, they will clearly explain to you the what, the why and the how of what they can do to help. They will have an efficient tool-box and will be ready to show you which methods or techniques are best suited and most pertinent to your situation. They will be **methodical** in their approach and will help you develop the action plans most likely to produce **concrete** results in the shortest time possible. They will first and foremost be preoccupied by your own interest and well-being by teaching you to be **optimal** and to adequately gauge your efforts. They will aim to, at all times, develop your autonomy in order to get you to take **responsibility** for your own change process. They will support you by guaranteeing a regular follow-up that will motivate your **patience** so you may progress regularly and steadily, little by little. Finally, they will encourage you and arouse your **optimism** throughout the course that carries you to the realization of your dearest objectives.

As you can see, the art of coaching cannot set aside the seven fundamental qualities of champions. These seven qualities will help you to go all the way toward your dreams and ensure you of an efficient follow-up to your change process. Without this follow-up, the risk is high that you'll lose sight of your strategic objectives and give up along the way. With the sixth key of success, you have in hand all the methods required to cover all the bases of such a follow-up and facilitate your own progression. And if ever you turn to outside help, assure yourself that you'll lucidly conserve leadership of your own strategy.

Putting it into Action

1. Choose the method you will use (logbook, yearly planner, computer program, etc.) for methodically following the evolution of your strategic process. Determine the major steps of this process by specifying your follow-up cycles and their duration: annual cycles, monthly cycles or macrocycles, weekly cycles or microcycles, etc., as a function of your needs.
2. Keeping in mind the **key factors** of success and the **critical concerns** forming your directional map (chapter 6), identify all your targeted objectives for your first annual cycle.
3. From the action plans of the specific projects you want to initiate at the beginning of your strategic process (chapter 7), set operational objectives for the first macrocycle or month of the year.
4. Considering all the tasks or operations planned within the action plans you want to start, establish your to-do-list for the first week (microcycle) of your strategic process while also keeping in mind your activities and regular responsibilities.
5. From your to-do-list, plan your timetable for each day of your weekly planner.
6. Plan, in your planner, some time for daily review where you evaluate and adjust your daily progression.
7. Plan, at the end of each week, a moment where you'll make an assessment and establish new operational objectives as well as

your new to-do-list, for the upcoming weekly microcycle.

8. Specify in advance an evaluation and adjustment period at the end of each of your macrocycles or monthly stages, to make a check up and carefully plan the targeted objectives and projects for the next stage to come.

9. Save yourself a period of transition at the end of your annual cycle to put your ideas in order, make an assessment of your evolution and adjust the major lines of your life strategy for the year to come.

Chapter 9

THE 7TH KEY:
SUSTAIN YOUR SPIRIT

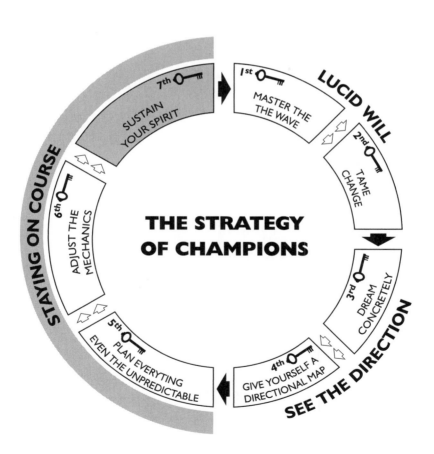

YOU'VE COME A LONG WAY since tackling the first key of success! You've taken the appropriate means to define your own coherent and lucid life strategy. You have transformed your most cherished dreams into a concrete and accessible reality. You've given yourself a progressive and methodical course of conduct to reach your ends. The only thing that remains to be done is for you to stick to your strategic planning and follow your course through until completion. Will you have the motivation and courage to stay on track and persist all the way to the end?

Despite your good intentions and in spite of the support provided by your strategy, your progress will sometimes be difficult. You will inevitably face ups and downs as well as moments of fatigue and boredom. On some occasions, setbacks or unexpected events will thwart your projects and force you to readapt or even, to start again from scratch. This might put your fundamental motivation and the very significance of your course of conduct to the test. You may then feel doubt, lose confidence and even experience the desire to let everything fall to the wayside.

Ups and downs are unavoidable yet completely normal. They drive many individuals to become discouraged and even abandon everything. However, nothing forces you to give in to them or to give up. They certainly represent risk factors to your progression but they don't condemn you to helplessness and failure. If you take the appropriate measures to encourage yourself and tame these difficult moments, there is nothing to prevent you from going all the way to the end with your life strategy and realize your dreams.

The seventh and last key of success enables you to properly adapt and be able to face every one of these ups and downs and setbacks that risk undermining your motivation and driving you to give up.

It will help you **SUSTAIN YOUR SPIRIT** throughout the course of your progression. From the perspective of corporate strategy, this last step corresponds to what I call **STRATEGIC SUPPORT**. In therapy, this is the moment where I ask the question: **WILL YOU KNOW HOW TO HANG ON?** In all these cases, this means identifying practical methods that will favor the maintenance of your dedication and **optimism** in the face of all the difficult moments, setbacks or delays likely to occur along the way.

All individuals, athletes, organizations or enterprises that go all the way with their strategies and reach their objectives, have never neglected this dimension of strategic support. Through experience, I have noted that all champions skillfully manipulate two fundamental factors to effectively **SUSTAIN THEIR SPIRIT**: they all know how to keep their motivation high and think in a constructive manner.

Keep Motivation High

Motivation is a complex phenomenon, which has been studied by numerous researchers from various disciplines like psychology, sport psychology, management, sociology and others. Considered from the perspective of a human being's mode of functioning, motivation is composed of many facets and components. Without going into every detail of this multidimensional process, it is still possible to grasp the essence of its influence with reference to a simple and concrete image.

In a very broad sense, motivation can be considered as a motor that drives us to develop, actualize and survive. From this angle, motivation is indistinguishable from the notion of well-being and "ill-being". In order to adapt and survive, our organism is fundamentally oriented towards a quest for well-being and the avoidance of "ill-being". As soon as there is the connotation of pleasure or displeasure, of comfort or discomfort, it sets in motion the effort to obtain one and avoid the other. The motivational motor is then activated to propel us to generate appropriate reactions and behaviors[14].

The motivation motor can be stimulated by internal or external incentives. Put another way, well-being like "ill-being" can be associated with external or internal factors. For example, we'll be attracted by a reward, a title or a medal, but we'll want to avoid a punishment or disagreement. In other circumstances, personal satisfaction and pleasure will incite us to pursue our efforts and maintain our commitment; conversely dissatisfaction and boredom will drive us to avoid a task or escape a situation.

The fact that external and internal incentives activate our motivational motor has led us to distinguish two fundamental components of motivation, the extrinsic and intrinsic[15]. The basic principle underlying intrinsic motivation relates to the notion that all human beings need to feel competent and self-determined. This constitutes one of the most powerful motives for action. It is because of this intrinsic element that we seek experiences to go through and challenges to overcome. Given this component of motivation, the activities that contribute to developing and maintaining our personal responsibility and competence arouse most our interests and involvement. The pleasure obtained from the accomplishment of a task itself as well as feelings of satisfaction represent powerful stimulants that contribute to maintaining our well-being and motivation.

The extrinsic component of motivation is associated with external reinforcements. Profits, rewards, enjoyable consequences and fame tend to stimulate our well-being and activate our motivational motor. Our attraction toward these incentives, our need to acquire them can make us produce the responses necessary for obtaining them.

The intrinsic and extrinsic components are two essential and complementary aspects of motivation. If you skillfully manipulate them and use them in harmony, you will successfully and effectively **SUSTAIN YOUR SPIRIT** all along the path toward the achievement of your life objectives. On the other hand, if you neglect the motivational aspects of your strategy and go against these basic principles of motivation, chances are strong that you'll end up quitting along the way. Whenever difficulties arise, whether results are late in coming or setbacks and obstacles have assailed you, you will no longer have the energy or the desire to pursue your progression. The effort required and the price to pay will appear more and more significant and, bit-by-bit, you'll loosen your vigilance, forget your aspirations, invent all sorts of excuses and return to your old reflexes. You'll become bogged down by your frustrations and dissatisfactions to once again rediscover the walls of your own prison.

To sustain your spirit throughout the course toward realizing your strategy for success, you can act on four parallel and complimentary levels. These four levels enable you to draw out the maximum profit from harmonizing intrinsic and extrinsic motivations. The more you know about playing with and effectively manipulating them, the more chance you'll have of overcoming the difficulties, obstacles and setbacks that will inevitably line your route.

Level 1 – Stimulate Involvement

The first important dimension to consider regarding maintaining your motivation and sustaining your spirit is stimulating your own involvement within your life strategy so you may develop a sufficient personal commitment.

Involvement and commitment enable you to travel the necessary road while conserving your energy and optimism even when faced with adversity. Involvement and commitment are not always innate talents or magical recipes that fall from the sky when we need them. These are qualities that can be learned and worked on by taking appropriate measures. These are abilities that we can develop while using and respecting the basic principles of intrinsic motivation.

To stimulate your involvement and maximize your motivation, never lose sight of three fundamental factors when putting your strategy of success into action. **First** ask yourself whether your objectives, your critical concerns or your projects will bring you pleasure and satisfaction. **Next** assure yourself that they take advantage of your competence and contribute to their enhancement. **Finally**, make certain that your targets and what you'll accomplish will make you more autonomous and independent.

If you deeply dislike the task you need to achieve, there's little chance you will persist even if your objective is fine and noble in and of itself. I knew a student who returned to her studies to complete her Ph.D. in sport psychology. She had long dreamed of completing this project. Learning to logically structure her thinking on the road of scientific research was, for her, an important ambition in her life. Whether it concerned taking a course or planning a research project, all went well and satisfied her. However, doctoral studies require more than that. You must also sit alone and synthesize your thoughts in writing a thesis that explains and summarizes all your work. For this student, the task of organizing her thoughts in writing was a strongly unpleasant activity and caused her great anxiety. She was unable to do it and tended to avoid occasions where she could work on it. Time passed and her deadline arrived without producing the required document. The more she put it off, the more her motivation decreased; she had to abandon her project despite all her efforts up to that point.

All projects and activities should bring you a minimum of pleasure and satisfaction to arouse your involvement and motivate you. If you want to control your diet in order to lose weight, it is important that you identify and develop new healthy, agreeable and stimulating dietary habits. People who want to be physically active in order to improve their health should choose a sport or form of exercise that will bring them pleasure and promote their well-being. If you need to play and interact for enjoyment, think of an activity for two rather than one or a team sport rather than throwing yourself into a physical preparation program for running the marathon! Even if it might be very effective, you will quickly get fed up.

This principle is valid everywhere: pleasure and satisfaction should be greater than the effort or energetic cost required by the activity or project. This doesn't mean everything you undertake should bring you total joy and bliss. There will always be two sides to any reality and rare are things that lead only to pleasure without a converse effort or a price to pay. I have already underlined this point in chapter 4 in discussing our natural resistance to change. To progress and persist, you must firstly assure yourself that the profit of change is greater than the energetic cost. If your strategic objectives, your critical concerns and your projects fail to respect this principle, your balance of pleasure/satisfaction will be insufficient and your intrinsic motivation will thus not be great enough to stimulate your involvement and favor your persistence.

Further to pleasure and satisfaction, another factor is just as important to consider when determining your strategic objectives, critical concerns and projects. In each case, keep in mind your feeling of competence. Make sure that what you undertake will lead you to success. The feeling of competence cannot be isolated from achieving concrete and satisfying results. I have already highlighted the importance of this factor in chapter 7.

Attained and satisfying results give you information, feedback on the effectiveness of your strategy. In bringing you satisfaction, they also pinpoint the pertinence of your efforts and the value of your capacities and abilities. Your feeling of competence increases and you thus develop the desire and motivation to pursue your course.

To guarantee yourself good results and an increase in your feeling of competence, it is most important to properly plan your projects and specify the concrete goals you wish to attain. In this sense, the fifth key of success (chapter 7) gives you all the means to facilitate your progression and favor the attainment of concrete and positive results.

In choosing your critical concerns and in putting your diverse projects into action, also try to benefit from your well-mastered abilities and qualities. You already possess expertise, potential and experience. Each time you can, rely on your accomplishments and exploit your resources. This will make your task easier and also enable you to feel more competent and at your best.

If a project requires capabilities or skills that you don't feel you've mastered yet, give yourself the time to develop and acquire them. Ask for help if necessary, but don't try to cut corners because then you risk having everything fail. If you go too fast, you'll never obtain the anticipated results and you'll often provoke effects that are negative and contrary to your expectations. It is better to progress more slowly and take the time to do things properly to obtain satisfaction and thus help your feelings of competence to grow and your motivation to persist.

A workaholic friend of mine was in great need of leisure activities to unwind, change pace and increase his quality of life. He'd always dreamed of playing the guitar. Thinking he had found the magic solution, he immediately bought himself an instrument, reference manual and private lessons. He could already see himself playing sonatas and amazing his wife and friends after only a few weeks of practice. This was not the case. This friend had no experience with a musical instrument and his ear for music was as good as a cracked bell! For a few weeks, he threw himself into practicing and neglected, for the first time in his life, his work. He finally had a hobby.

His enthusiasm was short-lived. The sum of his sonatas was *Row, Row, Row Your Boat* sprinkled with false notes. The embarrassed and polite encouragement from his wife and the more and more frequent grimaces from his professor left him with little doubt of his potential as a virtuoso. Discouraged and disappointed, he packed the guitar away at the back of his closet. He felt ridiculous, inadequate and incompetent. For him, leisure time was over and he blindly dove back into his work to forget about it.

It took several months for him to digest his failure and begin speaking once again of the possibilities of another hobby in his life. By going through all his interests and abilities, he remembered that, when younger, he had manifested a natural potential for all games with balls and engines. Further, one of the rare things he still appreciated today was walking outside with his wife or friends. Why then not try and learn to play golf? The idea made him smile, but this time he wouldn't try to become Jack Nicklaus or Tiger Woods in a matter of weeks. He took lessons and gave himself a progressive and realistic learning period. Little by little he learned his new physical activity, transforming it into an agreeable, satisfying and lasting hobby. By relying on his basic acquired abilities, by taking the time and necessary means to develop his new responses, he revived within himself a feeling of competence. He rediscovered the essential pleasure and satisfaction needed to maintain his commitment and motivation. Since then, he never diminished his participation in golf and his quality of life was greatly increased.

Further to pleasure, satisfaction and feelings of competence, you should never neglect a last important factor if you want to optimize your commitment. Whatever you decide to attain and realize should be done first and foremost by and for yourself. Your decisions and your choices belong to you.

If you have the impression that someone else controls your strategic choices, you will never have the feeling of self-determination. You will undertake activities and projects strictly for external reasons and you won't successfully stimulate your involvement. You'll only do what is strictly necessary as long as the source of control influences you and you'll end up disengaging yourself at the first chance or opportunity that presents itself.

Basing your strategic choices solely on the will of your father, mother or boss will never get you very far. This doesn't mean you'll never have to cope with constraints in your life and that you should reject all imposed obligations. There will be tasks or activities, as much in your professional, family, conjugal lives or other, on which you have no choice but facing them. However this doesn't signify that you have submitted your fundamental strategic objectives to the will of each and everyone. If you accept an assignment within your work context, this shouldn't strictly be done to please your boss or avoid looking bad. By functioning in this way, you will end up losing your identity and autonomy. Your motivation will melt like snow in the hot sun in the same way as your involvement and commitment inevitably will.

It is equally possible that with a mentality like this, you will follow the road toward exhaustion and *burnout*. You will be tossed about by the demands and requirements of others and you will continually lose control over your life. This sense of loss of control will gradually annihilate your feelings of self-determination. And without self-determination, chances are slim that you'll reach your ultimate goals.

When establishing your strategy of success, think for yourself. Define your own dreams, as a function of your values and needs. Make the effort to define your strategic motives and your mission before breaking them down into critical concerns and projects. In this way, when you will accept an assignment within your professional context or when you will respond to the demands of others, you'll do this under the light of your strategic orientation. Your compass will help you keep control over your choices and decisions. You'll be able to say no if you need to, because your direction, with the advantages and risks it involves, will be clear in your mind. You will persist in your life strategy because you will become more and more autonomous and independent. Like great champions, you will fully assume your destiny.

Level 2 – Use Goal-setting

The second level you need to work on for maintaining your motivation consists of proceeding by objectives within your life strategy. The pertinence of this factor was underlined in chapter 7. At this time Figure 3 adequately illustrated the place and importance that the determination of these objectives occupies within the scope of your strategy of success. The great majority of research focusing on goal-setting in psychology, sport psychology, management/administration and other similar domains pulls out the usefulness and effectiveness of this approach[16].

Going through the effort of defining objectives will help you consciously express your intentions; this will orient and motivate your future actions and behaviors. Doing this, you favor self-control in your life and increase your feelings of self-determination. This goal-setting process also has another important effect on intrinsic motivation: giving yourself targets as well as specific goals and subsequently reaching them, lead to the perception of greater competence. The positive impact of such a procedure thus reflects on your effectiveness and satisfaction. You are willing to make more efforts toward reaching your goals. You concentrate more on what you want to attain and your capability to persist grows. You become more motivated to develop the appropriate strategies for realizing your dreams.

In the domain of sport, athletes who set goals achieve the greatest success[17]. All champions who succeed and are able to sustain a high level have very precise career ambitions, which are translated into specific annual targets and clear and concrete daily training objectives. The most successful organizations and enterprises, where the rate of satisfaction is at its uppermost level, similarly know how to effectively implement the goal-setting process[18].

The concept of objectives is in fact found all throughout the elaboration of your strategy of success (chapters 5, 6, 7 and 8). It is one of the key notions guaranteeing your success. To be effective and bear fruit, the goal-setting process should nevertheless be used skillfully. Certain basic rules should be respected if you want to attain maximum benefits.

Firstly you should fully assume responsibility for each objective that you set as well as the consequences attached. Without lucid acceptance, you will neither commit nor give effort and will take the easy way out at the first opportunity.

Your objectives should then be formulated in a specific and precise fashion and not in a vague or general manner. Choose objectives on which you have total and direct control; not attaining your goals for reasons outside your control is discouraging.

Each of your objectives should be measurable so you may follow your progress. Also use a positive approach when defining an objective. "Learning to perfectly master this technical element" or "controlling my daily consumption of sugary foods to this level" have a more positive and motivating impact than saying "don't make that ridiculous technical error any more" or "don't eat as much sugary foods each day". Positive expressions favor constructive thinking and lead to more dynamic methods of tackling things.

Every objective should represent a challenge you can pleasurably and satisfactorily overcome. They should never be unattainable or unrealistic. Know how to properly gauge your expectations.

Determine in advance your deadline for meeting each of your objectives. Give yourself a reasonable timeframe. If your deadline is too far away, you will lose sight of your goal; the results will be late in manifesting themselves and your motivation will weaken. If the timeframe is too short, you create stress which will likely affect and limit your capabilities for success.

If you do not successfully attain your objectives within the set time limits or if they are too high or not demanding enough, make the required course corrections.

Take concrete and adequate means toward attaining your objectives. Methodically plan your operational procedure. Assign yourself priorities if you target many aims at once. Finally, meticulously follow the evolution of your progress because without an appropriate follow-up, your strategy risks fading with time; you'll drop your efforts, the desired results won't be obtained and you'll lose the motivation vital to sustaining your spirit.

Level 3 – Make Life Enjoyable

The seven keys of success respect and incorporate the basic rules of goal-setting. It's one of the sure advantages of the strategy of champions that favors the maintenance of your motivation. None-the-less, to maximize your chances of persisting throughout, it is also important to make your life more agreeable.

Always accomplishing the same tasks in exactly the same way, in the same order, in the same place and at the same time, may become boring and disagreeable. Routine instills habit along with its fastidious and monotonous side. We then repeat, without enthusiasm and without soul, the same activities or the same mode of life, while losing sight of the exciting aspects and incentives found at the beginning. Even our fundamental objectives lose their attraction and the temptation becomes strong to drop everything. To avoid this trap, it is important to take into account two complementary aspects: increasing the attractiveness of the task to accomplish and rendering the framework of your day-to-day reality more agreeable.

To make a task attractive, you need to break the monotony. If you are able to vary the execution of your activities, you enhance their agreeable and motivating side. In the domain of sport excellence, some coaches, however competent, disgust their athletes by forcefully imposing the same training routine. Athletes reach their saturation points where lassitude and monotony provoke physical and mental exhaustion leading to an ill-fated effect on performance. Their motivation thus plummets and some even abandon the practice of their sport in face of these unhappy conditions.

When I was teaching martial arts, I took great care to vary the content of training in order to arouse the interest and enthusiasm of my students. Regardless of the sport discipline, there are all types of ways to execute a task so as to increase its attractiveness and develop motivation. You can diversify, from one training to another, the exercises, as well as vary their order of execution, intensity, and number of repetitions or level of difficulty. You can create practice themes, contexts for evaluation, game situations, competition simulations or even invite competitors or other teams to participate in your training sessions. Sometimes you can break the rigid context of work by bringing in speakers or showing films or suitable documentaries, etc. With a little ingenuity and good intentions it is easy to break the monotony.

In the corporate world, it is also possible to bring variation within the context of work organization. Where the demands of production and the context of union agreement enable it, we will diversify the organization and execution of operations. In certain cases we will leave the employee or work team a margin for maneuvering when planning the schedule, arrangement of activities or distribution of responsibilities.

In acting upon the task to increase its attractiveness you will make your life easier. The first thing to do consists of properly defining the activities and operations you should undertake. The clearer your procedures are, the more precise your action plans will be, the more prepared you will be to be effective and efficient; the more pleasure and satisfaction you will feel at accomplishing your work.

Once your activities and projects have been adequately defined, try to incorporate flexibility and variety into your execution. Ask yourself if the organization of the task could be diversified. Be ingenious! Give yourself new, varied and agreeable habits you will follow for years to come.

You wish to spend more time with your spouse to strengthen your relationship. Does it necessarily always have to be the same night, around the same table or while doing the same activity? Use some imagination. Add color to your rhythm of life. A friend faced this difficulty in his own relationship. He and his wife had an original idea, adapted to their personal tastes and needs, for resolving this problem and giving themselves a more agreeable approach to reality. Together, they decided, at the beginning of the week, which evenings they had free. They also completed a list of varied activities that they liked and had dreamed of doing for a long time. Then they randomly determined which evening they would spend together and which of their activities they would undertake. In this way, from one week to another, they spent more time together without ever doing the same thing at the same time. This approach helped facilitate their change process and it became, for them, an enjoyable and stimulating game. This strongly contributed to strengthening their bonds. By skillfully acting on the activity to accomplish, their project was transformed into a source of pleasure and satisfaction.

If you need variety to stimulate or maintain your motivation, take the time to thoughtfully plan. You will realize the effort is minimal with respect to the motivational impact that you'll obtain.

Variation and motivation don't nevertheless mean the same things to everyone. A standardized and infallible magic recipe doesn't exist. Certain people need a lot of variety or diversity to feel stimulated and motivated to persist. For others, a little change or sporadic freshness is enough to effectively maintain their motivational motor. It is up to you to find the appropriate dose and adapt it to your tastes and needs. The important thing is to not let yourself sink into a paralyzing habit that will make you lose sight of your foremost objectives and push you, little by little, to abandon your dearest projects.

Besides variation, you can also act upon the task along other avenues to render it more agreeable. If one activity is composed of difficult facets or tiring or boring operations, you can undertake them first when you are fresh and re-energized or spread them over a longer period of time. Another important aspect is being able to know when to stop when fatigue or reluctance set in. You will never benefit by bringing yourself to the brink of exhaustion. You will be less effective as a result and you will always have to correct or redo work. I know very well what I'm talking about as I have sometimes fallen into this trap while writing this book. Each time I pushed the machine too hard, at the end of the day and in a state of fatigue, I paid the price: whether I had to redo work that didn't satisfy me, or whether I was unproductive due to accumulated fatigue the next day.

The human machine is not without limits. You need to know how to work with it to get the best results possible out of it. You must be skilful at varying and adapting your activities and your projects to sustain your motivation at its most favorable level. It is just as important to keep in mind your framework of life, your work or leisure environment, if you want to optimize your motivation.

A tri-athlete asked himself how to make his training sessions more interesting and feel more motivated. He always biked the same course, ran the same circuit and swam the same lane at the same pool. By working on his training framework, by modifying his courses, by choosing different circuits and changing pools from time to time, this athlete was able to skillfully embellish his external environment. These simple modifications made his life more enjoyable and facilitated his involvement, his efforts and his persistence.

Getting out of the habitual practice environment is a good way to boost motivation. Training in another place or in another context facilitates diversity and stimulates interest. It is also possible to play with the training environment to vary its arrangement or modify the décor. Within an organizational context, many companies and organizations focus special attention on this factor. The external scope – décor, color, lighting, neatness, etc. – is also a primordial factor in facilitating pleasure at work and stimulating interest and motivation.

When you have a task to accomplish or a project to bring to term, ask yourself if the environmental context is favorable to its realization. For the example of Bruno who wished to reduce the number of meals eaten at restaurants with his coworkers, it wouldn't be wise for him to shut himself in his office every lunch hour, alone with his lunch box. He soon would have had enough and easily returned to the habit he wished to modify. He thus planned a more agreeable strategy by carefully choosing more varied and satisfying places, moments and styles of lunch.

Choose somewhere conducive to realizing the tasks you wish to accomplish. You want to talk with your spouse or children, make the effort to choose an agreeable and appropriate context for this action. Perhaps checking in with your son demands more than a table corner, at the end of breakfast, just before he leaves for school. You want to start an exercise program at home, thus arrange a favorable workout area for yourself rather than scattering this and that throughout your home. You'd like your employees to interact more, maybe it's pertinent then to set-up an attractive and relaxing space for taking coffee breaks. Each activity or each project can require a particular framework that favors its realization.

Arrange your office, workshop, kitchen, garage or any other place to make yourself feel comfortable and effective in executing your tasks. Poor arrangement, disorder or dirtiness, these all have a negative impact on your desire to even begin your work. Take the time to clearly see and organize your space before throwing yourself into action; it sometimes takes a bit longer to get going but the positive repercussions worth the trouble. Everything will seem easier and simpler, your results will be quicker in coming and your level of satisfaction will be increased.

When you have the opportunity, now and then, change the place or context where you pursue your activities. Writing a book like this one is a long project that requires lots of discipline and can become fastidious and tiresome. One of the things that helped me break the monotony and maintain a good production rhythm was to change, from time to time, the place and context where I wrote. Each time, I felt a certain relief or alleviation with respect to the task to accomplish. It was as if I put aside or left behind me an old restraining collar that had held me from seeing the positive and agreeable aspects of the work I was performing.

Without necessarily changing the place you can still embellish your context of work or of life by sometimes making certain modifications to your environment. Offer yourself a bouquet of flowers, display your motto or personal mission on the wall, play background music, etc. There are all sorts of ways to vary and improve your environmental context. Try to be creative; don't hold back your imagination.

Add unexpected elements to your rhythm of life. Give yourself hobbies and free time to allow yourself the chance to breath. Have the wisdom to incorporate release valves into your schedule for letting off tension and fatigue. Don't always try to productively use each hour and every minute of the day. Many people become so obsessed by the absolute efficiency of their use of time that they are unhappy if they face ten free minutes in a day.

Don't fall into this trap which I call *overbooking* your day. You run the risk of sinking into fatigue, anxiety, restlessness or inefficiency. Set aside moments of relaxation to give your system the chance to recover. Learning to let go in order to refresh your inner self, will benefit you in the medium and long term. A very effective and productive businessman that I knew, used to set aside for himself, every two weeks, a day for "not doing". Regardless of all his other concerns and obligations, this day was sacred and belonged only to him. For this particular day he planned nothing in advance. He wanted to step out of his well-organized box and stay in contact with his needs, his feelings and his tastes of the moment. During this "not doing" day he decided what he wanted to do as he went along. He took his time, reclaimed contact with himself and gave himself the chance to catch up with the simple life again.

Knowing how to embellish your life context is a question of dosage, of needs and of personal tastes. Miraculous recipes don't

BLOW AWAY YOUR LIMITS

exist. When you plan your daily and weekly schedule, take the care to assess the attractiveness of your tasks and your external environment. Put color and charm into your use of time. Make your life agreeable, as this is one of the most effective and indispensable methods for maintaining your motivation.

Level 4 – Know How to Reward Yourself

In working on the three preceding levels of motivation, you have stimulated all the intrinsic components of your motivational motor: pleasure, satisfaction and the feeling of competence and self-determination. The fourth level of intervention more particularly addresses the extrinsic aspect of motivation.

By placing the accent on this dimension of motivation, you enter the world of external consequences associated with your behaviors, whether they are positive or negative. This is the domain of prizes, medals, money, applause, recognition, setbacks or negative evaluations. The basic principle is relatively simple. When an individual issues a response or behavior, it can be augmented or diminished if it is followed by the appropriate consequence. When a result is attained, it can equally be increased, maintained or reduced as a function of the ensuing consequences. Despite the validity of this general principle, reality is however not always so simple.

The psychology of motivation has taught us that the extrinsic and intrinsic components of the motivational motor can interact in a positive fashion one moment and in a negative fashion the next. At certain times, a reward can increase the tendency of a person to act and persist but, at other times, it can have the contrary effect.

A simple story illustrates this paradoxical aspect of extrinsic motivation[19]. A group of noisy youngsters enjoyed playing near the home of an older gentleman. This man, annoyed, couldn't figure out a way to get them to play somewhere else. One day, he came up with a brilliant idea. He gathered the youngsters together and offered them each a dollar if they'd come back the next day and play near his place. As he expected, the enthusiastic boys returned the next day to collect their pay. At that time, he offered them each 75 cents to return the following day. When they returned, his offer went down to 50 cents for the next day and he added that for every day after that, he could only afford to pay them 25 cents each. The youngsters started to grumble and discussed the situation between them; they decided that a meager 25 cents was not worth all their efforts. They warned their "sponsor" that from now on they would no longer play near his place!

This story fully demonstrates the paradoxical relationship that exists between extrinsic and intrinsic motivation. At the beginning, the compensation encouraged the game. But, little by little, the focal interest of the youngsters passed from their games' inherent pleasure to external compensation. The activity itself gradually lost its attractiveness and their intrinsic motivation dropped and was replaced by an extrinsic component. But, as the reward diminished, the extrinsic motivation also declined and they abandoned their activities.

If we look at professional sports today, the central interest of many athletes, which once had been the simple pleasure of playing, has been replaced by the enormous salaries they're paid. What would happen if these high salaries disappeared one day? How many of them would continue practicing their sport?

Using external rewards comes with a certain risk. They are double-edged swords. Positive consequences could have a stimulating impact on our motivational motor and behavior. Nevertheless, they could also produce the contrary effect. To obtain an optimal impact, you must find a synergy between both the extrinsic and intrinsic components of motivation. It is necessary to take care in considering the perceptions provoked by external compensations. If they are perceived as valuing excellence or competence, they will have a positive effect. If they become more important than the activity itself and the pleasure received, they can become unfavorable and diminish intrinsic motivation[20].

In sport, awards, medals and trophies contribute toward boosting motivation, but they can sometimes also hinder its positive effect.

In certain forms of martial arts, it became customary to give bigger and bigger trophies according to the importance of the competition. Imagine a three-foot tall youngster receiving a trophy three and a half feet high! I have known teenagers who mostly sought after the importance and magnitude of the external reward above and beyond the pleasure brought by the activity itself. They would skip competitions where the trophies were not as big and once they had obtained all sorts of awards and recognitions, they became totally disinterested in practicing their sport.

Rewards, medals and trophies don't need to be enormous to stimulate the motivational motor. If these external consequences convey a notion of excellence, competence and achievement, they will arouse interest and persistence. In the great majority of sports, the Olympic medal leads to very few important financial repercussions. However, this small medal placed around a neck stimulates the motivational motor of thousands of athletes around the world. It symbolizes the ultimate accomplishment, the pinnacle of excellence, mastery and supreme competence. It works in synergy with the pleasure brought by practicing the sport itself and inspires athletes to travel the entire supplementary road necessary to successfully surpassing their limits.

I have experienced, within corporations and organizations, two situations that adequately illustrate the paradoxical influence rewards exert on people's motivation and mode of functioning. Both cases involved organizations where we had implemented programs for optimizing efficiency. The employees worked in teams to solve production problems or inefficiencies of administrative processes. The programs both employed systems of recognition which emphasized the employees participation and supported their motivation.

In one of the companies, management absolutely wanted to associate a monetary reward with program performance. The impact of each project, of each solution brought by the teams of employees was evaluated from an economic standpoint and a percentage of the engendered benefits was returned to the participants responsible for its results.

At the start of the project, the employees became involved due to their interest and the satisfaction experienced in improving their work conditions. However, once the custom of monetary rewards had taken on its full amplitude, the employees develop a tendency to join problem-solving teams only to get the best possible benefits. The external consequence had become more important than the activity itself. Many people even started to question our method of evaluating the economies each project produced. Criticism was more and more frequent and nobody wanted to attack the less "lucrative" problems, even when they were important to improving work conditions. In reaching this extreme, the company had to halt application of the recognition system and it took time before they could restart the program on a more positive basis.

Within the other company, the recognition system was defined another way. The accent was placed on the participants' competence, effort and involvement. Once a team had completed a project, they presented their results to those responsible for the follow-up and implementation. Positive feedback, appreciation of work quality and thanks for the accomplished effort was transmitted to the team members. A project report was printed in the company's internal journal and charts illustrating the obtained results were hung on the walls. The results were also presented whenever the management group, responsible for coordinating the whole program, had a meeting. Everyone then received a small souvenir to underline his or her involvement and effort, from the hand of the Chief Executive Officer himself. The implemented projects were published in regional newspapers listing the names of all participating employees.

The impact of this recognition program aroused such pride, such feelings of competence from the employees that everyone absolutely bought into participating in a work team. They all impatiently waited their turn and each studied project was as interesting and useful as the next. The work atmosphere and the organization's efficiency greatly improved. The positive external consequences enhanced the impact of intrinsic motivation and further stimulated the interest and persistence of everyone within the enterprise.

Using rewards or positive reinforcements can be just as constructive and profitable if appropriately employed. Whether it's about stimulating your own motivation or someone else's, you need to respect certain basic principles to obtain real positive results without provoking contrary or unfavorable effects. You must first ensure that the reward has a real positive signification for you or for the people for which it was destined. You can decide to reward yourself with a meal out at a restaurant or a nice perfume once your task has been accomplished. Nevertheless, if you aren't greatly attracted to these types of things, the compensation will have little effect on motivating your behavior. You can promise to take your teenagers on a family camping trip one weekend in order to try and encourage their persistence in performing certain household chores. On the other hand, at this age, if all they dream of is being with their friends, there's a very slim chance that camping with the "old folks" will be sufficiently enticing.

Choose a reinforcement that is out of the "ordinary" and not something you would still offer yourself regardless of the obtained results. If you choose a night out at the movies or a concert as compensation and, in any matter, you go regularly two times a week, how could there be any real impact with such a consequence? Compensations should be desired, out of the ordinary, unaccustomed or a bit unique in some way to truly stimulate interest.

If you are very comfortable with offering yourself anything you desire, you should try and be a little more imaginative. Maybe you should use negative reinforcements to motivate your efforts. You can thus plan to deny yourself of an agreeable habit (for example eating out at a restaurant or drinking your favorite cocktail...), so long as you haven't achieved a certain level of success with your efforts. Once your objective has been attained, you will feel satisfied and proud on top of rediscovering your pleasurable habit. By acting in this way, you give significance to the consequences you've decided to employ. You have assured they will pull at your heartstrings and will be more likely to activate your motivational motor.

When selecting your reinforcements, be creative and diversify your methods. Always using the same consequence in the same manner becomes monotonous and loses its attractiveness.

Reinforcements can come from diverse sources and may be used in conjunction to obtain maximum motivation impact. With corporations, for example, an effective recognition system will draw out its "rewards" from all four types of consequences. There is the category of material or financial character where we find gifts, monetary gratification, individual meals or with the group, certain outings or leisure activities paid by the enterprise, bonuses, stock options offered by the organization, etc.

A second type of reinforcement touches more psychological or social aspects. It relates to positive feedback, honor, official recognition ceremonies, titles, attestations or diplomas, public recognition either displayed or published in local publications and more of the same. A third type of positive consequence concerns the advantages offered to individuals or groups like training sessions or development opportunities that could, in turn, improve the person's standard of living or lead to eventual promotions. Finally, the domain of job responsibilities offers a fourth type of reinforcement likely to stimulate motivation. Everything that touches the functions of job-related authority, responsibility or control is within this sphere.

By using these four sources of reinforcement to inspire you, you should be ready to vary your positive consequences and, if desired, to multiply their impact by skillfully combining them. By carefully selecting the gratifications, they should shine light on your competence or the competence of others. A reward should clearly value a person's ability, effort, persistence or other qualities. It is preferable that it not strictly be awarded as a function of the final result. You could simply pay your child to mow the lawn, but you could also make him manager of part of the family garden. The responsibility itself could motivate him. When supervising his work, tour the garden with him and highlight the quality of his work. Give him feedback that shows how much you appreciate his efforts and involvement. Pay him a monetary reward in accordance with the criteria of excellence you've established in advance. You can also include in your approach a symbolic gift or small bonus that stresses the value of his persistence, work consistency or the important role he plays within your family.

Your project is to lose those 20 extra kilos and you decide to offer yourself a trip to Europe if you can attain your objective. It is a nice reward, but it is far in the future and it only focuses on the final result, which is difficult to attain. You will be confronted with multiple difficulties along the way, so you risk losing sight of its attraction. You will obtain a stronger motivational impact if you value the quality of your work and effort needed to attain your target. You can associate a positive consequence with successfully maintaining, throughout a whole week, your average number of daily calories under 2,000. Another gratification could recognize your ability of preparing a satisfying healthy daily meal for yourself over so many consecutive days. A positive reinforcement could reward your perseverance in maintaining three periods of physical activity each week. You should know how to attribute your stars, trophies and medals so that they value your abilities, efforts and persistence in your progression.

When you use reinforcements, you need to adequately define the rules of the game – be it for yourself or for others – right from the start. Exactly specify in what circumstances, following what conditions and why a reward is awarded. Assure yourself that the rules of the game are properly understood, interpreted and accepted. Next, be consistent in the application of these rules. If you go against the pre-established principles, the positive consequences take on an uncertain, arbitrary or even coercive significance. Or else they simply lose their motivational effect, if they are obtained at any moment, in any way, whether the criterion of acquisition was attained or not. A reward should facilitate evaluation of the quality or lack of quality of the work accomplished.

If meant for someone else, reinforcements should be specific and precise. To have the full desired effect, it should clearly target a single person or a small group of individuals. The more vague it is and the more people it addresses, the less chance it will have for arousing motivation in each and every person. If you thank or congratulate your five children at once for participating with the household chores, you display your recognition. Nevertheless you will never develop their intrinsic motivation as well as if you'd highlighted one child's particular effort with this chore, the attentive care demonstrated by another with that operation and so on. The more people feel directly recognized for personal qualities or skills, the more satisfaction or pride they will feel and the more involved they will become in further pursuing the task.

Finally, it is important that a consequence be awarded as soon as possible following the attainment of an established criterion. If compensation comes too far in time, it will lose its impact on the reaction or behavior we had wished to reinforce. You promise to go shopping with your young daughter if she puts forth the effort to properly perform a pre-established task. The moment arrives but you can't find the time to fulfill your promise. Of course, you don't absolutely back down, but you delay application of the planned reinforcement by a week or two. You thus provoke disappointment and frustration. Your child's motivation won't be stimulated and she could even perceive her reward as a simple manipulation on your part. Her enthusiasm will diminish as well as her involvement and persistence with accomplishing the task. You provoke an undesired effect because you failed to respect one of the basic rules for using positive reinforcements.

If you utilize and respect the principles I've explained, you will favor complicity, a synergy between the extrinsic and intrinsic components of motivation. The rewards will become effective tools for arousing interest, involvement and persistence in the realization of your projects or the accomplishment of the tasks you demand of others. Like everything that touches motivation, an effective use of rewards requires time, thought and care. You should properly prepare and plan your approach to harmonize it with your different action plans and your follow-up mechanism. If you know how to do this, the rewards will have a more positive impact and will beneficially propel your diverse initiatives along the three other levels that can help you support your motivation (stimulate your involvement, proceed by objectives and make your life agreeable).

Think Constructively

Your manner of thinking, interpreting the world and seeing yourself in day-to-day reality, shapes your way of acting and behaving in life. If you learn to develop constructive and positive thinking, you increase your chances of properly adapting and succeeding. You become more creative and will know how to transform your tough times into challenges to better overcome them. You develop your dynamics of functioning in a way to stimulate and boost your motivation.

Thinking constructively and **keeping motivation high** are two factors that work together to help you **sustain your spirit** right to the end. Keeping your motivation high helps you remain positive and look on the bright side of life. Thinking in a constructive manner gives spirit and dynamism to your motivational motor. These two factors are the inseparable elements of the seventh and last key of success.

So they could think in a constructive fashion, all champions have learned to be optimistic, to talk to themselves in a positive manner and to develop happy memories.

Be Optimistic

Being optimistic doesn't mean going through life with a constant smile while stupidly pretending that all is well at all times, that nothing touches you and that paradise exists here on earth. Optimists are not blind. They take a realistic look at the world without ever forgetting the positive aspects that enable them to construct, create and realize themselves.

Optimism is a quality that can be developed and learned. It is linked to the way we perceive and interpret the events in our life. Each and every one of us has known past successes and failures. Each and every one of us has hopes for realizing certain dreams or certain projects in the future. Each and every one of us has to face, in our present, the unexpected as well as annoying setbacks that may block our progress. If we consider these past, present or future events with a lucid and positive eye, we will develop our optimism and make it a reliable ally throughout our whole life.

Your view of the past, how you interpret your successes and set-backs is fundamental to orienting your frame of mind within your strategy of life. The reasons you give or the causes you use to explain events that have touched you will determine your capacity to persist and bounce back in the face of adversity[21].

If you tend to attribute your successes to stable and internal caus-es, you will develop greater confidence in your capacities and will be more ready to confront your difficulties. An internal cause refers to, among other things, your abilities or efforts. Your abili-ties nevertheless represent a more stable and permanent factor than your efforts. In other words, your efforts can vary from one competition to the next whereas your abilities are more stable and difficult to change. By firstly attributing your successes to person-al abilities, you will feel like you have everything needed to suc-ceed again. You thus boost your confidence, your feeling of com-petence and your motivation to pursue your goals.

If you continually attribute your successes to chance or tell your-self that the task was just easy and simple, you are recognizing few of your own merits. You turn to external factors that are stable (simplicity of the particular task) or unstable (luck) to explain your good results. You fail to consider that you truly have control over what happens to you and you will then feel even more powerless in the face of obstacles. Your chances to go all the way with your plans and projects will thus be less promising.

Your interpretation of your setbacks or past difficulties is just as important toward conditioning your optimism. If you condemn yourself for your disappointments and constantly attribute your misfortune to a lack of skill, weakness or stupidity on your part, you will develop a negative and fatalistic image of yourself. You will feel powerless and not be tempted to confront new difficulties or persist with your ventures.

If you consider rather that bad luck or a task temporarily too difficult is responsible for your setback, you will never completely close the door. Things could eventually change and improve. There is still hope that next time everything will turn in your favor and you'll realize success. You thus will be driven to charge ahead once again to try your luck.

The attributions you use to explain the positive and negative events you've lived through thus condition your way of reacting, of facing conflicts, of adapting yourself and of sustaining your spirit. Research has shown[22] that as a general rule, in sport, winners will more often attribute their successes to stable internal causes within their control than losers do. The more motivated athletes also use more internal attributions to explain their successes.

When you experience success, take the opportunity to recognize the role your abilities, capabilities and competence played. This will arouse your optimism and feed your motivation. When you encounter failure, learn to detect the unstable causes that could be at the source. Don't lose sight of the effect of bad luck, accidental events or a fluctuation in your own effort level. This will help you cultivate hope and favor your capacity to regain control of yourself, to adjust yourself and to pursue your progression.

Developing your optimism nevertheless doesn't mean that you sink into exaggeration or illusion. People who continually and exclusively attribute their successes to themselves forget other important aspects of reality. They fall into egocentrism, thinking only of their little "me" and isolating themselves within their ivory tower. In a similar manner, invariably and strictly attributing your failures and setbacks to external factors is also egocentric. This is a self-protective strategy that causes us to avoid our responsibilities by always placing fault onto the shoulders of others or blaming the external reality.

These two forms of exaggeration are illogic and unrealistic. The successes and positive events of your life could also be linked to the help and competence of other people. Luck or accidental events can sometimes favor you. You can experience failure because you didn't do enough work or make the necessary effort needed to succeed. It could be that you didn't know how to exploit all your abilities to reach your goals. If you fall into the trap of an egocentric attribution strategy you will fail to see the game as well as the important influence of all these other factors. Your vision of the world will not be sufficiently global or shaded. Arrogance, excessive confidence and blindness will become your guides to transform your strategy into a weapon that will turn on you.

When looking at the positive or negative events they've experienced, optimistic people never lose sight of their competence or the good side of life. They nevertheless know how to remain lucid and coherent so they won't sink into the blind egocentrism likely to lead to failure.

By learning to interpret your past successes and setbacks in an optimistic and realistic manner, you develop the ability to face daily hassles and unexpected events. If you appreciate at their true value your competence and capabilities, you will be able to get through any temporary annoyances. You will know how to interpret them for what they are, that is accidental events not meaning failure or unhappiness for the rest of your life. You will be able to channel your energies and count on your resources to rebound positively. You will transform temporary annoyances into stimulating challenges emphasizing your resources and the dynamism of your mode of functioning.

On a beautiful alpine autumn morning, I was to lead a strategy session for a multinational corporation. As planned – or at least as I believed – I arrived at the company's head office at 9h30. Upon entering the meeting hall, I saw, seated around the table, a dozen members of the executive management with scowls and disappointed looks on their faces. The discontentment and aggressiveness was palpable. At once, I was seated and I asked myself what could have happened. They had been waiting for me to start the meeting since 9h and each was frustrated because of the time lost due to my delay. There had been a misunderstanding. The person who organized my schedule had forgotten to advise me of the change made to the day's agenda.

Needless to say my adrenaline got me going. I was facing a huge problem that could compromise the effectiveness of the strategic process we needed to undertake. At this point I could easily have thought that all was lost or that I didn't have the ability to fix the situation. I could have stupidly frozen in place or blamed the incompetence of others. But what would this have solved?

I believed I could do it, despite this annoyance. I told myself I wouldn't be overwhelmed by such an unfortunate event. I focused on the challenge. I decided then that I would salvage everything before the end of the morning: the positive attitude of those sitting before me, along with their esteem, their respect and their collaboration. I assumed the blame by explaining the misunderstanding then I began the session with enthusiasm, a smile and dynamism. Two hours later, everything had changed. A positive atmosphere had returned and it was one of the most interesting strategy sessions I'd ever conducted.

Assuming your responsibilities, believing in your potential and attributing temporary annoyances to simple coincidences will help in developing a positive vision and optimism. Never let the unexpected throw you off. Accept it, try to get a better grasp on the situation and find the solutions to change things for the better. The more successful you are at doing this, the more confident you'll become and you'll learn to look at life in a constructive fashion.

Your disposition toward optimism will also be intimately linked to your vision of the future[23]. If you see yourself in a positive manner, you'll tend to believe that the future has good things in store for you. All your expectations will be within your reach and you'll believe in your ability to attain them. You will thus be ready to give all the necessary efforts to get there, even when these efforts might, at times, prove demanding and costly.

If straight off you have doubts and lack faith in your ability to realize your dreams, you will diminish your efforts at the first sign of difficulties. Your expectations will appear inaccessible to you and your motivation will decrease. You will nourish your disposition toward pessimism and be less ready to confront stressful events and eventual problems. You will be less committed and will not give your best in trying to lead your strategy for success to term.

What methods can we take to develop our optimism? Visualization or mental imagery is one of the most effective techniques I frequently use with my clients. With athletes, for example, we use mental playback to make a detailed review of their last performance or entire competition. By making them replay the "movie" of these events in their head, they can calmly and lucidly evaluate what happened. They can analyze their strengths and weaknesses by learning to distinguish the relevant causes of their successes as well as their setbacks. They examine all the external circumstances without losing view of the internal factors within their control. Did something happen to undermine or help their performance? Did they try hard enough? Did they respect their competition strategy and exploit all the abilities they possessed? They review all the facts on their internal "movie" so they won't neglect anything and will consider all the pertinent elements that will help them make the needed course adjustments. All this revision is done under the light of optimism and constructive thinking.

It is the same with all unexpected events and annoyances that could arise during the heat of action. Here I use a technique of mental reorientation that helps people transform setbacks into positive reactions or challenges. When athletes make a mistake or an unfortunate unexpected event happens, they immediately recognize it on their internal "movie" and put it aside to get rid of it. They could, for example, visualize the error or fortuitous event as if it was unwinding on a computer screen, accumulating these images on their hard drives for later examination and then shut their computer to erase it from the present; then, they use their mental imagery to immediately see the alternative solution – the correct action, the right movement, the proper tactic – to make it present and attainable in their spirits. This favors an adaptive reaction, which is rapid, effective and dynamic.

To develop a more optimistic and constructive vision of your future, you can employ a technique of mental self-assertion. Many athletes use this technique to motivate themselves and encourage their persistence. It simply consists of visualizing themselves succeeding and attaining their most cherished objectives. Such a technique should, certainly, coincide with a realistic, methodical and gradual goal-setting approach. To develop their optimism and motivate themselves, athletes see themselves succeeding in their discipline as they'd hoped, being congratulated by everyone and climbing onto the podium at the closing ceremony to get their medal. Using this same idea, I knew a motocross champion who adored his sport; it was his main reason for living. At one point, seriously injured, he had to spend several weeks in the hospital not knowing if he'd even be able to walk again. For his part, he held the unshakeable belief that not only would he walk again but that he'd also return to the competitive circuit. On the wall, facing his bed, he hung his competition shoes. Each time he opened his eyes and saw them, he'd imagine himself once again on his bike, winning a competition then receiving the trophy that crowned his victory. His internal "movie" was clear and precise and he visualized it each day, without fail, to sustain his optimism. What he'd wanted so badly was realized, to the great astonishment of his doctors and admirers.

Visualization is a tool accessible to anyone. It is neither complex nor costly. It just requires time and effort. Whether it concerns your successes or failures, setbacks or dreams, you need to know how to exploit your internal "movie". If you look at the bright side of life at all times and always do so with optimism, everything will become more accessible and attainable.

Talk to Yourself Positively

Visualizing the facts and events in your life in an optimistic manner helps you to think constructively. Your vision of reality, your interpretation of the world does not, however, rest solely on images. It is also associated with affects (feelings, sensations, emotions, etc.) and a constant internal dialogue that translates the reality of what you experience into various cognitive notions (concepts, ideas, judgments, reasonings, etc.). These internal components of your mode of functioning play a fundamental role in your way of behaving and adapting to your surrounding reality.

The causal attributions you use to explain your successes and failures denote the image you entertain of yourself in particular circumstances. You will see yourself, for example, as clumsy, awkward or unfit; you won't perceive the accidental circumstances that could hinder you or you'll ignore the inconsistency of your efforts. Your internal film will be neither complete nor exact.

This internal representation of your reality could be accompanied by feelings of guilt or shame. You might feel angry with yourself or temporarily depressed. And, in your heart of hearts, a small voice will continually repeat how stupid and unskilled you were;

it even will try to convince you that you no longer have value, that you were born to fail or that your life no longer holds any hope!

All optimistic or pessimistic visions undeniably include an internal dialogue and positive or negative affects. This constitutes your interpretation of reality, your perception of the world that has been developed and constructed since you were young. The causal attributions you use to explain your successes and failures have roots that probably trace back to your childhood. You have been instilled with the optimism or pessimism of your parents and other significant people around you. This influence implanted itself within your system through the mediation of images, affects and internal dialogues. To effectively develop your optimism and constructive thinking, it is thus important that you adequately adjust these images, affects and internal dialogues.

One effective way of doing this is to bring your attention to the small internal voice that constantly speaks to you. By what it says to you, this little voice will stir up positive or negative emotions or feelings within you; it will also cause you to play images in your head, which are more or less exact, that will orient your vision of the world in an optimistic or pessimistic way. In short, this little voice is a key element of your interpretation of reality.

I often explain to my clients that the brain is a marvelous machine but, from time to time, it can be a stupid machine. It believes what you tell it. If you spend your time telling it you're clumsy, incapable and incompetent, it will end up believing you. It will program awkward reactions and behaviors in your system and that will give proof of your supposed inability. If you talk to it in a positive fashion and tell it you possess all you need to succeed, it will also believe you. It will try to develop reactions and behaviors that will help you realize your dreams.

Certainly, this is neither magical nor miraculous. Even if you repeat to yourself that you're a magnificent bird and you can fly, chances are slim that you will survive after throwing yourself off the top of a skyscraper! Talking positively to yourself is learning to distinguish the good side of things in a reality that is neither all black nor all white. It is creating within you a state of confidence, the belief that you are capable of actualizing your potential and realizing your desired dreams with your strategy of life.

Talking to yourself in a positive fashion is very different from what too many "licensed motivators" have tried to make you believe with flowery discourse. It is not enough to say to yourself: all is good, life is beautiful and I will succeed! This is just a flash in the pan that will die out as fast as it was sparked up. Talking positively to yourself consists first of taking a clear look at yourself, in a complex reality, with the support of an effective strategy of life. Without this solid base, your nice positive phrases will ring false and will pass through your heart of hearts without leaving any traces of the optimism they should nourish.

Learning to develop a positive internal dialogue requires that you become aware of all your abilities and qualities. You must wake this potential, make it conscious into your mind and chosely link it to your desired dreams and objectives. It is also important to never lose sight of all the good results and successes you've obtained up to now. Also take into consideration all the work and efforts you've consented to do as well as the positive effects of your preparation or training.

Within all human beings, there exists a unique potential, innumerable and rich achievements that, in the heat of action or faced with the difficulties of life, we are ready to lose sight of. What you have to do is to allow this potential and these accomplishments to surface from your unconscious so that they can permeate your field of consciousness. Learning to speak to yourself in a positive fashion, it is precisely this: developing an internal dialogue that places value on your real potential and your achievements. By means of using this positive internal dialogue, your unconscious will spontaneously reproduce it and constructively orient your perception of yourself and your interpretation of reality. As I have mentioned, your brain is a marvelous but stupid machine. It will believe whatever you tell it. If you endlessly remind it of your potential and your attainments, it will have confidence in your capabilities and will make you act according to your true value.

To develop the positive side of your internal dialogue, take the opportunity to look at yourself. Draw up a list of all your qualities and abilities; write down your past successes and the good results you've obtained; take into account your efforts, your work, your preparation and all that could help you attain your objectives. Then, from this material, create a series of sentences that will draw out your accomplishments and your potential. It could be affirmations like:

- ° With my problem-solving ability, I have all I need to face this situation and attain my objectives.
- ° I know how to find the means to succeed because I have the patience and ingenuity to do so.
- ° With my training, I have given myself all the tools to succeed.
- ° I work methodically and consistently; I did everything in my power to make my dream come true.
- ° I have already successfully accomplished something similar; I have all that's needed to succeed again. Etc.

These sentences are just simple examples to illustrate what a positive internal dialogue means. There are numerous ways to formulate your affirmations. What is essential is that they are realistic and positive. They should have a personal significance to you, this means they refer to important aspects of your potential and your achievements. Express them in the present tense to favor their impact on your confidence and your present optimism. Be on the watch for new ideas for renewing your affirmations from time to time, so your brain won't be put to sleep under the effects of routine or boring habits. Finally, use them frequently if you want to obtain a satisfying impact.

With experience, I have observed that it is ideal to define about fifteen positive affirmations. Then, on a daily basis, you need to take the time to read them and repeat them. I suggest doing this three times a day, at pre-established periods, in a quiet place where you can concentrate. Repeat them slowly taking the time to integrate them. You will see, with time, that you will start to spontaneously express them, without even making a conscious effort, in many circumstances of your life. It is then that you will become aware that you have started to think positively.

You can also write some of your positive sentences onto small reminder cards you can post in different places within your environment. Each time you see them, you'll repeat them internally. This will help you generalize your constructive thinking to your daily life.

Another way of developing your constructive thinking and your optimistic vision of reality is to include your positive internal dialogue into your visualization. When you use mental imagery to properly interpret your present reality or to be optimistic about your vision of the future, don't hesitate to incorporate positive affirmations. You will thus enrich your internal film, make it more fertile and effective and, at the same time, stimulate positive affects; your interpretation of the world will take on a tinge of optimism and motivation.

It is possible that through defining your positive affirmations you will become aware of the negative ideas and phrases already rooted in your subconscious. You will thus have the impression that the negative persona within you continually tries to prevail over the positive dimension you're trying to put in place. This is completely normal and can be overcome. Take the time to listen to what this negative persona is saying and try to uncover your internal enemy's logic. Note all the negative sentences that this incorrigible pessimist repeats within your mind. Analyze them properly and understand his game; beside your list of negative ideas write down then the positive affirmations you will use to attack them to counteract their effect. The more your affirmations act as antidotes to your negative ideas, the more they'll be able to put your pessimistic persona in its place. The more you use them, the more importance you give to your optimistic side and the more force you'll give to your constructive vision of reality.

The experience of Jean-Louis, a member of the Canadian national martial arts team, illustrates this point well. The previous year, he had won the gold medal at the world team championship in Brazil. The same championship was about to take place, this time, in his hometown, in the presence of his parents and friends. About two months before the competition, anxiety started to surface and Jean-Louis began losing confidence and became seriously afraid for his performance. In examining his pessimistic vision of the future, we observed that his negative persona never stopped tormenting him. It repeated continually to him that he had been lucky the previous year and that nothing guaranteed his success this year. All his parents and friends who considered him a champion would be in attendance. If he didn't perform well, the entire world would see that he was nothing more than "wind" and undeserving of his reputation. He would look like a complete idiot and shame would follow him without respite.

After gaining an understanding of his internal enemy, Jean-Louis composed a list of all those negative ideas and phrases. Then we worked on reinterpreting his causal attributions and pessimistic projections of the future. We identified an internal dialogue that would be the antidote, capable of counteracting the influence of his negative persona. We taped his positive affirmations onto a cassette and Jean-Louis listened to this cassette three times a day, for three weeks. With those who are interested, I frequently use this technique instead of the simple reading of your positive internal dialogue. The advantage is that you can hear your cassette at any moment of the day, while driving your car, walking outside or at any other appropriate occasion.

Already, by our next meeting, after only one week of practice, Jean-Louis had noticed significant progress. He told me that each time a negative idea came to him, the positive antidote surfaced at the same time to attack and replace his repetitive thoughts. After only three weeks, Jean-Louis's problem had disappeared. He had rediscovered his dynamism, his confidence and his constructive way of thinking, which had always enabled him to give his best to each and every competitive performance.

Speaking to yourself in a positive manner is thus an ability that can be learned, with many different concrete methods for doing so. If you take the trouble to use them and, more particularly, to associate them with your mental visualization, you will develop constructive thinking which will enable you to dynamically and effectively enhance your motivation and sustain your spirit without fail.

Develop Happy Memories

I sometimes hear people say: "It is very easy to be optimistic when you are happy and have everything!" Is this how it works? Are we optimistic because we are happy or does happiness touch us because we know how to be optimistic? Certain people think this is the old problem of the chicken and the egg...and which came first?

For my part, this dilemma doesn't exist. Happiness is not given; it is taken, learned and tamed. I am happy if I succeed in life, which means if I realize my dreams and reach my objectives. However, this is not an absolute win at all times. There are highs and lows, but lows do not signify unhappiness. When we expect this as normal, when we know and accept that the game of life is a perpetual adjustment, fluctuations become part of a sound evolution and happy progression.

The big difficulty is that we sometimes lose, even frequently, the happy background of our life. In the heat of action, facing our problems or our persistent difficulties, we tend to forget this. It's as if the memory of our successes, of our value, of our abilities and our qualities blur themselves to make room for the worries of the moment. We lose sight of our achievements and our potential. Further, we even forget all the well-being that surrounds us and inhabits us, our health, our agreeable dwelling, our love for our spouse and all the other things that satisfy us but don't touch us anymore. We center our attention on our momentary difficulties, letting them dominate us just to tell us that we are unhappy with our situation or our fate. We have lost happiness along the way and, nevertheless, so little is needed to remind us that it always accompanies us.

Optimists have developed a sixth sense to detect happiness. By learning to see and speak to themselves in a constructive fashion, they leave no room for unhappiness. All momentary setbacks, snags or annoyances are interpreted at their true value, without losing sight of the positive dimensions surrounding them. Optimists remember. They do not forget their victories, their successes, their well-being and their achievements. They do not lose sight of the shore they wish to reach nor the dreams they want to realize. They know how to nourish their consciousness with all the attractive aspects of their life. They have learned to develop happy memories.

To sustain your spirit right to the end, you should also know how to feed the flame of happiness in your daily life. Don't wait for well-being and fortune to fall from the sky. Happiness won't come from outside, as if by enchantment. You will find it within you by learning to maintain its seeds and favor its growth.

You can use different concrete methods to cultivate and keep up your sense of happiness. The first important thing is to ensure that you don't lose sight of your potential and your attainments. In this sense, all the affirmations you've developed for learning to speak positively to yourself will be of great assistance. Even if you renew them regularly, don't get rid of them along the way as if they were old useless debris. They represent steps in your evolution toward mastering your constructive thinking.

I suggest to my clients that they use their logbooks to record their traces of happiness in memory. Keep a section in your journal to write out your affirmations. In this way, when your horizon seems more somber, you can reread these positive phrases and observe all the efforts you've committed and the progression you've followed along the way of optimism. You will thus revive your confidence, your satisfaction and your pride, to rediscover your courage in the heart of the momentary storm that assails you.

Another interesting and effective method for cultivating happy memories is to make a note of all your happy events and successes. Don't neglect any sphere of activity in your life. Each time you attain a satisfaction, a joy, a realization or a success, write them down in your logbook. When you have the impression that your life is nothing but difficulties and setbacks, you can return to this material as proof of happier days. You will observe thus that the great adventure of your life is not just full of annoyances. You will regain hope and stimulate the sense of happiness that escaped you.

If you make note of your positive affirmations and your happy events, don't just wait for stormy days and heavy winds before rereading them. We quickly become used to well-being or happiness and we lose sight of either just as rapidly. When in good health and fine form, how many of us are conscious of the gift life is. Unfortunately it is when we are suffering that we are conscious of the importance of our physical well-being. And then we say: Things were good when I wasn't sick... I had forgotten! To really keep sight of the traces of happiness, be pro-active and periodically refer to your list of happy events. Refresh your memory from time to time in order to sustain the flame of your optimism.

You can be even more proactive and learn to better read and detect the presence of happiness in your daily reality. At the end of each day, my wife, this marvelous optimist, thanks heaven for the gifts of life. She makes note of the little things that satisfied her or made her happy. This doesn't imply great victories or resounding successes. Rather, she tries to acknowledge, within her daily life, all the little facts and acts that favored her well-being and made her appreciate life's fullness. Even when she is sick or suffering, she doesn't forget the sun's warmth, the gentleness of rain or the simple fact that we benefit from running water, fresh for drinking and hot for washing ourselves. By thinking in this way, each day, she takes steps toward happiness. She has learned to cherish happy memories out of the smallest things and, no matter what, for her, life has become synonymous to joy, well-being and recognition.

Try to do the same thing for a little while and you'll see, your vision of the world will gradually change. You will forget your small unhappy "me" to open your consciousness to the marvelous gift of life. Take the time, for example, to write down in your logbook, each night, three positive events, acts or facts of the day. Open your eyes wide, take everything into consideration. You will become aware that with time your sense of happiness will awaken and your life will become a satisfying, unforgettable and unique adventure.

Finally, to optimally stimulate your positive vision of reality, don't ever lose sight of the shore of your dreams. Return frequently to your strategic objectives. Keep ever-present in your mind your strategic line of action, your mission and your directional map. Refer to this material, as you would refer to a road map to properly recall the itinerary ahead and the road already traveled. By acting this way, you give dimension to your daily life and remind yourself that your existence is a fascinating strategic process, full of challenges and happy outcomes.

By becoming aware of the favorable events in your life, of the gifts that each day brings and the marvelous dreams you embrace, you develop happy memories. You learn to think constructively to enhance your motivation and effectively sustain your spirit all throughout your journey on the way to success.

Putting it into Action

1. Ensure that your critical concerns as well as your action plans will truly bring you pleasure and satisfaction; also look to see if they value your competence and promote your autonomy and independence.
2. Verify if the objectives you've set for your critical concerns, your action plans and your step-by-step progression (macrocycles and microcycles), within your annual cycle, properly respect the basic rules and principles of goal-setting.
3. Try and make your life enjoyable by increasing the attractiveness of the tasks and operations planned within your action plans or daily use of time.
4. Arrange your weekly and daily schedule so you won't overload yourself and try, from time to time, to break the routine of your rhythm of life.
5. Don't neglect rewarding yourself by planning certain positive reinforcements with respect to your projects and action plans, so you'll optimize your motivation, extrinsic as well as intrinsic.
6. Learn to see yourself with optimism by developing appropriate visualization or mental imagery: attribute the relevant causes to your past successes and setbacks (mental playback); transform the annoyances of your daily life into challenges (mental reorientation) and maintain, for your projects, a positive vision of the future (mental self-assertion).
7. Positively orient your way of thinking, your internal dialogue: identify positive affirmations adapted to your needs and use them in your daily life or incorporate them into your practice of visualization; positively restructure your internal dialogue if the latter is negative or inconvenient.
8. Develop your sense of happiness by recognizing, each day, two or three events, acts or facts that had a positive meaning for you.

PART 5

LIVING STRATEGICALLY…

Chapter 10

...THE TRUE MEANING OF SUCCESS

MANY EXPRESSIONS have been used to convey what we experience in life. When we've endured hard times or feel as if life's hassles will never come to an end, we're likely to say that life is cruel, that it's a valley of tears, that it's not a garden of roses. More pessimistic individuals will even state that it's nothing more than a poisoned gift, filled with suffering and torment.

When the sun is shining or when hope comes alive once again, we will say that life is a wonderful adventure, filled with promise and joy. We look upon it as a fantastic voyage that holds a wide range of surprises and discoveries. Indomitable optimists will vow that life is the most precious gift of all.

All these images are connected to our personal experiences. They reflect our way of seeing and interpreting the events in our lives.

But, in reality, what if life would simply be life; a collection of facts, events or circumstances crossing our path and being neither carriers of unhappiness nor pledges of happiness?

They present themselves as they are, unassuming, in the same way the sun, wind, waves or storm come to meet a ship's captain. They then become what we allow them to be, a danger, a test, a pleasure or a challenge.

Life takes the form we wish to give it. The only ultimate constraints are that we are born and must die. But, between these two limitations, everything else is up to us. We can do whatever we want. I have known people who've transformed illness, pain, infirmity or reversals of fortune into opportunities to grow and surpass their own limits. I have met others who, due to the smallest frustration, have become losers or transformed themselves into tyrants. I have crossed paths with people who appeared to have it all, health, beauty, intelligence and a promising future; however they failed to see this. They favored their own pessimistic view of life without ever escaping from it or getting to anything that was positive or creative.

Life brings us what we take from it. In and of itself, it is neither good nor bad. It offers us a vast array of possibilities and it's up to us to profit from them. I like to see life as a giant chessboard where the game is played between reality and us. Sometimes, we make better moves and the game goes in our favor. Sometimes, our opponent's tactics annoy us and undermine our progress. In each case, the outcome will depend on the quality and efficiency of our own strategy.

All champions I've been associated with have truly grasped this inescapable truth. Success didn't magically fall to them from the sky. They have all experienced happier times as well as setbacks or failures. For them, it's all part of the game. The most important thing is that they learned to live strategically and surpass the limits of the moment.

I'm not suggesting that they all elaborated a life plan by following, word for word, the strategic progression outlined in the preceding chapters. Living strategically means implementing an appropriate process for attaining your objectives and finding satisfaction. Strategic individuals are satisfied and happy people, who feel comfortable as they are and at ease in their environment. They feel comfortable that way because they are consistent with themselves and sound-minded in their way of behaving.

If you prefer a bohemian approach to life and consider yourself to be allergic to planning, but on the other hand you are fatigued, stressed and dissatisfied with life, in some sense a contradiction exists. If you are extremely well organized, with very precise action plans and a full agenda, but discontentment and disappointment are part of your daily life, discordance also exists. Organized or not, you lack consistency as well as a strategy. In order to be a happy bohemian, you must still assume responsibility for yourself, find inner harmony and take the necessary methods to be comfortable inside yourself. In order to be satisfied with a structured life, you must also accept yourself and have a way of living that is in accordance with your beliefs and fundamental values. Lacking this, in one case or the other, there will be tension, contradiction and dissatisfaction; I have often observed that a dissatisfied person lacks both consistency and a life strategy.

No matter what difficulties they encounter, champions appreciate life; they are satisfied and comfortable with themselves. They have found inner harmony and have defined for themselves a consistent way of functioning for realizing their dreams. This way of functioning, even if it doesn't follow, point by point, every detail of the success strategy presented in this book, at the very least it will respect the fundamental principles. To fulfill your potential, you must first lucidly **WANT** to progress, next clearly **SEE** the direction to follow and then know how to **STAY** on course throughout the entire journey. Regardless of which methods you use, these three principles are the basic truisms of a successful life.

To lucidly **WANT**, it is essential that we look at ourselves full in the face, without batting an eyelid. We must be capable of understanding our most basic motivations and our mode of functioning. We need the courage to make an honest, lucid and judicious self-assessment. This is essentially the target of the first two keys of success of the strategy of champions. A summary of this strategy (page 311) lists the seven keys of success with, in the next two columns, their counterparts in business as well as in the therapeutic process.

To clearly **SEE** the direction we must properly define the shore we hope to reach as well as equip ourselves with a directional map to orient us throughout the length of our journey. The third and fourth keys of success are effective guides for this. To **STAY** on course, it is necessary that we accurately plan the details of the road to travel, that we are prepared to make any necessary adjustments along the way and that we can sustain our motivation right to the end. The three last keys of success provide us with the appropriate means to avoid losing our way and enable us to persist, without giving up, right to the end of our voyage.

By respecting these fundamental principles, by following the example of champions, you will succeed at providing yourself with a life strategy. By working to develop an intelligent and harmonious progression, you will promote and preserve your internal consistency. By relying on these solid foundations, satisfaction and success will occupy a bigger and bigger place in your life.

THE STRATEGY OF CHAMPIONS:
The keys of success and their counterparts in the business world and in the therapeutic process

KEYS OF SUCCESS LUCIDLY WANT	STRATEGY FOR CORPORA-TIONS/ORGANIZATIONS	THERAPEUTIC PROCESS
LUCIDLY WANT		
1st Key: Master the Wave	**Phase 1:** Portrait of Strategic Functioning	**1st Question:** What is the problem?
2nd Key: Tame Change	**Phase 2:** Appraisal of Strategic Functioning	**2nd Question:** Are you ready to change?
SEE THE DIRECTION		
3rd Key: Dream Concretely	**Phase 3:** Strategic Orientation	**3rd Question:** What do you want to be?
4th Key: Give Yourself a Directional Map	**Phase 4:** Strategic Priorities	**4th Question:** What do you choose to do?
STAY ON COURSE		
5th Key: Plan Everything Even the Unpredictable	**Phase 5:** Strategic Deployment	**5th Question:** How will you do this?
6th Key: Adjust the Mechanics	**Phase 6:** Strategic Follow-up	**6th Question:** Will you go all the way?
7th Key: Sustain Your Spirit	**Phase 7:** Strategic Support	**7th Question:** Will you know how to hang on?

But, do we really have to do all that?

But... do you really have to respect all these principles to be satisfied and succeed in life? Do you have to be this methodical? The strategy of champions is not a set of directions or magical recipes that you must follow absolutely, word for word, in order to find success. It is a personal way of functioning that must respect certain fundamental principles to be effective and produce the fruits of its labor. All champions respect these principles, but each in their own way. In many respects, their approach to life is similar in its logic and in the way they all behave. Nevertheless, they all bring to it their unique color, their personal methods and their individual experiences.

With this book, I wanted to give a concrete, practical and comprehensive form to the mode of functioning of those men and women who have succeeded in standing out from the crowd. My target was to give you access to the abilities they've mastered and the methods they've used to achieve their goals. I attempted to demystify what appears to many as their innate talents, their gifts from heaven or their jealously guarded secrets. I sought to convince you that going beyond your limits is just as possible for you and that all it takes is a decision to take action.

Start to act as a function of your needs and in correspondence with your potential. Try not to do it all overnight. From now on you now know the basic principles of success. Master them gradually, while taking appropriate and concrete means to change and progress. Use the strategy of champions like a reference point to guide your own evolution, but also leave room for creativity. The most important thing is to start. Don't wait; don't put it off until tomorrow... start to take your life in hand and to act by and for yourself.

Give yourself the time and opportunity to gain experience. Don't wait until you're perfect and know everything before putting it into action. Instead get into action and work toward eventually knowing everything and, little by little, increasing your level of perfection. If, at first, you only want to learn how to use methodical action plans, to give yourself priorities or to develop your motivation, then go right ahead. Start by making use of some of these strategic principles but, at least, start. With experience and practice, you will enrich your way of functioning. Bit by bit, it will become more refined, coherent and effective.

With experience, you will discover that the loftier and more demanding your objectives are, the more your success will have to rely on the basic principles of the strategy of champions. The more an athlete respects these principles of excellence, the better his or her chances for success; the best of them are those who incorporate a greater number of these principles into their preparation and competition strategy[24]. However, an athlete does not become a world champion overnight. It takes time and experience to implement a winning strategy. This doesn't stop the athlete from starting to train, even though he or she may be far from perfect at the beginning. Just like an elite athlete, dare to try; start somewhere and use the strategy of champions as a guide so you may gradually but effectively experience progress. As illustrated by the circular diagram found at the beginning of each chapter, this strategy is a progressive and evolutionary process but it nevertheless has a point of departure.

As too many people tend to do, don't bow your head before the challenges of your life. Don't fall into the trap of escapes and loopholes. If you're the type to snap back "I have never done that and I am no worse off", maybe you're totally satisfied with yourself and with your life. This is not always the case with the majority of people who seek refuge behind this illusory evasion. Someone I know often uses this type of argument whenever he is given a suggestion. He responds by saying, for example: "I have never made a budget and I always managed" or "I have never planned anything in advance, I won't start now!" He likes to think of himself as a "bohemian" and is very proud of this image. The other side of the coin is not however rosy. He has trouble making ends meet. He is often fatigued and not always happy with his life inside this insecurity and disorder. The future worries him and makes him anxious. Faced with this inconsistency, he has no other choice but to find an honorable way out. The external reality or the events of his past have become responsible for his unhappiness. He doesn't want to modify a thing, but his dissatisfaction persists and he turns in circles, going nowhere.

Another typical evasion is the tendency to swagger, saying: "In any case, I don't believe in those types of things!" Thus the door closes and, to your great relief, you won't need to make any effort to change. Nevertheless your dissatisfactions are ever present, but you still hope that a lucky coincidence or a stroke from the magic wand of destiny will fix everything. Your beliefs lead you by the end of your nose.

My young neighbor seems to have it all: good-looking, intelligent, sociable, honest and sincere. His only difficulty is his belief that life is a lottery. One day he'll end up winning the whole jackpot. He embraces many dreams, but has never taken the step from imagination to reality. If the effort to do something is too great, he drops it. He doesn't try to adapt himself, to start modestly or to take the necessary measures to attain his objectives. He's waiting for life to serve him his opportunity on a silver platter. His beliefs allow him to avoid facing reality, but in the meantime, he grows older and accumulates, in his life, feelings of both dissatisfaction and helplessness.

Don't let your beliefs put you to sleep and surround you with illusion. Be honest and critical towards yourself. Take a lucid look at the results they enable you to obtain. These results are the objective and impartial witnesses to your effectiveness. If you are not satisfied and feel that life is not going in your favor, sound off the alarm. Don't place blame for everything on other people's shoulders, on your past or on the external reality. Stop waiting for the lottery and take things in hand. Don't allow your beliefs to fool you and let you waste your life.

One of the best excuses and probably the one I hear most often is time: "If you think we have the time to take care of that when we are stuck in the heat of action..." This excuse is particularly popular in the world of business. Very often overwhelmed by the demands of production, middle management and business executives have the tendency to brush aside any suggestion or procedure likely to question their acquired habits. Nevertheless, how much energy and money are just lost in production defects and work redone.

In private organizations, ineffectiveness of administrative and production processes cost a fortune. All the same, we prefer to shut our eyes and not worry about it. If everything were done properly from the start, if the strategy was well thought-out and adequate, the results would speak for themselves. But, we don't have the time... except for redoing work that was poorly executed the first time, wasting thus a lot of money!

The business environment also lets itself be fooled by unrealistic beliefs and magical thinking. The world tendency today is cutting manpower (downsizing) and organizations are regrouping or joining together (merging). Those who make the cuts have the attentive ear of shareholders and executives. I don't mean you shouldn't rationalize or reorganize in order to survive in the business world, but you need to know how to do this lucidly, within the framework of a coherent strategy that includes the global vision of the environment in which we evolve.

Recent studies in the business environment[25] have highlighted the negative impact of decisions made by management. In more than 60% of the cases where personnel was cut, nothing significantly changed regarding the levels of the economy of worthless costs, the quality of production and the ineffective functioning of the companies in question. This is without speaking of all the human resource problems created by these cuts.

Personnel cuts and mergers don't solve anything unless the true problems are first identified, tackled with appropriate means and resolved. Without a strategy, the real weaknesses will unquestionably resurface. The studies cited above concluded that managers were too often reactive and lacking in vision and dimension. Also, their decisions are not very effective and if nothing changes by itself, they don't know how to face the situation except by making even more cuts!

We also blindly use the argument of a lack of time. Tossed about by our rhythm of life and our demands at work, we no longer have the time to take care of our health, of our nutrition, of our budget, of our household chores, of what goes on around us and even... of our children. And, when problems do arise, we are completely surprised. We then need to find the time to make repairs or even, overwhelmed by circumstances, we bow our head and just give up. In each case, the bill is high and the price to pay can even mean the destruction of what we have so dearly dreamed of achieving.

Rather than having to fix the broken pots, before our small universe blows up in our face, why don't we take the time to prevent, plan and properly build? Why don't we stop for a few hours each year to add dimension and vision to our lives? What is the cost of taking a few minutes each day to take our bearings and adjust before our machine breaks down or journeys onto a path without end or a way of no return? To save time, sometimes you need to know how to take the time!

One final excuse frequently used for avoiding taking our control of our lives is a lack of confidence: "In any case, I don't have enough self-confidence to throw myself into such an adventure..." We thus pretend that we don't possess the potential, the abilities or the competence required to succeed in our lives. In this way, we don't even have to put forth the effort to take responsibility for our destiny. We have acknowledged in advance that success is not for us and we lower our arms before ever trying.

For some, they made an effort, but they came across bad experiences, disappointments or setbacks. They held onto the bitter memory or sense of failure and they won't dare risk themselves again. They claim their confidence was destroyed and they can't find the energy or courage to start over.

No matter what we've experienced and what our excuses are, the pretext of no confidence is nothing but an illusion, a phantom that takes pleasure in placing shackles around our legs. Self-confidence is not a "magic box" localized somewhere in the brain, that suddenly breaks down, becoming impossible to repair or even useless. Confidence is nothing but a concept, a name we attribute to a whole collection of reactions that we manifest and are responsible for. Like with any reaction, we can adjust it, correct it, develop it, acquire it, sustain it or strengthen it. But we can also weaken it, undermine it, sabotage it or destroy it. We are not at the mercy of a mysterious component of our system that tosses us about according to its will and pleasure. We are this component and we can shape it according to our own desire. Unfortunately, too many people believe they depend upon their confidence when, it is rather their confidence that depends on them.

Champions understand this reality and have learned to develop their self-confidence. They all share a profound desire for self-actualization, to become "competent"; they are also capable of properly evaluating their current aptitudes. They can lucidly regard their abilities and performance capacities. Success is part of their lives because they set realistic objectives that they're prepared to attain through appropriate effort and work.

With the experience of success, they gradually progress and improve themselves; they thus develop a feeling of effectiveness and a perception of competence. If they suffer some setback or hard times, they can correctly identify the causes and make the appropriate adjustments. They don't lose themselves in defeatist explanations or pessimistic attributions. They force themselves to correct and control their internal dialogue. They are capable of talking positively to themselves, to encourage themselves and to use optimistic mental imagery. In summary, they take appropriate means to maintain their motivation and think constructively. They use a methodical strategy that leads to concrete results within a reasonable and acceptable delay. By behaving in this way they develop their self-confidence. They don't delude themselves and wait to feel confident before starting. They first think strategically and act accordingly. Confidence is one of the consequences of their way of functioning that will, accordingly, nourish their motivation and sustain their spirit.

Don't allow yourself to become fooled by the excuse of a lack of confidence. To become strategic, you must make the decision to start and put in the necessary time and effort. Don't ever forget that the longest voyages, as well as the greatest, always begin with those first humble steps. You simply need the courage to do it.

The Unavoidable Necessity of a Strategy

Using a strategy doesn't just enable us to optimize our mode of functioning and go all the way toward our dreams. It also guarantees our own survival as human beings, as well as the survival of the social organizations we've developed and the enterprises we've created. If we place ourselves within the context of the theory of evolution, we are forced to recognize that the stronger and more adaptive species have survived. The law of natural selection states that the more powerful systems last the longest. This undeniable reality is expressed well by the concept of *survival of the fittest*, which means those more able will survive.

In an evolutionary context where human beings seem to have more or less dominated the planet, this concept can be translated to the *survival of the brightest*: the future as well as survival will increasingly belong to the brightest, to those individuals or social systems that will best know how to make use of a strategy. I have observed this in the world of international elite athletes. I have often asked these great athletes as well as their coaches what, according to them, made the difference between those who last and those who are less successful among the best elite athletes. Each time, I received the same answer: "The difference lies between their two ears… it's all played in the head." That small difference of a thousandth of a second or a hundredth of a point that continually maintains the athlete on the summit relies on the psychological strategy he or she uses. This doesn't just mean concentrating well in the starting blocks or at the very moment of striking the ball. This requires an extremely well-elaborated, carefully planned and sensible preparation, with both a training strategy and a lucid, global and coherent life strategy as a backdrop.

During the Olympic Summer Games in Atlanta, I listened to an interview with an athlete who had just won a gold medal. The young girl talked about all the training, work and effort she'd committed to during the last few years preceding the Games. The journalist appeared flabbergasted and, eventually, he couldn't stop himself from asking her if she regretted having to make so many sacrifices and putting in so much energy to win "such a small medal"? The young athlete had a very pertinent response. She calmly made him understand that it wasn't just about the medal. Above all, she had discovered, through her sport, a way of life. She had given her life meaning and had learned that to realize your dreams and maintain yourself at the summit, you have no choice but to shape your own destiny.

In the business context, the survival of the organization essentially depends on its foresight and its strategy. I have always been surprised, in this tough and often relentless milieu, to what extent success was fleeting. I like to take different *Fortune 500* lists, over an interval of a few years, and compare the successful companies listed. If you do this exercise you'll observe, that after only five years, a remarkable number of companies have completely disappeared from this index of excellence. Many others have fallen off to find themselves at the end of the list, at the end of the honor roll. Everything looks like if success is only rarely maintained.

Natural selection is a strong influence in the business world. The free market will swallow you quickly unless you continually seek to progress and reaffirm your position. The great majority of entrepreneurs, men or women, think that a corporation's only valuable strategic objective is to turn a profit. This is true in the sense that all organizations with a lucrative purpose attempt to be profitable and improve their financial situation. Nevertheless, as I have repeated to these same entrepreneurs: "Since the whole world is trying to make a profit, what will differentiate you from everyone else on the market? What will be your distinctive strength? What will enable you to distinguish yourselves and to assure your own success and survival?"

This is where we find the difference between those corporations that last and those that disappear. The best know how to find a strategic orientation that will lead them to the right port despite market pressures and fluctuations. Like the greatest athletes, brilliant entrepreneurs have learned that to be champions and stay on the summit, the only alternative is to think and act in a strategic manner.

We live in a world where the laws of natural selection have always played a role and will continually wield their influence. Each day we are likely to be confronted by multiple demands from our environment, by the inevitable constraints of the social organizations in which we live and by the pressures or threats exerted by our own kind. If we wish to get the most out of our marvelous system, if we want to realize our dreams and persist in a world where natural selection exerts its constant influence, we have no choice but to be proactive and shape our own existences. In this context where we live, with the reality that is ours, strategy becomes an **unavoidable necessity**.

The Challenge of the 3rd Millennium

This need for a strategic approach is not only for that brief period of time representing the duration of our lives. There are more important things than just our own individual survival or that of an organization or enterprise. Acting strategically obliges us to think globally. For the life span we are granted, we need to keep in mind the survival of the system in which we have inserted ourselves.

Short-term advantages and profits without consideration for ill-fated consequences, rarely escape the real costs they too often ignore or camouflage. In this sense, you just need to think of the

American tobacco companies that generated incredible revenues over many years while ignoring the noxious effects caused by their products. The repercussions on the well-being of the population have collectively cost us hundreds of millions of dollars in all kinds of health care, without even talking about the lives destroyed by tobacco use. Right to the end these companies refused to recognize their responsibilities but were finally confronted with compensations that could equally cost hundreds of millions. And nevertheless, despite this lesson, the problem is not solved. I am not at all convinced that they won't keep on going with the same pattern until the next bill we will have to pay and force upon them once again.

Considering this example, it sometimes seems like human beings are shortsighted. Very often we forget the implications of our actions and lose sight of the fact that one day or another we'll have to pay the "full bill". We act as though we're immortal and will benefit from unlimited resources. We think in the short-term without consideration or respect for the global system that has assured our survival.

However, we live on a planet that has offered us everything. As "modern man[26]", we've been established for around 35,000 years. During this period, we've succeeded at profoundly transforming our planet to shape it and adapt it to our needs. We have influenced it and exploited it like no other species before us. Many among us even fear that we have brought it to the limit of its capacities and have reached a point of no return.

At the end of the twentieth century, many doomsday prophets were predicting the end of the world. Each turn of the century has always brought out its share of soothsayers and seers of all kinds, who are quick to tell us about the bad things that deservedly await us. It's a normal phenomenon, all the more apparent as we also enter a new millennium.

We like to pay attention to everything that goes wrong. Newscasts on television continually report on accidents, conflicts and catas-

BLOW AWAY YOUR LIMITS

trophes. The airtime allotted to contentment, happy events or positive achievements is relatively small compared to the amount of sensational news that endlessly display our misfortunes before our eyes. It's as if we have a certain natural propensity for distress, adversity and even, morbidity.

We should definitely not hide our weaknesses, errors and lack of vision. However, we shouldn't forget that there are two sides to a coin. Strategic living and thinking should inspire us to globally consider all dimensions of reality. The century has gone out and the millennium has toppled over and nothing has changed. The planet continues to turn and we pursue our path with the same questions in our head, the same problems to resolve and the same challenges to surpass.

All throughout the brief history "of modern man" we haven't only been exploiting, wasting and destroying our environment. We have also learned to know it better, understand it and preserve it. We are more and more conscious of the problems we create. Never in the history of humanity have we ever been as sensitive to the fragility of our ecosystem. Never did we have such a precise and global portrait of the functioning of our planet. Never did we take so many measures nor put as much effort into rectifying and improving our situation.

Certainly, we have an enormous amount of mistakes to correct and we still continue to make many more. For some, our decadence has reached a point of no return. I would rather say that our planetary consciousness has reached a level of irreversibility. We can no longer close our eyes, go back and act as if nothing has happened. We have set in motion a process that can only drive us onto the way to improvement and optimization of our planetary situation.

Many feel that, more and more, our politicians have become liars and incompetents. Their only perspective seems to be holding on to power at any cost and the art of governing giving the impression of a return to favoritism, patronage and the encouragement of "politics of interest". Pressure groups have become more and more powerful and are often able to control the governmental machines.

This is quite possibly a true image of reality. Power and its abuse have always existed, in all civilizations, throughout the history of humanity. This phenomenon is not about to change. This is part of our shortcoming as humans, like our tendency to inconsiderately exploit the planet we inhabit. Tyrants are part of the history of man and, sadly, will continue to endlessly exert their influence. But we shouldn't think that only they exist. Champions have also occupied their place in the sun and equally, have always exerted a beneficial influence throughout the course of history. Our era is no exception to this rule. We have our champions, in all domains, including leaders and politicians.

There are more and more men and women, in positions of power, who are aware of the global problems of our planet. There are more and more international forums that examine our planetary difficulties to try to find solutions. Never in the history of humanity have we had this opportunity to globally think and shape our future.

Compared to the period of evolution where civilizations were born, knew their height then began their decline to finally disappear into the fog of history, we live in an era where the basic facts are radically different. We have reached a point where the territorial configuration of our planet and the division of its states tend irrefutably toward worldwide stabilization. As a community, we visibly attempt to maintain and protect the existing zones of influence. More and more, we possess a global vision of the distribution of space and the control of power within a planetary context. There will always be, undoubtedly, numerous jolts and adjustments. Nevertheless, despite the racial and cultural differences that divide us, we are less and less a juxtaposition of civilizations confronting each other to survive. We are, on the contrary, on the way toward becoming, little by little, **the civilization** emerging from years of evolution, conflict and great upheavals.

We speak of a global community that wants to survive, bloom and progress. We think about an immense and complex social system that should shape and create its own destiny. But we also face global problems engendered by such a situation. For the first time in our history, we are all at once confronted with the common limits imposed by our global system. For the first time ever, we need to overcome a challenge that no other civilization had to face: the rational and coherent development of the planet or else it will gradually become extinguished, no longer able to support the survival of the human race.

This is a huge challenge that will stimulate our creativity and force us to develop a strategic vision like never before. The phenomenon of globalization is a complex conjuncture and we should not underestimate its degree of difficulty. The idea of globalization has aroused much enthusiasm, but at the same time, seeded many false hopes. It has too often been associated with the notion of wealth and abundance for all. We too easily over hype this "miracle" of the future as the end to our suffering and the answer to all our problems. Certainly, with free-trade and market globalization, the door of prosperity will open, more and more, to each and everyone on our planet wanting to seize the opportunity. However, such a situation will be neither magical nor miraculous. In this context, as global as it may become, we will always have to work, create and maintain an optimal functioning to merit and preserve a comfortable place in the sun.

The United States of America probably represents, for the time being, one of the closest examples of the future socio-economic picture of the planet in a context of more extended free-trade and globalization. The European Union will probably become another example shortly. In the United States, there already exists a very extensive form of free trade between constituent States. This country, with all its cultural diversity, internal dynamism and prosperity circulating throughout, represents the pre-eminent dream of a host of immigrants wanting to move there. Now, despite this free-trade, this smaller scale "globalization" along with all the opportunities offered to everyone, there are still enormous disparities within the American frontiers. Certain States like certain regions are much wealthier than others. Crime and poverty are worse and more evident in certain places. Hope might be available to everyone and the opportunities, in principle, accessible to all citizens, but it is known for a fact that the American miracle belongs to those who are clever enough to create and seize the opportunity.

On a planetary level, with the perspective of globalization and the emergence of a worldwide civilization, the picture will be no different. Regardless of the amplitude of free-trade and the global equality of opportunities, there will undeniably be those organizations, enterprises, regions, societies or States that will be more brilliant and prosperous. This doesn't mean that abundance, wealth and success will forever belong to these privileged regions or these particular organizations.

Success will persist as long as humans who have made it possible, will continue to work on developing and promoting it. The very moment men and women responsible for this success will relax their vigilance, there will be people elsewhere, within different enterprises, organizations, regions or societies, who will see their opening and profit from the opportunity. In this context of the globalization and international free-trade of **our civilization** which is about to emerge, there won't be any more favors and free gifts than there were before when various cultures and civilizations had to battle each other for survival. Lowering the arms, even just a little, will be enough within such a context, to lose grip on a comfortable place in the sun. When elite athletes let themselves go, as when businesses relax their vigilance, immediately there is someone else ready to profit from the occasion and rise to the summit. Only the more brilliant enterprises and athletes can maintain their supremacy, for as long as they are able to use a lucid and coherent strategy.

It's the same in all spheres of human activity. The principle of natural selection influences everything and along all dimensions. Globalization and the emergence of a worldwide civilization won't change anything, except to make us more and more conscious of the complex constraints imposed on us by the demands of our survival. Within this global context, human intelligence and capacity will be the prevailing factors. Future trend specialists[27] have predicted that the major breakthroughs of the twenty-first century will not firstly depend on technological progress but on our consciousness of the place and role we occupy as human beings. In the competitive atmosphere of a global economy, the difference will be our capacity to innovate in order to favor and develop the quality of our human resources. Corporations and large organizations will increasingly need more and more men and women capable of critical thinking, who can adapt themselves to change and, above all, manifest a strong capacity to plan and act in a strategic manner.

This vision of our evolution describes the future that awaits us during the next few years. It values, in a very relevant manner, the place and role we will occupy in the beginning of this century. The importance of this role will not be limited to the next few decades alone. We need to put a lot of time and effort into taming this new context of a **global civilization** confronted by the restrictions and constraints of limited and finite time and space. We need lots of worldly wisdom and discernment to protect our survival in an evo-lutionary climate where natural selection will continue to influ-ence our relationships as well as our dynamics of functioning.

Intelligence and strategy will enable individuals, organizations, regions, provinces or States to better distinguish themselves and merit a comfortable place in the sun. Nevertheless, we need to ensure that this sound and normal competition will not undermine our conditions for survival as a human community. It will also be important for us to develop a whole strategy, a global vision that will endlessly be refined as we go along with our evolution as a **planetary civilization**.

We've already begun the movement in this direction. There are increasingly more international forums and supranational organizations that study our problems and try to orient our collective future. These forums and organizations still often have the innate impulse toward national supremacy and racial or cultural domination. We are only slowly starting to think in a global manner and we still have much to learn. We need to come up with a conception, a way of seeing things, where the well-being of the whole and the perpetuation of our planetary habitat will be preponderant.

Those supranational organizations, whose objective is to create, adjust and implement such a vision, will be confronted with a huge problem. That being how to allow the individual's dynamism and creativity to blossom, while defining and enforcing certain standards essential to our survival and common well-being. This will require shrewdness of mind and a sharp intelligence just like never before, in order to ensure proper guidance without overly being controlling. The global game will thus resemble a colossal three-dimensional chess game where the supra-planetary component will harmoniously contribute to and promote dynamic interactions and creativity on the level of organizations, societies, regions or States.

Such an enterprise represents the most impressive challenge we have ever had to face throughout our common historic evolution. Therefore we shouldn't expect to achieve perfection overnight. A few hundred years probably still separate us from an optimal level of global management and collective well-being. This level can only be reached if we decide to add strategy to our lives and allow the cleverness and brilliance slumbering within each of us, to bloom. The twenty-first century should become a time of increased awareness of our significance as human beings; I believe that the third millennium will keep going on in the same direction and bare witness to the blossoming of the **strategic human being**.

NOTES

1. This anecdote was taken from an article written by Alice Park found in the October 2, 1995 issue of Time Magazine.
2. ORLICK, T., PARTINGTON, J. (1988). Mental links to excellence. *The Sport Psychologist, 2,* 105-130.
3. ORLICK, T., PARTINGTON, J. (1988). Mental links to excellence. *The Sport Psychologist, 2,* 105-130.
4. RYCHTA, T. (1982). Sport as a human personality development factor. In T. ORLICK, J. PARTINGTON, J. SALMELA (Eds.), *Mental Training for Coaches and Athletes* (p. 101-102). Coaching Association of Canada.
5. Homeostasis is a concept developed by the American physiologist Walter CANNON (See: Cannon, W.B. *The Wisdom of the Body,* New York: Norton, 1939). Impressed by an organism's capacity to maintain its physiological equilibrium and well-being, Cannon created this expression from two Greek words meaning "remain constant". Since then, the notion of homeostasis has obtained general recognition and holds an important place within cybernetics as well as with systemic approaches.
6. In psychology, the importance and effectiveness of social support has been widely documented by such authors as:
BERKMAN, L.F. & SYME, S.L. (1979). Social networks, host resistance and mortality: A nine-year follow-up study of Alameda County residents. *American Journal of Epidemiology, 109,* 186-204.
BILLINGS, A.G. & MOOS, R.H. (1981). The role of coping responses and social resources in attenuating the stress of life events. *Journal of Behavioral Medicine, 4,* 139-157.
BROWN, G.B. & ANDREWS, B. (1986). Social support and depression. In M.H. Appley & Trumbull (Eds.) *Dynamics of stress – Physiological, psychological, and social perspectives.* New York: Plenum Press.
COBB, S. (1976). Social support as a moderator of life stress. *Psychosomatic Medicine, 38,* 300-316.

COHEN, S. (1988). Psychosocial models of the role of social support in the etiology of physical disease. *Health Psychology, 7,* 269-297.

REVENSON, T.A., WOOLMAN, C.A. & FELTON, B.J. (1983). Social supports as stress buffers for adult cancer patients. *Psychosomatic Medicine, 45,* 321-331.

SCHAEFFER, C., COYNE, J.C. & LAZARUS, R.S. (1981). The health-related functions of social support. *Journal of Behavioral Medicine, 4,* 381-405.

7. This 80/20 principle was suggested by the Italian economist and sociologist PARETO, who lived from 1848 to 1923.

8. Symbolization in psychoanalysis refers to the internal representation we have of the world and of ourselves. This representation is subjective, personal to each individual and, therefore, it constitutes a transformation of reality. For a psychoanalyst such as René ROUSSILLON, for example (see his two works appearing in PUF, one in 1991 – *Paradoxes et situations limites de la psychanalyse* – and the other in 1995 – *Logiques et archéologigues du cadre psychanalytique*), therapy can be viewed as a method for optimizing the patient's symbolization capacity. Therapeutic activity consists of analyzing and fully understanding how individuals have symbolized their reality through their personal history. This reflection can then lead those individuals to rework their symbolization; therapy then becomes a way of symbolizing or of transforming the act of symbolization itself.

    When, within the context I have presented, I speak of restructuring our definition of the world, of putting our memory in order, it is this type of transformation that I refer to. Nevertheless, to achieve an effective transformation, I do not consider that analysis and becoming aware of our "historical symbolization" is sufficient. The learning of a new way of symbolizing should also be put into concrete action, in the same way that our first experiences of symbolization were developed through experience. In other words, becoming conscious of our symbolization is essential to its own transformation, but at the same time, to ultimately become effective, it is inseparable from the concrete learning of this same transformation process in reality.

9. COVEY, Stephen R. (1989). *The Seven Habits of Highly Effective People: Restoring the Character Ethic.* New York, Simon & Schuster.

10. Fundamental motives and basic values that constitute what I call

the "guiding system" of the human being approximate the notion of "fundamental reinforcements" advanced in psychology by Steven REISS (motivational theory of sensitivity). According to this researcher, each person can have a different vision of what he or she wishes to attain or avoid. Contrary to FREUD'S idea, sexuality is neither the only nor the ultimate motivator of human functioning. There are other needs or fundamental motivators of our actions like, among others, curiosity, independence, physical activity, prestige and so on. For those wishing to go further into this, consult the following reference:

REISS, S. & HAVERCAMP, S.M. (1996). The sensitivity theory of motivation: Implications for psychopathology. *Behavior Resource and Therapy, 34,* 621-632.

11. Meanwhile, don't lose sight that the pursuit of your dreams doesn't always demand or require a detailed deployment procedure as complex as the one illustrated in *figure 2* and for the case of Bruno or the example of the "windows". I have used these examples to fully define all the possible steps of a deployment procedure in reality. Nevertheless some of your critical concerns don't necessitate being defined in more detail or subdivided into more precise components. It could also be that they don't imply any problematic or unsatisfactory situations. In these cases, you are ready to go directly to identifying the targets for your action plans.

12. In briefly describing the toolbox that is accessible to us, in this text, I referred to various intervention techniques used in psychology and sport psychology. I have not gone into the details of these modalities or the use of these techniques. Explaining the *modus operandi* of each technique would require numerous explanations, going beyond the objectives and perspectives of the present book. Above all, it is important to be aware that these techniques exist and that they can be used if needed. For the reader interested in going even further, there are diverse works in psychology or sport psychology with detailed explanations and reviews of these more specific subjects.

13. ORLICK, T., PARTINGTON, J. (1988). Mental links to excellence. *The Sport Psychologist, 2,* 105-130.

14. This way of looking at motivation is related to the notion of achievement motivation and to the explanatory model of motivation developed by McClelland and Atkinson:

McCLELLAND, D. (1985). *Human motivation*. Glenview, Il.: Scott, Foresman.
McCLELLAND, D., ATKINSON, J., CLARK, R. and LOW-ELL, E. (1953). *The achievement motive*. New York: Appleton-Century-Crofts.

15. The concepts of intrinsic and extrinsic motivation have been fully discussed and explained by:
DECI, E.L. (1980). *The psychology of self-determination*. Lexington, MA: Lexington Books.
DECI, E.L. (1975). *Intrinsic motivation*. New York: Plenum Press.

16. The effects and usefulness of goal-setting, in sport as well as in an industrial and environmental context, have been well presented and discussed by:
LOCKE, E.A. and LATHAM, G.P. (1990). *A Theory of Goal Setting and Task Performance*. Englewood Cliffs, NJ: Prentice Hall.
LOCKE, E.A. and LATHAM, G.P. (1985). The application of goal setting to sports. *Journal of Sport Psychology, 7,* 205-222.
LOCKE, E.A., SHAW, K.M., SAARI, L.M. and LATHAM, G.P. (1981). Goal setting and task performance: 1969-1980. *Psychological Bulletin, 90,* 125-153.

17. Refer to the research conducted by:
ORLICK, T., PARTINGTON, J. (1988). Mental links to excellence. *The Sport Psychologist, 2,* 105-130.

18. See the volume published by Richard Durand where you can note that objectives and favorable results are two inseparable allies on the way to success:
DURAND, R. (1997). *Objectif: réussir sa vie et dans la vie*. Montréal: Un monde différent.

19. This story was reported in the publication of:SIEDENTOP, D. and RAMEY, G. (1977). Extrinsic rewards and intrinsic motivation. *Motor Skills: Theory into Practice, 2,* 49-62.

20. This important detail related to the perception of external rewards was fully explained and illustrated by Cox with respect to sport psychology:
COX, R.C. (1994). *Sport Psychology: Concepts and Applications*. Madison, WI: WCB Brown & Benchmark.

21. In psychology, as in sport psychology, the reasons we use to explain our successes and our setbacks, the positive or negative events of our lives, have been methodically analyzed and studied within the context of what we call attribution theory. This

theory is complex and tries to explain how the causal interpretations we make of our successes and setbacks can influence our actions, our emotions, our confidence as well as a part of our motivation.

The theory was first developed through the works of Heider and later enriched by the contributions of such significant authors as Weiner and Russell. By using this theory as a base, Seligman formulated his concept of optimism to explain the human's capacity to effectively confront difficult situations and "bounce back" in the face of adversity.

For those interested in a better understanding of these theoretical notions, here are basic references:

HEIDER, F. (1958). *The Psychology of Interpersonal Relations.* New York: John Wiley and Sons.

RUSSEL, D. (1982). The causal dimension scale: A measure of how individuals perceive causes. *Journal of Personality and Social Psychology, 42,* 1137-1145.

SELIGMAN, M.E.P. (1992). *Learned Optimism.* New York: Knopf.

WEINER, B. (1972). *Theories of Motivation: From Mechanism to Cognition.* Chicago: Rand McNally.

22. The research relating to the role and impact of the causal attributions in sport were very well summarized and presented by: COX, R.C. (1994). *Sport Psychology: Concepts and Applications.* Madison, WI: WCB Brown & Benchmark.

23. The relationship between optimism, the expectations that we hold for our future and our capacity to succeed was examined in research performed by Scheier and Carver: SCHEIER, M.F. & CARVER, C.S. (1992). Effects of optimism on psychological and physical well being: Theoretical overview and empirical update. *Cognitive Therapy and Research, 16,* 201-228. SCHEIER, M.F. & CARVER, C.S. (1985). Optimism, coping and health: Assessment and implications of generalized outcome expectancies. *Health Psychology, 4,* 219-247.

24. This refers to the research performed by:ORLICK, T., PARTINGTON, J. (1988). Mental links to excellence. *The Sport Psychologist, 2,* 105-130.

25. Televised report presented by Radio-Canada, April 1st, 1996, on the show "Le Point".

26. "Modern man" is a variety of Homo sapiens, hominidae with a larger brain who probably appeared about 250,000 years ago.

27. NAISBITT, J. & ABURDENE, P. (1990). *Megatrends 2000: Ten New Directions for the 1990's.* New York: Avon Books.

ANNEXES

Directional Maps (Tables 1.1, 1.2 and 1.3)

Action Plans (Tables 2.1, 2.2, 2.3 and 2.4)

TABLE 1.1: DIRECTIONAL MAP FOR

CRITICAL CONCERNS: ° PROJECTS ° INITIATIVES	FIRST YEAR									
	MONTH									
	1	2	3	4	5	6	7	8	9	10
PROJECT 1	▓	▓	▓	▓	▓	▓	▓	▓	▓	▓
PROJECT 2	▓	▓	▓	▓	▓	▓	▓	▓	▓	▓
PROJECT 3			▓	▓	▓	▓	▓	▓	▓	
PROJECT 4				▓	▓	▓	▓	▓	▓	▓
PROJECT 5				▓	▓	▓	▓	▓	▓	
ETC.										

THE PRIORITY *CRITICAL CONCERNS*

		SECOND YEAR									
		MONTH									
11	12	1	2	3	4	5	6	7	8	9	...

TABLE 1.2: DIRECTIONAL MAP AS A FUNCTION OF THE *KEY*

PRIORITIES	KEY FACTORS OF SUCCESS AND CRITICAL CONCERNS	FIRST YEAR								
		MONTH								
		1	2	3	4	5	6	7	8	9
KEY FACTOR 1										
4	PROJECT A									
1	PROJECT B									
6	PROJECT C									
2	PROJECT D									
KEY FACTOR 2										
3	PROJECT A									
5	PROJECT B									
7	PROJECT C									
KEY FACTOR 3										
9	PROJECT A									
10	PROJECT B									
8	PROJECT C									
	ETC.									

FACTORS OF SUCCESS AND THE PRIORITY *CRITICAL CONCERNS*

			SECOND YEAR								
			MONTH								
10	11	12	1	2	3	4	5	6	7	8	...

TABLE 1.3: SEBASTIEN'S DIRECTIONAL MAP: *KEY*

PRIORITIES	KEY FACTORS OF SUCCESS AND CRITICAL CONCERNS	FIRST YEAR — MONTH								
		1	2	3	4	5	6	7	8	9
IMPROVE MY HEALTH		██	██	██	██	██	██	██	██	██
1	STOP SMOKING	▓	▓	▓	▓	▓	▓	▓	▓	▓
3	CONTROL MY EATING HABITS			▓	▓	▓	▓	▓	▓	▓
2	START FITNESS PROGRAM			▓	▓	▓	▓	▓	▓	▓
4	KEEP HIKING ON THE MOUNTAIN					▓	▓			
GIVE MYSELF A SOLID FINANCIAL STRUCTURE								██	██	
5	PAY BACK MY DEBTS							▓	▓	
7	INVEST IN RETIREMENT SAVINGS PLAN									
9	SAVE FOR A HOUSE									
BECOME A RESPECTED AND RECOGNIZED PROFESSIONAL									██	
10	TAKE A POLITICAL ROLE WITHIN THE ASSOCIATION									
6	CONTINUE WITH MY TRAINING								▓	
8	START WRITING ARTICLES									
	ETC.									

FACTORS AND THE PRIORITY *CRITICAL CONCERNS*

			SECOND YEAR								
			MONTH								
10	11	12	1	2	3	4	5	6	7	8	...

TABLE 2.1: TABLE OF ACTION PLANS AS A
CAUSES OF EACH COMPONENT

○ **CRITICAL CONCERN (WHAT):**

○ **COMPONENT (what):**

TARGETS / CAUSES	OPERATIONAL OBJECTIVES	HOW (methods/operations)	WHEN / WHERE

FUNCTION OF THE TARGETS AND/OR
OF YOUR CRITICAL CONCERNS

° **OBJECTIVE:**

° **OBJECTIVE:**

WHO	REQUIRED RESOURCES	COSTS	DESIRED RESULTS (when)	OBTAINED RESULTS (when)

TABLE 2.2: ACTION PLAN ELABORATED
JOINT OIL LEAK PROBLEM

○ **CRITICAL CONCERN (WHAT):** Eliminate leak defects of the manufactured engines.

○ **COMPONENT (what):** Upper sealant joint oil leak of the type X motors

TARGETS / CAUSES	OPERATIONAL OBJECTIVES	HOW (methods/operations)	WHEN / WHERE
Tightening procedure of the bolts for the motor head.	100% use of this new tightening procedure within 10 weeks form now.	**Establish a new tightening procedure** ○ Select resource people	Week 1
		○ Schedule study meetings	Week 1
		○ Determine the procedure with the help of a flow chart	Week 2 Room J Building B
		○ Verify and adjust on the floor	Week 2 Assembly line #3
		Inform and train the personnel ○ General information meeting	Week 2 Central lecture-room
		○ Divide into teams	Week 2
		○ Select the trainers and a coordinator	Week 2
		○ Train the teams (1-hour duration) and schedule planning	Weeks 3-10; Building B
		Verification and follow-up of the application	Weeks 11-12
		Etc.	Etc.

342

BY BERNARD FOR THE UPPER SEALANT
OF THE TYPE X MOTORS

° **OBJECTIVE:** To go from x to y leaks within one year from now.

° **OBJECTIVE:** Total elimination (zero) of this type of leak within 3 months from now.

WHO	REQUIRED RESOURCES	COSTS	DESIRED RESULTS (when)	OBTAINED RESULTS (when)
Bernard and his team			New procedure established for the end of the 2nd week	As planned
Bernard and his team				
Resource people	Trained employees pulled from the assembly line	Amount X re: time, salary & replacement on the production line		
Resource people	Meeting room	No cost for the room	25% application & leak reduction end of week 4	30% end of week 4
Bernard and his team	Reservation of lecture-room	No cost	50% application & leak reduction end of week 6	60% end of week 6
Bernard and his team			75% application & leak reduction end of week 8	85% end of week 8
Bernard and resource people	Employees taken from the production line	Amount Y re: time, salary & replacement on the line	100% application & leak reduction end of week 10	100% end of week 9
Trainers with their coordinator	Room for team meetings	No cost for rooms		
Bernard, his team and the trainers				
Etc.	Etc.	Etc.	Etc.	Etc.

343

TABLE 2.3: PARTIAL ILLUSTRATION OF AN
CONTROLLING ACTIVATION AND COMPETITIVE

° **CRITICAL CONCERN (WHAT):** Better control my competitive anxiety
° **COMPONENT (what):** Learn to reduce my activation level during the waiting period before my event

TARGETS / CAUSES	OPERATIONAL OBJECTIVES	HOW (methods/operations)	WHEN / WHERE
Global muscular tension is too high	Reduce tension level from 9/10 to 5/10 within six weeks	**Muscular relaxation through control of breathing** ° Identify the best technique for breathing control	Week 1
		° Practice at home	Week 2; my room
		° Home and in daily life	Week 3; room, car, lockers
		° Include within training	Week 4; before each execution
		° Test it during the waiting periods at competitions	Week 5; waiting periods in Vancouver
		° Adjust and stabilize at international competitions	Week 6; Calgary, China, Korea
Habit of looking around at other competitors during waiting periods	Never look at others during waiting periods	**Plan a behavioral routine to occupy my time** ° Choose the activities for the routine	Week 3
		° Practice them with visualization	Week 4; room and training
		° Test them during the waiting periods at competitions	Week 5; at Vancouver
		° Adjust and stabilize them at international competition	Week 6; Calgary, China, Korea

ELITE ATHLETE'S ACTION PLAN TOWARD
ANXIETY WITH REGARDS TO THE OLYMPIC GAMES

° **OBJECTIVE:** Reduce anxiety from 80% to 40% within 6 months from now

- -

° **OBJECTIVE:** Reduce level from 9/10 to 5/10 within six weeks from now

WHO	REQUIRED RESOURCES	COSTS	DESIRED RESULTS (when)	OBTAINED RESULTS (when)
With the psy-chologist Alone and adjust with the psychologist		Amount X for consultation	Control of 8/10 by the end of week 2 7/10 for week 3 6/10 for week 4 5/10 for week 5 Stabilize at 5/10 in week 6	8/10 for week 2 6/10 for week 3 5/10 for week 4 Week 5: return to 6/10 Week 6: 6/10 then stabilized at 5/10
With the psy-chologist Alone and adjust with the psychologist		Same amount X for consultation	Week 3: set the routine Week 4: mental practice Weeks 5 and 6: no looking around during the waiting periods	As planned

345

TABLE 2.3 (CONTINUED): PARTIAL ILLUSTRATION OF AN
CONTROLLING ACTIVATION AND COMPETITIVE

○ **CRITICAL CONCERN (WHAT):** Better control my competitive anxiety

○ **COMPONENT (what):** Learn to reduce my activation level during the waiting period before my event

TARGETS / CAUSES	OPERATIONAL OBJECTIVES	HOW (methods/operations)	WHEN / WHERE
Negative thoughts during the waiting periods	Reduce the number of negative thoughts during waiting periods by 75% within six weeks from now	**Stop and restructure the negative thoughts** ○ Identify the negative thoughts and their positive opposites	Week 2
	Stop and willingly get rid of the 25% that remain or can surface	○ Practice stopping the negative thoughts with visualization	Week 3; my room
		○ Visualization for stopping and restructuring the negative thoughts into positive ones	Week 4; room and training
		○ Make an audio cassette of positive thoughts to listen to during the waiting periods	Week 4
		○ Test the cassette and restructuring in competition	Week 5; in Vancouver
		○ Adjust and stabilize at international competitions	Week 6; Calgary, China and Korea

346

ELITE ATHLETE'S ACTION PLAN TOWARD
ANXIETY WITH REGARDS TO THE OLYMPIC GAMES

° **OBJECTIVE:** Reduce anxiety from 80% to 40% within 6 months from now

° **OBJECTIVE:** Reduce level from 9/10 to 5/10 within six weeks from now

WHO	REQUIRED RESOURCES	COSTS	DESIRED RESULTS (when)	OBTAINED RESULTS (when)
With the help of the psychologist		Amount X for consultation	Week 2: identify positive dialogue	Week 2: OK, done
Alone and adjust with the psychologist			Week 3: reduce negative thoughts by 25%	Week 3: reduced by 20%
With the help of the psychologist	*Walkman*; Sound system for recording	The cost of a *walkman* and a cassette	Week 4: reduce by 50%	Week 4: reduced by 40%
Alone			Week 5: reduce by 75%	Week 5: reduced by 65%
			Week 6: maintain at 75% and control the rest	Week 6: reduced by 75% and good control
			GENERAL After 6 weeks:	**GENERAL** After 6 weeks:
			° Activation stabilized at 5/10	° Activation OK at 5/10
			° Anxiety reduced to 60%	° Competitive anxiety reduced to 55%

TABLE 2.4: PARTIAL ILLUSTRATION OF BRUNO'S
BY WORKING TO CORRECT HIS

° **CRITICAL CONCERN (WHAT):** Lose my excess weight

° **COMPONENT (what):** Eating too much

TARGETS / CAUSES	OPERATIONAL OBJECTIVES	HOW (methods/operations)	WHEN / WHERE
Eating lunch with colleagues and remaining in an atmosphere of work and pressure	Go from 5 to 2 lunch hours per week with colleagues within 3 weeks	Schedule in advance which days I will eat lunch at a restaurant	Week 1
		Prepare a "normal" lunch to eat in my office the other days	Prepare lunch at home the night before
	Eat only with x, y and z, who are not stressful		
		Plan "excuses" so I won't insult those people when I don't eat with them	At least one day ahead
	Maintain this for 2 months		
		In 3 weeks, gradually eliminate the stressful individuals	
		The days when I eat in my office, plan a relaxing activity (reading the paper, a book and breathing exercises)	Also plan this the night before

ACTION PLAN FOR CONTROLLING HIS WEIGHT
BAD HABIT OF OVER-EATING

° **OBJECTIVE:** Go from 90 to 75 kilos within six months from now

----

° **OBJECTIVE:** Go from 3,000 to 2,600 calories/day within two months
from now

WHO	REQUIRED RESOURCES	COSTS	DESIRED RESULTS (when)	OBTAINED RESULTS (when)
With my wife			Week 1: 2 of 4 lunch hours with stressful people and 4 times at a restaurant	Week 1: OK, as planned but 3 of 4 with stressful people
			Week 2: 1 of 3 lunch hours with stressful people and 3 times at a restaurant	Week 2: 3 times at a restaurant and 1 of 3 with stressful people
			Week 3: 2 times at a restaurant with x, y and z only	Week 3: OK, as planned
			Weeks 4 to 8: maintain	Weeks 4 to 8: OK, except for weeks 5 and 7 where stressful people could not be avoided 1 time out of 2

TABLE 2.4 (CONTINUED): PARTIAL ILLUSTRATION OF
WEIGHT BY WORKING TO CORRECT HIS

° **CRITICAL CONCERN (WHAT):** Lose my excess weight

° **COMPONENT (what):** Eating too much

TARGETS / CAUSES	OPERATIONAL OBJECTIVES	HOW (methods/operations)	WHEN / WHERE
The type of restaurant chosen for lunch	Within 3 weeks from now, eliminate fast food and buffets and maintain thereafter	Determine in advance in my schedule the type of restaurant I will go to	Also plan this the night before
Eat too quickly without giving my stomach enough time to feel when it is full	Go from ° 10 to 25 minutes to eat breakfast ° 15 to 30 minutes for lunch ° 20 to 50 minutes for dinner within 3 weeks and then maintain for two months	Use a stopwatch to mark the start and finish of each meal Chew each mouthful slowly Breath between each mouthful If the time is not respected, no dessert with the next meal	Morning and night at home Weekends at home Lunches at the restaurant and office
	Never take more than one helping in each case from hereon	If these objectives are attained every day, eat out at a restaurant on Saturday night, if not no wine on the weekend or eating out at a restaurant	
Etc.	Etc.	Etc.	

BRUNO'S ACTION PLAN FOR CONTROLLING HIS
BAD HABIT OF OVER-EATING

° **OBJECTIVE:** Go from 90 to 75 kilos within six months from now

- -

° **OBJECTIVE:** Go from 3,000 to 2,600 calories/day within two months from now

WHO	REQUIRED RESOURCES	COSTS	DESIRED RESULTS (when)	OBTAINED RESULTS (when)
			Week 1: 2 fast food Week 2: 1 fast food Week 3: 0 fast food	OK, as planned and maintained
My wife will help me remember to chew and breathe and only take one helping	A stopwatch	Amount X for the watch	**Week 1:** ° 10 to 15 minutes for breakfast ° 15 to 20 minutes for lunch ° 20 to 30 minutes for dinner ° One helping each time **Week 2:** ° 15 to 20 minutes for breakfast ° 20 to 25 minutes for lunch ° 30 to 40 minutes for dinner **Week 3:** ° 20 to 25 minutes for breakfast ° 25 to 30 minutes for lunch ° 40 to 50 minutes for dinner **Week 4 and beyond:** ° Maintain ° Always only one helping	**Week 1:** ° 3 meals where objectives not attained ° Unpleasant consequences applied to correct this **Week 2:** ° OK as planned with reward Saturday night **Week 3:** ° OK as planned with reward Saturday night **Week 4 and beyond:** ° Quit in week 5 ° Negative consequence applied ° Maintained since then